T0351638

HOW WE
VOTE

HOW WE VOTE

INNOVATION IN AMERICAN ELECTIONS

KATHLEEN HALE • MITCHELL BROWN

GEORGETOWN UNIVERSITY PRESS / WASHINGTON, DC

The publisher is not responsible for third-party websites or their content. URL links were active at time of publication.

Library of Congress Cataloging-in-Publication Data

Names: Hale, Kathleen, author. | Brown, Mitchell, author.
Title: How We Vote : Innovation in American Elections / Kathleen Hale, Mitchell Brown.
Other titles: Public Management and Change.
Description: Washington, DC : Georgetown University Press, 2020. | Series: Public management and change | Includes bibliographical references and index.
Identifiers: LCCN 2019035435 (print) | LCCN 2019035436 (ebook) | ISBN 9781626167780 (hardcover) | ISBN 9781626167803 (ebook)
Subjects: LCSH: Voting—United States. | Elections—United States.
Classification: LCC JK1976 .H255 2020 (print) | LCC JK1976 (ebook) | DDC 324.60973—dc23
LC record available at https://lccn.loc.gov/2019035435
LC ebook record available at https://lccn.loc.gov/2019035436

♾ This book is printed on acid-free paper meeting the requirements of the American National Standard for Permanence in Paper for Printed Library Materials.

21 20   9 8 7 6 5 4 3 2 First printing

Printed in the United States of America.
Cover design by Spencer Fuller, Faceout Studio.

For our mothers, Dolores and Melinda

CONTENTS

LIST OF ILLUSTRATIONS

FIGURES

TABLES

FOREWORD

The year 2019 marked my fiftieth year in elections. When I started out in this business in Buffalo at a pretty-good-sized local board in 1969, there was no innovation. Voter registration was a laborious process; we had to hire one hundred extra people to shuffle cards, put them in heavy binders, and then put them in heavy canisters. The voter registration list was done on an old IBM punch card Univac system. Polling places were literally booths we put in the middle of the street with a potbellied stove on one end and the lever machine on the other.

Several things that happened along the way turned the tide. Certainly, the Voting Rights Act of 1965 and the court cases that followed it were significant. Lowering the age of voting from twenty-one to eighteen was another. The next big one was the National Voter Registration Act (NVRA). This was followed by the passage of the Help America Vote Act (HAVA).

The NVRA changed the way voter registration was conducted and list maintenance was done, and it changed the structure of authority in election administration. We still have confusion and court opinions about list maintenance and how to do this the right way because the law was written in a way that could be interpreted in different ways. This is true for much of election administration legislation because of the political involvement in the development of legislation.

The NVRA was the impetus for the first big expansion of innovation in election offices because it mandated that local offices learn to do these things better and utilize new and emerging technology. The NVRA opened up the door to mail registration, expanded outreach to various public service entities, and mandated a federal form—all of which increased numbers of voter registrations, in turn meaning that boards had to find ways to capture and manage these data. A number of us worked hard with the Federal Election Commission Clearinghouse on Election Administration, which was the predecessor to the Election Administration Commission, to redesign the registration forms through their advisory board, and we worked with literacy experts to figure this out. This was the beginning of innovation in election offices in the contemporary era.

The next major event that changed the business of election administration was the election of 2000. Before that election, media and most advocacy groups, and even most voters, did not know much, or care, about the election administration process. But the 2000 election exploded this. Every news organization in the country was trying to find out how elections were run, and they were all asking similar questions: What was happening with punch cards? Was my voting system OK? Why was everyone not allowed to cast a provisional ballot?

The period from 2001 to 2004 marked the politics of the development of HAVA. During this period, the US Senate flipped party control, and because of the makeup of Congress, when the HAVA bill was written, the senior members on both sides of the aisle wanted a piece of the pie. They all wanted their own initiative as part of the bill (which is not unusual for a piece of legislation). There were provisions and sometimes fights about voter identification, punch cards and lever machines, provisional ballots, voting systems for people with disabilities and the ability to vote independently, and the creation of the US Election Assistance Commission. There were more than twenty-five other projects given to the commission to complete in a short period, including standards for voting machines. This spurred much innovation. And for the first time in the history of election administration, states were given substantial money to create new systems, buy equipment, and use their resources to support other parts of the election administration system. Together, the NVRA, the 2000 election, and HAVA fostered major innovation and improvement in elections.

Education and training were another change that spurred innovation. I was part of the first Election Center Certification in Election and Registration Administration (CERA) board—the impetus for creating this certification was to enhance the professionalization of election administrators across the country through a partnership with Auburn University. This partnership has led to well over a thousand graduates, and it continues to be the only professional certification that is specifically for election administrators. By increasing capacity and spurring ideas and change, CERA has become the leading force in training-based innovation.

But there is a point at which innovation plateaus, and one needs to concentrate on others things. Many things can be done with computers and technology, but there continue to be critical aspects related to people. People's problems need to be supported through dialogue and working directly with them; innovation will not solve these issues. This is where education and training remain critical. Elections are and will always be a business that must relate to people. You need communication skills, and the ability to work in the community, to reach out, and to build and use the resources around you. You need to be able to collaborate, work with advocacy groups, and engage with the legislature—all within a political system and environment.

People should care about innovation in election administration as a projection of what is going to happen in the future, even with the current slowdown in technological changes as people respond to and worry about cybersecurity. Innovation happens where there are resources and an inclination to take risks—the real pioneers in our business are the jurisdictions and their leaders highlighted in this book. Innovation also drives away the "I like it just the way it is" crowd. You can have tools, but without people to operate them, you do not have anything.

To spur innovation, you need resources, people with foresight and vision willing to take a risk, and opportunity. Some of the major periods of innovation in election administration since the start of the twentieth century in America have happened because the federal government provided the opportunity through the passage of major legislation—the Nineteenth Amendment, the VRA, the Twenty-Sixth Amendment, the NVRA, and HAVA. And amazing people have been there to grab these opportunities and use the resources at their disposal to make positive change happen.

This book shares the work of those people who have the vision, foresight, and zeal to tackle new initiatives and take the risks that others may not have taken. I am very, very proud of my relationship with the people at Auburn University and the authors of this book. In my fifty years in this business, they have been a real shining light. They have been opening doors to the election community and offering this community opportunities to grow knowledge and increase professionalism, and by extension enhance innovation.

Thomas R. Wilkey
Albany, New York, and New Smyrna Beach, Florida
April 26, 2018

ACKNOWLEDGMENTS

This book became possible only with the assistance and support of many people. Election officials across the country opened their doors to us, and we owe them our greatest acknowledgment. We are grateful for every opportunity to visit election offices and to talk with election officials during Election Day and on all the other very busy days of the year. We are especially honored to have the opportunity to serve with many fine public servants of elections on task forces, boards, and working groups, and to work with them through Auburn University's partnership with the Election Center and the CERA professional certification program. In writing this book, we reflected many times on the incredible wealth of knowledge and skill that so many bring to running elections.

We owe our deep appreciation to our graduate student team—Election Center Fellow Tyler St. Clair, PhD students Lindsey Forson and Jan Hume, and master's of public administration students Emily Hale and Shaniqua Williams—for their continued enthusiasm in pursuit of our many questions and in search of countless details for this and many other projects, and to Mary Afton Day, also an Election Center fellow, for her initial work on several of the graphics in this book.

It is our honor to be included in the Public Management and Change series, and we extend special thanks to Beryl Radin and Don Jacobs for their belief in this project. Thanks are also due for the manuscript readers, and to the rest of the production team at Georgetown University Press for their careful attention to detail. All errors belong to us.

We hope that this work will help others learn more about the significance of the work of thousands of public servants who work tirelessly to improve American elections, and about the lessons that apply to all sorts of innovations that occur across public service in areas of complex, interdependent networked arrangements.

LIST OF ABBREVIATIONS

AVR	automatic voter registration
CEO	chief election official
CERA	certified elections/registration administrator
CIO	chief information officer
DHS	Department of Homeland Security
DOJ	Department of Justice
EAC	Elections Assistance Commission
EAVS	Election Administration and Voting Survey
EPB	electronic pollbook
ERIC	Electronic Registration Information Center
HAVA	Help America Vote Act of 2002
LEO	local election official
NIST	National Institute of Standards and Technology
NVRA	National Voter Registration Act of 1993
OVI	online voting initiative
OVR	online voter registration
SOS	secretary of state
SSN	Social Security Number
UOCAVA	Uniformed and Overseas Citizens Absentee Voting Act of 1986
USPS	US Postal Service
VBM	voting by mail
VRA	Voting Rights Act of 1965

Introduction:
Innovation Drivers and the
Unique American Context

The most recent American elections have been historic events. In the presidential and general elections in November 2016, the presidential candidates themselves were larger than life. Hillary Clinton ran—and lost—as the Democratic Party's nominee and the first female presidential candidate from a major political party. Donald Trump ran—and won—as the Republican Party's nominee and as a populist reformer and political outsider. Election systems and the infrastructure of elections were called into question in new ways. The Trump campaign sounded the drumbeat that elections were "rigged" all across the country and established a narrative that many votes were cast by ineligible voters; this narrative persists today. An avalanche of media reported that foreign interests, probably Russian, breached electronic security protocols to gain access to the Democratic National Committee's records and election databases in some states, giving rise to widespread concerns about election security.

The architecture of federal–state election relationships also made the news. Trump won the election by prevailing in the Electoral College, although Clinton led the popular vote by nearly 3 million votes. This was the first presidential election held without the force of the Voting Rights Act of 1965 (VRA) requirements for prior federal oversight of state and local changes to election practices, which had been in effect since 1965; this prior review was intended to prevent discriminatory practices that effectively disenfranchised entire minority populations in some states, until they were dismantled in 2013 by the US Supreme Court in the *Shelby County v. Holder* ruling. The results of the presidential election were widely discussed in the media, and especially among Clinton supporters; however, the new institutional approach to federal oversight—which does not include prior review—received little, if any, public attention.

The 2018 elections themselves were by almost all accounts free from any cyber intrusion, although the political debates raged about the interaction of foreign nations (i.e., Russia), and deliberate disinformation was promulgated and amplified through Facebook, arguably the largest social media platform in the world. Administrative conditions in states with superheated political races seemed frayed. In the run-up to Election Day, questions were raised in places like Alabama, Georgia, and Kansas about the propriety of elected secretaries of state interpreting election rules for elections in which they were also candidates. At the close of Election Day, close races in states such as Florida and Georgia highlighted recount procedures and deadlines that are rarely in the public eye. Media interest was drawn to process questions about state postmark requirements for the receipt of absentee ballots and other ballots returned by mail, lengths of canvass periods, and instructions given to voters who were issued provisional ballots.

Since the 2000 election, *Bush v. Gore* in 2000, and the Help America Vote Act of 2002 (HAVA), election officials in the nation's over 8,000 election jurisdictions have operated in an intergovernmental environment of constant change, including wide swings in political control at both state and federal levels as well as heightened partisanship at the national level and within states. At the same time, interest in election administration has expanded, and has been reflected in thousands of state legislative proposals and executive initiatives intended to control the times and places in which elections are conducted, as well as who can vote and how. Proposals that range from methods of identification to voting technology to periods of early voting continue to be hotly debated in all fifty states, the District of Columbia, and US territories. Established administrative responsibilities, routines, and relationships have been altered by judicial interpretations of long-standing national laws, including the VRA, the Americans with Disabilities Act of 1990, and the National Voter Registration Act of 1993 (NVRA). New statutory methods of voting for military and overseas voters are bringing some registration practices into the electronic age.

During this period, dueling presidential commissions have come and gone. In 2014, the Presidential Commission on Election Administration reported its recommendations for addressing numerous election administration issues and reflected a sense of the field at the time. In 2018, the Presidential Advisory Commission on Election Integrity attempted, without success, to collect voter registration data from the states in order to investigate unspecified claims of voter fraud; the commission was dissolved after states refused to provide confidential information, among other factors.

Today, news accounts continue to suggest that elections are in need of drastic overhaul in some regard or another. The popular wisdom is that American elections are either in need of serious repair or are completely broken. We disagree, and we set forth a strong contrary position in this catalog and analysis of change within the context of the American political system and its unique intergovernmental arrangements that grind many good ideas to a halt and helps to spread others, both in the field of election administration and otherwise.

In this highly complex and closely monitored policy environment, election administrators face clear challenges as they execute an increasing number of responsibilities, and do so with significant success. Election administrators are also at the mercy of policy prescriptions that they are largely unable to influence. Understanding these challenges and how election administrators address them is important, because elections are the way that America measures and reflects the quantity and quality of its democracy. The evidence about election performance as a public administration function and as a measure of public management is, in fact, quite positive, despite much media coverage, punditry, and public opinion that suggests otherwise. Perhaps even more significant, the issues that election administrators face in trying to measure performance and success are indicative of larger themes in performance measurement and accountability in public service.

This book extends emerging scholarship about election administration by considering election operations as a matter of public administration, and by examining *how* election offices innovate to address complexities, interdependencies, and accountability issues against a fluid political environment. We use the lens of public administration and public management theory to examine the conduct of elections as a contemporary intergovernmental enterprise. We use a mix of data sources and analysis techniques to reflect upon and draw conclusions about the networks of organizations that operate in this critical aspect of American democracy.

The book draws upon the essential public-sector themes of cooperation, collaboration, governance, and measurement to examine how election officials are meeting the challenges of implementation and compliance in a network of intergovernmental and cross-sectoral interaction, and how these officials conceptualize success. Substantive topics include changes that election administrators have initiated to address challenges in establishing and maintaining voter registration methods and voting options, improvements in voter convenience, support for voting in languages other than English, the integrity of the voting process, and voting system technology. We also focus on the concept of measurement as an overarching and essential dimension of the way that network innovation occurs.

State and local election officials are at the center of each configuration and are influenced by political and policy dynamics among national officials, equipment vendors, nonprofit groups, and interested citizens. In each topical area, the configurations of elected officials, appointed staff, back-office civil servants, and street-level bureaucrats, including poll workers, vary with the types of nonelection offices and organizations that are involved. These include both elected and appointed government officials and mainline civil servants. These range across the US Postal Service, vendors, language advocacy groups, motor vehicle offices, and more. In some areas, state lawmakers have been particularly active, and in at least one (voting for military and overseas citizens), Congress has recently played a leading role. And courts at all levels are always present and have been highly influential during the period of this study.

Collectively, these topical areas present a holistic, though not exhaustive, view of administrative challenges across a range of different intergovernmental and cross-sectoral organizational arrangements, and they offer ground-level insight into the ways that public offices utilize different methods of cooperation, collaboration, governance, and measurement to address their challenges. The solutions crafted by election administrators illuminate the process of public-sector innovation and change under persistent conditions of high visibility, public scrutiny, legal review, and limited resources.

THE COMPONENTS OF INNOVATION

This is a book about innovation—change—in America election administration in the modern era. Innovation is a complex phenomenon, and as we attempt to reflect the nuances about innovation in practice, we model innovation through the consideration of four interconnected public-sector concepts. These factors support and facilitate change, and they also inhibit it.

The first factor is politics. In what we consider to be the modern era of election administration—post-2000—the politics of election operations and voter registration have been highly partisan for the most part, and policy choices have focused on administrative practices in particular. Students of the history of election administration and the VRA in particular know that, in very important ways, it took nearly two hundred years to achieve this singular piece of legislation, which occurred essentially a century after amendments to the US Constitution established the right to vote for all men regardless of race, color, or previous condition of servitude. The politics of voting also extends far beyond the implementation of technical requirements and implicates the meaning of citizenship as a fundamental consideration of American governance. In a nation of immigrants, the concept of citizenship has always been a creation of law and judicial interpretation. The ability to vote is an essential element of what it means to be a citizen. White men born outside the United States were granted citizenship and given the right to vote in 1790 through the Naturalization Act. Voting rights were later extended to naturalized nonwhite men in 1870 and to naturalized women in 1920.

Students of the federal system of government writ large understand that the intergovernmental framework of modern American election administration was cast long ago, at the nation's founding, in divisions of authority between states and the new national government, and descriptions of entitlement to the franchise and definitions of citizenship. The successes and failures over time along the way to the VRA were intertwined in the back-and-forth of party politics in the United States' two-party system and strong regional preferences for states rights. From the nation's founding, political power to control the parameters of elections was established firmly in the states. Yet, at times, national authority held sway at key inflection points to establish national principles—including the abolition of slavery, the concept of equal protection under the law, and the expansion of citizenship and the right to vote beyond white men born in the United States first to naturalized white men, then to all men, and then to women. Voting rights are still limited primarily to citizens, although noncitizens are permitted to vote in some local elections. And in most states, criminal convictions carry the loss of voting rights for at least some period, and permanently in some states.

Changes were forced by court and public challenges advanced by advocacy organizations and other nonprofit groups. This political give-and-take continued as new federal laws such as the NVRA and the HAVA were passed and brought new questions alongside old issues. In the modern era, partisan battles have been waged over such questions as methods of voter identification, whether to classify voters as inactive and how to remove them from voter rolls, whether a criminal conviction removes a voter from the rolls, how to draw district lines, and whether election jurisdictions were bound by the conditions of federal review and approval established under the VRA half a century earlier. Federal courts have waded into these and other questions, and their decisions continue to shape the election landscape.

The few major federal laws that regulate election systems, and more critically the absence of unifying federal law for most areas, provide the backdrop or platform for much of the innovation in election administration. Unlike other areas of American public policy, election administration exists without significant federal regulatory oversight. In the breach, local election administrators and their state-level counterparts have developed new and improved methods of operation, based on their own desire to do good work; public desires for more accessible, current, and convenient practices; demands from parties through state legislatures; and court prescriptions imposed on complex practices that have always been locally driven. Driven by the political decisions of federal lawmakers and state legislatures that form macro-level election policy, local election officials have forged new administrative ground through innovation in smaller administrative policies and practice. Their proposals and techniques must survive in a partisan political environment, and as a result have taken hold in some places and not others. It is also important to note that legislatures are not the only policymakers under the American federal system. Citizens in nearly half the states can exercise direct democracy to bring about political change; one example is Florida Amendment 4, which was approved by a strong majority of voters and restores voting rights to convicted felons.

The second factor is professionalism.[1] Professionalism in public administration writ large has evolved with the nation's bureaucracy, especially since

the early part of the twentieth century. Professionalism in election administration is a latecomer, relatively speaking, but as it has evolved it has had an
impact on innovation across the states in important ways. Today's election
administration workforce of public servants and seasonal staff is charged with
extraordinary responsibility. For both seasoned veterans and newcomers to
the profession, forces are at work to promote and further develop the necessary knowledge, skills, and abilities to do their jobs effectively. Professionalism in election administration, as we demonstrate, has been fostered in
significant measure by network interactions among various levels of government and professional and other nonprofit organizations.

The third factor is resources. Although rarely statistically significant in
the quantitative analyses of innovation presented in this book, the availability of resources is a clear seed for many of the most important innovations
that we chronicle. Even the most populous (and presumably the wealthiest)
election jurisdictions compete for local resources with every other county,
township, and state service. By any estimate we have made, the average
election fraction of local jurisdiction resources is significantly less than a
half of a percent (0.005) of the total funding of the jurisdiction, even under
the most generous calculations. These local resources are critical because
election administration is not supported by federal funds in any significant
way. Election jurisdictions typically depend upon revenue decisions made
by other government units (i.e., counties and states), and it is an understatement to note that election office staff are experts at stretching a dol-
lar. All the innovations described in this book result from the stewardship
of always-limited public funds. And to be clear, resources are about more
than money. Resources, in our conception, include people—well-meaning,
visionary, hard-working leaders, some of whom are able to leverage financial
resources, some of whom are able to bring people together, and some of
whom are able to see solutions to problems well before the problems themselves were commonly understood.

The fourth factor is need. The phrase *necessity is the mother of invention*
is nowhere better exemplified than in election administration. Although
underresourced, election administration is fundamental to conducting elections. Need in election administration specifically and in the larger environment generally is spurred by the pressures of voters, community members,
advocates, candidates, courts, and legislative mandates, which must be met
regardless of available resources, levels of professionalism, and political climate. The story of innovation is also a story about dedicated election officials
responding to these conditions. The needs that drive the innovations that we
have observed include administrative needs within offices, needs within specific communities, and the overall needs of voters.

The innovations in this volume are bookended in many respects by federal voting rights laws, beginning with the VRA, and influenced by political

and administrative responses to the presidential elections of 2000 and 2016. Of these two recent election cycles, the first served as the impetus for the wholesale introduction of electronic voting systems and electronic voting records generally. The second prompted considerable exploration of security for online and electronic election systems. The changes that have occurred over more than fifty years illustrate the vigilant attention of public servants both inside and outside government among the increasingly diverse citizenry.

Any analysis of innovation engages the past, the present, and the future. Each of the innovations presented in this book evolved along a unique arc in time. Some took decades to come to fruition in response to federal law, some developed only as new technology became more widely accessible and understood, and still others emerged in moments of crisis (whether anticipated, perceived, or actual). Some of the innovations we explore reflect the practices of local election jurisdictions that were seen as best practices and in turn were incorporated into the recommendations of the Presidential Commission on Election Administration (2014). There is no truly unified approach to these innovations across election jurisdictions. This suggests that there are multiple influences at work, and that differences in local and state priorities remain. We expect that the factors at work—politics, professionalism, resources, and needs—will manifest themselves differently in each area, and at different times in the process. As is the case for election administration generally, one size does not fit all.

CONSIDERING THE UNIQUE AMERICAN CONTEXT OF ELECTION ADMINISTRATION

It is also important to consider the American federal context and how its unique features support the modern election administration structure. The administration of elections in other federal systems is often less complicated than in the United States. The problems that election administrators face in the United States are different, and the solutions are different as well. Understanding the comparative complexity of all election operations requires delving into constitutional structures, electoral systems, and electoral procedures (Norris 2004). Election characteristics derive from such elemental factors as the structure of government and decision-making (direct democracy, republics, or autocracies, federated versus unified structures); for republics, the approach to representation (single-member versus multimember districts); electoral rules (first past the post, rank choice, etc.); qualifications for electors and candidates; the administrative structure for running elections (independent electoral bodies, governmental electoral bodies, or mixed approaches); and the amount of authority of these bodies to make, enforce, and adjudicate rules.

The US system is a federated republic with primary authority for election administration constitutionally established at the subnational level and implementation vested at the local level. Local and state practices across the country evolved largely independently over time within states, and with a few exceptions primarily related to suffrage rules; these units continue to exercise relative primacy over the process today. This structure means that the national government may expand or constrain the political opportunity structure that supports innovation, but the state governments also have significant influence over innovation as well.

Local and state practices are the heart of American election administration, but such a distribution of power and authority may appear to present significant drawbacks when seen from a comparative perspective. Catt and others (2014, 17) write that "devolving electoral powers and responsibilities to local authorities without appropriate oversight may make it more difficult to maintain electoral consistency, service, quality and—ultimately—the freedom and fairness of elections. The Unites States is a good example of this difficulty."

We note that the use of the term "devolving" in the quotation above is a bit of a misnomer because it implies that power and authority were previously held by the national government, which is not the American case. And students of American elections, including ourselves, also beg to differ. We believe that subnational autonomy brings experimentation and innovation, and, to a degree, also protects elections at the national level from external threats like cyber tampering.

However, from a comparative perspective, innovation can mean a lot of things—from new laws to changes in institutional arrangements to the mechanics of registering voters, balloting, and counting. Indeed, transparency, efficiency, and accuracy can, in and of themselves, be innovative. In some of these ways, the United States leads the field. In others, particularly innovations that relate to the use of technology for voting, the US lags behind other countries and will likely continue to do so.

Finding comparable countries to use as benchmarks for the US is fraught with problems. If we were to focus on federalist countries, we might look to places like India, Mexico, or Germany. India and Mexico have independent election boards, and Germany has a national election board with power over disputes. Among countries with governmentally based election boards or offices like those in the US, there is variance over the location of that authority within the federal system. Some, like Brazil, operate at the national and state levels, and some operate at the national and province levels, like Australia and Canada. In others, the local level responds to both national and regional authorities, as in the Russian Federation. Perhaps the only country structurally similar to the US today is Switzerland, but it differs vastly in size and heterogeneity (for more detail, see Catt et al. 2014).

International norms may affect American election administration in the future. Like many countries, we are likely to move toward automatic (or more highly automated, electronic) voter registration as technology makes it easier to create voter files from other population data in government offices. But in other ways, the US is unlikely to innovate in similar ways, at least not quickly. For instance, Internet-based voting and the use of biometric identifiers for verifying voter eligibility may seem to be just around the corner, given the ubiquitous and visible use of similar technology in other fields where security is an essential concern, such as banking and airline travel. In election administration, security concerns and cultural and political norms will slow or stall the adoption of these innovations. In this way, innovation in election administration depends in part on wealth (and the availability of related technology), political will, and culture.

ELECTION ADMINISTRATION AND PEOPLE

On Election Day, hundreds of thousands of people express their opinions on politics and policy by casting ballots, in some places in a polling place near their home, in others by mailing in their ballot in advance of the election, and in some by going to a central community voting center. Not all people have the same experiences, and some of them encounter problems or have questions raised for them through the process. In this section, we describe some of these people and their problems and questions, all of which pose challenges for election administrators. We use composite case studies to feature the problems encountered by prospective voters and election administrators and the ways in which innovations have helped or not. These cases synthesize experiences that we have observed and that have been reported to us, and do not represent any particular person or office or jurisdiction; based on our research, we feel that the cases fairly represent the range of issues posed by the innovations we discuss in this book. In chapters 3 through 8, we go into detail about the how and the why these problems are (and in some cases are not) resolved through election administration innovations. In the conclusion, we come back to these prospective voters and election administrators and discuss the future of innovation to improve their experiences.

Maya Martinez and John Smith

On Election Day, Maya Martinez goes to her local polling place. Shortly after the last election, Maya married, and recently she and her husband moved across town. When she checks in at her polling location, she shows her driver's license, and a poll worker looks up her name on an electronic tablet computer. She learns that she is listed on the voter rolls by her new last name but still listed at her former address. Because her new address is connected to different local races than her former address, she is at the wrong polling location for this election.

John Smith is next in line to vote. He shares a first and last name with more than 44,000 others in the United States; his last and first names are statistically the most common, respectively. John shows his driver's license in order to check in to vote, which is required in his state as a form of voter identification. His license bears his full name, John James Jeremiah Smith, but his signature appears as John JJ Smith in the pollbooks used by the election office.

John is also afraid that the state's new voter identification requirement is a barrier to participation targeted at members of minority groups like him and his family. He remembers family stories from the civil rights years about how hard it was to register, about violent intimidation, and how many people simply did not try to vote. His grandmother has a hard time getting around and does not have a driver's license (nor has she ever). However, she is very invested in voting. She was not able to register in time for this election because she could not get a ride to do so in person. The folks at the election office she called suggested she register online through the state portal, but she does not have a computer or Internet access at home, and could not get to the library to register there. She wonders what kind of documentation she will need in order to register, even if she can find a computer and go online—she was born at home and, in addition to not having a driver's license, does not have a birth certificate.

George Markus and Martha Pendleton

George and Martha are codirectors of their local county's election office, which is led by a bipartisan team appointed by the board of county commissioners. With more than 100,000 registered voters, the county is at the midpoint of election jurisdictions in terms of size. The responsibilities of the office include maintaining lists of registered voters and coordinating these data with the state's electronic database. George oversees the integration of voter registration data coming in to the local election office, which collects data from the county's bureau of vital statistics, the federal and state criminal justice system, the US Postal Service, and county agencies that issue driver's licenses and provide public services to people with disabilities. Martha oversees voter outreach programs that help voters know where to vote, and she oversees the training program for poll workers who use the voter registration lists on Election Day. Martha's training program addresses what to do when prospective voters' names do not appear on the precinct list, and the many reasons that eligible voters appear in the wrong voting location. This training also directs poll workers in the steps to take when responding to voters such as Maya and John. George and Martha have spent the last year meeting with vendors, other local election officials, and with representatives from the state election office to develop proposals to adopt electronic pollbooks and online voter registration; these proposals are now pending before the state legislature.

Claire Michaels and Paul Randolph

Claire suffers from anxiety and depression and sometimes finds it difficult to leave her house to do anything, much less take the chance of having to wait in long lines with strangers to vote; voting also seems stressful because Claire has moved frequently and her polling place is typically in an unfamiliar location. Despite these negative factors, she feels passionately about politics and expresses her opinions on social media and through her online communities. She also wants to be a part of the democratic process through voting, but sometimes it is just not possible for her to get to the polls. Across town, Paul has recently bought a new house. He moved from a town about an hour away but still works in his old hometown and commutes there four days a week, working extra-long hours on those days so he can avoid the commute one day a week. Election Day is almost always on a Tuesday in his state, which is one of his workdays; he wishes he could still vote in his old precinct so he could go there from work at lunchtime, but that is against state law. Paul has heard about vote centers in other states, but his state does not have these either. He has yet to transfer his registration to the new county because it is so inconvenient for him to get to the polls at what would be his new precinct.

Jessica Sadie and Anthony Smith

In the same state where Claire and Paul live, Jessica, a local election official, wants to be able to implement voting by mail (VBM), but she is working in a state with traditional precinct-based voting and excuse-based absentee balloting. She has gone to every state association meeting for the last three years and expressed her opinions about this, and although some of the other election officials across the state agree with her, there has been no traction in the state legislature to move to VBM. Her cousin, John JJ Smith, has mentioned his worry about their grandmother and thinks she would be more willing to get involved if she could vote at home. Jessica wants to make this change happen for everyone like her grandmother in the state.

Halfway across the country, Anthony works in a state election office that has been at the forefront of VBM, vote centers, and other election innovations. And though he is proud of the work they have done, he is also deeply concerned that though VBM seems innovative now, it may not in the future. In speaking with young people in his community, he has become concerned that, as people become more technologically sophisticated, they will be less likely to use VBM, and will instead prefer email, social media, and other Web-based applications or apps. Anthony would love to be able to move to Web-based voting. However, the election security threats associated with that are significant, so in the meantime he feels he needs to work to continue the state's VBM efforts while also making it attractive to younger and more technology-savvy voters.

Sylvia Moreno and Jim Smith

In 2016 Sylvia, a newly naturalized US citizen, moved to a new state for a job and was considering whether to register to vote in the upcoming election. Her accent is very strong—she wonders whether the election office will actually allow her to register if she speaks. She wants to have information provided in the Spanish language for registration to ensure that she can follow the instructions properly. She worries that if there is no translator to help her register or when she votes, she will not be able to understand what to do, and she does not know if she is allowed to ask for help, or what will happen if she does. Unbeknownst to her, her new county of residence had just been covered for Spanish heritage language under Section 203 of the Voting Rights Act using US Census estimates; but because they had just been covered under Section 203, these materials were not yet available. At the same time, across the country, Jim, a Native American, was trying to talk with his grandfather about voting. A Navajo speaker at home, Jim worked to convince his grandfather about the importance of his vote, especially because so many of the other elders have been passing away and the voice of his generation is so important. He was finally successful when he told his grandfather that he would be able to vote in his native language instead of English.

David Chen and Mary Bledsoe

At the same time that Sylvia and Jim were attempting to engage in the voting process using languages other than English, and in advance of the 2016 election, David, the election director of a jurisdiction with about 700,000 registered voters, discovered that census estimates added Vietnamese as a new language to its elections. However, these estimates just missed requiring that the jurisdiction include its local Korean local community, which has a sizable population and much activism. As the election director, David wanted to go ahead and provide Korean language services as well, but there was pushback related to what he thought were marginal expenses from part of his elected elections board. Media coverage of the need for, and interest of Koreans in, having language assistance has been intense. Media interest has expanded to cover Polish speakers, who want the same consideration.

In advance of the same election, Mary, the election director of a jurisdiction that had no requirement for language coverage, was meeting with a community group of citizens who were interested in having information translated into Spanish about the upcoming election that would be available for use in community meetings and on radio stations. Through their meeting, she pondered whether and how her staff of three full-time employees could take this on.

Jane Walker and Lamont Jackson

In advance of the 2016 presidential election, Jane was trying to decide if she was going to take the time to go vote. She had heard from one of her friends after church one day that ballots for presidential candidate Donald Trump would not be counted—that even though she voted on a paper ballot, when she put her ballot into the machine, the machine was secretly programmed to not count her ballot. She did not feel like the possibility of a long wait in line with her children would be worth it if her ballot would not be counted anyway, and she knew that Hillary Clinton was just going to win the election. Elsewhere, Lamont, a first-time candidate in a local election, was trying to understand the process of what happens after the ballots are cast. He had heard from a friend that when that friend ran for office, the count was so close that it took weeks to determine the outcome of the election. Are the results reported on television on Election Night not enough? What is a certification period? How will he know if he should ask for a recount? Is it true that provisional ballots are only counted if the election is close? How close is that?

Joe Stevens and Sonia Rios

Some weeks after the election, Joe, an election administrator, was working long hours going through the process of certifying the results from the most recent local election, which was close. One of the candidates was sure that there was a problem at a precinct where voters were more likely to be in support of her, but the result seemed in favor of the rival candidate, Lamont. In addition, the number of ballots cast in that precinct was unusually high. She sent her lawyers to the election office to argue to the board for an investigation, and Joe is waiting on the board's decision so he can complete the certification process. Meanwhile, at the state capital, Sonia, who works in the state election office, is trying to develop an auditing program for the state and is in negotiations with a statistician about a sampling procedure to use for selecting counties and ballots. She feels that moving to a statewide audit will enhance the confidence of her state's voters in their elections and will improve people's trust in government. Although she would prefer that all counties in the state participate in the auditing procedure, it is being mandated by the state office; and because the initial budget is not large enough to support a full census of counties, they have to engage in a sampling procedure.

Micah Bensen

Micah is a college student who spends considerable time on social media, following the threads posted by people he knows on a variety of issues. Since the 2016 presidential election, he has been particularly concerned about election security. Public accounts continue to document that Russians are clearly involved in "influence campaigns" to target the US and destabilize its democracy, and the question he is currently struggling with is "to what extent?" It is possible that many of the memes he saw on Facebook before the election were generated to further the divide in the country and are part of a coordinated disinformation campaign. He has also heard that Russia penetrated some state voter registration systems. He believes, as do many of his friends, that this is far from the whole story. If Russia can hack a statewide voter registration list, surely this means they can change it. And if Russians or other bad actors can do that, this has to mean that they can also get in through a backdoor and access the counting machines in his county as well as in other counties around the country, potentially changing the results of our elections. And he knows that bad actors have been successful in denial-of-service attacks on election websites. This must also mean that they can change the results of the elections at the end of the process and report whatever they want. When he went to vote in the last election, the poll workers signed him in on a tablet. He received a paper ballot, but then it went into a machine for counting. How does he know that his name will be on the tablet next time? How does he know his ballot was actually counted the way he intended? The questions Micah most wants answered now are: What is next? And how does he know that anything he is told is true?

Alan Parker

Alan was excited when he learned that the US Election Assistance Commission was distributing $380 million in remaining HAVA funds released by Congress to the states, primarily for election security. The commission's notice stated that the funds would come to state chief election officers like Alan, and that the funds would need to be spent rather quickly—perhaps as quickly as within the next few years. He sets up a meeting with his senior staff and also with the president of the state association of election officials. He plans to talk with them to determine who should reach out to the state's three different voting system vendors. Local election officials have been very involved through their association in talking with vendors about the next generation of voting systems. Local election officials also have their fingers on the pulse of local emergency management efforts that are deployed in case of a disaster.

With the 2020 presidential election cycle rapidly approaching, Alan's chief election officer's office has a few full-time dedicated information technology staff members, and he may need to call upon the state information technology staff for assistance in order to understand more about what election security needs might look like. He has more questions than answers at this point. How can he determine how secure the state and local systems are? What does that actually mean? How expensive will it be to address these things? Will the remaining HAVA funds be enough? And who will know how to address them? Alan remembers an election association conference session from a few months ago, and he recalls a speaker noting that technology security consultants are out there but may not know much about elections. He thinks that if there are any security consultants who are familiar with elections, they will be swamped with requests for proposals and assessments. He thinks he will need to address at least some of the security issues with in-house staff, and he wonders what skills they will need to possess.

Steve Evans and Mandy Rogers

Steve and Mandy are graduate students enrolled at universities in different states. They meet at a conference, and they discuss their experiences voting in the presidential election in 2016. As they talk, they realize that their experiences at check-in were completely different and the time it took was also different. Mandy had to show her identification; Steve did not. Steve waited in line for check-in for 5 minutes; Mandy waited for 45 minutes. They both registered through the department of motor vehicles when they changed their licenses as part of their moves to their respective new schools, and were curious about why they had such different experiences when they had that in common. Mandy decides this is an incredible area for research. She suspects that the differences in their experiences are related to the fact that she lives in a poor, primarily minority community, and that Steve does not. She suggests that she and Steve work on a new project together to understand both the similarities and differences in their experiences. Both were unaware that there is a significant and growing body of literature on this topic, with scores of researchers trying to understand these similarities and differences as well as their effects at a much more granular level.

Donna DiAngelo

After the most recent election, Donna, an elected county election director, has been asked to provide information to respond to a media request about how much the most recent election cost the taxpayers. She remembers being asked for data about election costs a few years before. She also recalls very clearly that, some months after she provided the information, legislators from her district were up in arms because it had been reported in the newspaper that the cost per voter in her district was twice what it was across the state. The information she had provided was used to rank each of the counties, and those rankings were then made publicly available. It took her months to convince the legislators connected to her county, as well as her voters, that she was not spending money frivolously and that there was no good way to compare costs per vote across the counties. She was sure to this day, despite her best efforts, that many residents did not believe her; because of the negative reactions from voters, she was secretly surprised when she won the last election. Now she has been asked by a research team to provide similar data, and she is concerned that if she does so, it will eventually open her up again to unfair comparisons, criticisms, bad media, and pushback from citizens.

PLAN OF THE BOOK

This book is not a history lesson, but history matters in order to set the stage. The election administration innovations that we see today would not be possible without the institutional architecture laid down decades before, and they are also shaped by those institutions. This book is also not about election mechanics, per se. Fundamentally, however, the operational details that flow through that architecture and that constitute American elections and the work of election administrators are largely absent from public, political, and academic deliberations about what "should" happen. The contemporary state of the judiciary and its interpretations of these different approaches is also a critical component. It is only through the details that the innovative nature of the work of public servants in this field can be revealed.

We begin our discussion by situating American election administration in its political environment and the intergovernmental system of regulatory and judicial constraints. Chapter 1 looks at the critical requirements of the federal system's intergovernmental architecture that has evolved over more than half a century. This architecture is constructed by the VRA, NVRA, and HAVA, which together define how Americans register to vote. An intricate intergovernmental network of public offices within elections proper interacts with the US Postal Service and other private organizations that support state and local data management efforts to create and maintain accurate voter registration lists.

Our ideas about how innovation occurs in complex systems are grounded in a theory of change that we apply to the election administration system. This theory is presented in chapter 2. It casts innovation in election administration systems as interactions through cooperation, collaboration, and governance arrangements that are characterized by complexity and interdependence and are constrained by requirements for public and political accountability.

Voter registration is the first step in American elections. Chapter 3 examines voter registration in the modern era and how it has been shaped by federal legal requirements and evolving innovations, including online voter registration, automatic voter registration, and the use of technology to gather and manage large data sets.

Chapter 4 presents the story of how voting by mail, the most common alternative to in-person Election Day voting, has evolved. Voting by mail has served as a springboard for other methods of convenience voting, and it has also become a more nuanced method of election administration in many jurisdictions.

Chapter 5 illustrates the role of collaboration in developing similar approaches for working with voters who do not speak English well. Each jurisdiction has a unique complement of voters; however, the challenges of finding voters who need assistance, providing accurate assistance, and forecasting when and how language assistance will be required are similar across the country. There are strong similarities in the solutions and approaches that have been successful.

Chapter 6 addresses innovations implemented in evaluating election processes. One focus is on the nationwide requirement for provisional ballots that are cast on Election Day and counted separately from other ballots. The chapter also examines the emerging role of election audit practices.

Chapter 7 focuses on how election jurisdictions are addressing the challenges of voting system technology, including the adoption of a common data format, online voting, the development of new voting systems, and strategies to address cybersecurity issues.

Chapter 8 chronicles the efforts of various government agencies and nonprofit groups to conceptualize and measure the success of election performance. It presents various approaches to measuring success, and it discusses their benefits and drawbacks. Two case studies are presented that illustrate efforts to build upon extant approaches and the questions that arise in exploratory research. We conclude by exploring the enduring relationships between organizations in the election administration environment, the current role of partisanship, and the questions raised by considering professionalization and innovation in tandem.

In any research project, choices are made about what to focus on, and what to set aside for another day. The innovations that we consider cover a wide span, and are representative of the most innovative practices in the field. The cases and topics reflect a range and depth of methods for meeting the needs of voters for access and participation while also addressing the challenges of interoffice requirements, massive data sets and data transfer, old and new technology, and threats posed by bad actors. Some aspects of election administration are evolving rapidly, and the issues and solutions presented here can only represent a slice in time. Technology continues to advance, as election offices all across the country are poised to acquire new voting systems. Judicial decisions episodically alter the landscape. Executive branch determinations also have effects; for example, the institutional infrastructure for election security did not exist at all until 2018. The challenges to public administration principles of accountability are apparent—who is actually responsible for an output or outcome, and who has the authority to get the job done? The way that we think about measuring success in public programs is critical, and yet it is elusive in the election administration arena.

The methods we used to collect data for this book also include a wide array of original and secondary sources, which we detail in appendix C. In short, over several years, we observed elections and non–Election Day administrative functions through site visits, we interviewed officials from various counties and state and federal offices, we read both formal and informal reports on reform, we perused proposed legislation and court rulings, and we collected existing data from a variety of sources and quantified them. From all these, we developed a mixed-method analysis of the drivers of innovation in US election administration. We use this collection of methods to weave a detailed story of how innovation arises in election administration in the US context, and to analyze how the different facets important to innovation work.

Innovation is a function of politics, professionalism, resources, and need, and nowhere is this clearer than in US elections. The complex interplay of factors that make change happen in one place but not in another is challenging to model. Our purpose here is to examine an array of areas in election administration where innovation has emerged (or not), with the aim of process improvement, and to examine why, in order to add to the conversation about how elections should be administered.

NOTE

1. Throughout we refer to professionalism to indicate a condition or state of being, and refer to professionalization as a process of achieving professionalism and perhaps other goals.

1

The Federal System and Politics: How the US Intergovernmental Architecture Shapes the Ways We Vote

The 2016 US presidential election mobilized 142 million registered voters, thousands of election jurisdictions, tens of thousands of polling places, hundreds of thousands of voting machines, and millions of poll workers. Nearly 40 million people voted at a polling place on Election Day, using one of more than 500,000 electronic voting machines of various types. Across the country, nearly 300,000 machines scanned paper ballots, and more than 200,000 machines presented ballots on a touch screen for voters to make their selections. Roughly 100 million people cast their ballots early or by mail. Voters were citizens of all races, colors, and genders. They were citizens by birth, or had become naturalized after migrating from around the world. Some had experienced periods of incarceration, some could speak English, and some could not.

Contrast this with the elections held two hundred years ago. In 1816, the eighth presidential election was held over thirty-four days, from Friday, November 1, through Wednesday, December 4. James Monroe, a Democratic Republican, was declared the winner with 183 electoral votes, over Rufus King, a Federalist, who had 34 electoral votes. The popular vote was not yet tracked uniformly across states as a method of choosing presidential electors; however, the estimate is that roughly 80,000 ballots were cast. Voters in nineteen states around the country used paper ballots that they created themselves, or voted viva voce, declaring their candidate preferences out loud and in public.[1] No government election office created ballots or provided equipment. Votes were neither from women nor people of color. Across the states, various requirements were imposed on white men in order to exercise the franchise, including land ownership, residence, and religious allegiance, among others.

Fast forward one hundred years to the presidential election of 1916. A popular vote total of slightly more than 18.5 million was reported, and Woodrow Wilson, a Democrat, won with 277 electoral votes over Charles Hughes, Republican, who had 254 electoral votes. Punch card machines and mechanical lever machines were used in many locations; the first of these had been introduced just before the turn of the century. By 1896, thirty-nine of the forty-five states used secret ballots printed by local governments, reflecting the adoption of the Australian ballot format. The proportion of the population going to the polls had also increased, as the rules for ballot access had also changed over time. The ratification of the Fifteenth Amendment to the Constitution in 1870 permitted males to vote without regard to race, color, or previous condition of servitude; in practice, many states effectively excluded nonwhites from voting for nearly the next 100 years. In 1916, women were partially enfranchised; some women could vote in some elections, and these rights were most expansive in states that began as Western territories (e.g., Colorado, Utah, Washington, and Wyoming), although the Nineteenth Amendment was not yet a reality (Keyssar 2000).

More than a hundred years later, elections have changed even more. The franchise has expanded to include most all citizens age eighteen years and older. Voting today involves complex electronic equipment for registering to vote, for casting and counting ballots, and for transmitting results. Ballots are cast by various methods, including by mail, on days before Election Day and on Election Day, and in traditional polling places or vote centers. Voters register in person at election offices, at a host of other venues, or online.

What began as a somewhat simplistic and individualized event using pebbles, voices, or raised hands has evolved into a significant administrative apparatus. Election administration today means designing and implementing new methods of voter registration and casting ballots and using new techniques to monitor results and ensure transparency. Election officials implement new methods of voting, address cybersecurity concerns, and make it possible to vote in languages other than English. They verify voter eligibility and resolve issues raised by incomplete or contestable identification. Across all these operations, election administrators seek indicators of election success that demonstrate operational accuracy, security, and transparency— regardless of how many voters decide to vote and in which manner.

Approaches to implementing election administration activities are shaped by the American federal system and the intergovernmental environment; they are also prompted and accompanied by shifts in political winds, changes in voter perceptions and needs, and resource levels. Universally, technological change is a cross-cutting force. Local election offices carry the weight of election operations and related administration. State election offices have gained authority in recent decades, as major policy decisions about methods of conducting elections are made by state legislators. The role of federal agencies in elections is largely advisory; significant regulatory authority rests only with the US Department of Justice (DOJ) to enforce the federal requirements for voter access and participation. Federal courts serve as a backstop on equal protection issues but have not overturned many recent state political decisions that define election practices. Among these are the requirements for various methods of identification, including government-issued photo identification, the requirement for additional proof of citizenship in voter registration, and hyperpartisan state redistricting configurations (i.e., partisan gerrymandering) that effectively limit the influence of voters in one political party or the other.

In the American intergovernmental system, the administrative dynamics are characteristically interactive and collaborative, and reflect significant interactions with the private sector and with government offices that are not devoted to election operations. Many organizational relationships are voluntary, and through these, election officials can seek resources and technical support. Local election officials have considerable latitude to experiment to address local conditions, although they often lack resources and may, in some cases, lack policy authority.

To set the stage for understanding innovation, this chapter introduces the institutional context of election administration, including considerations of the federal system, intergovernmental relationships, and major political developments. Innovation in public service occurs within a changing environment that reflects shifts in politics, organizational arrangements, rules, technology, and public opinion.

ELECTIONS AND THE AMERICAN FEDERAL SYSTEM

The American election administration environment is perhaps the most intractably complex policy environment in which public managers operate. This complexity stems from the constitutional imperatives that invest authority for aspects of elections in both the national government and the states. It also stems from the evolution of election administration as a matter that has been left to local governments for much of the country's history. Moreover, not least because elections are the way we measure democracy and are a key element of the American political system, the institutional architecture of election administration also reflects the geography of American politics.

The federal system of American election administration is embedded in the country's origins. The American federal system matters particularly in the case of election administration because of the constitutional imperatives that establish institutions at the national level and in the states. Political institutions, in turn, define the boundaries of political participation. The American history of participation is deeply rooted in race and citizenship in at least three dimensions. First, our governing documents at both the national and state levels define who can participate and in what ways. The franchise has always been a limited concept; and though it has expanded over time, its expansion has been episodic and fraught with controversy within states and between the states and the national government about who should be eligible to vote, and who has the authority to make this decision.

Second, our national and state institutions prescribe what we need to do in order to participate. In the past, for example, some of us were asked to pay a poll tax or pass a test, each made illegal by a variety of court decisions and the Voting Rights Act of 1965. Since the 2000 election, more and more of us are being required to possess particular forms of identification, including government-issued photo identification and proof of citizenship.

Third, our institutions have typically tied our participation to where we live. Historically, voting based on geography has allowed patterns of exclusion and inclusion to be reinforced within political institutions. This can mean that votes cast in some places matter more than those cast in others. This can also mean that methods making it more convenient to vote may or may not be available, depending on geography.

These same governing documents also prescribe which levels of government can make decisions about participation. Election administration evolved from local practices that became codified at the state level over time. The national judiciary has allowed state practices to hold sway for long periods, as the chronology given in table 1.1 illustrates. Federal action has occurred only rarely, although in rather sweeping ways. These federal actions have also been answered by new challenges from the states. Across time, the pendulum of federal intervention has swung between deference to states' political cultures—which tended to restrict the franchise, first to white male citizens and over time to all citizens—and waves of national social, political, and cultural change accompanied by shifts in public opinion and legislation in support of efforts to act on a national sense of equality and equity.

The original construction of the franchise promoted states' independence in determining voter qualifications; by and large, those entitled to vote were white, male landowners, and in some states they were also members of particular churches not associated with immigrant groups. State practices strained the Union to the point of secession and were answered, after the Civil War, with constitutional amendments that abolished slavery, established a measure of equal protection and due process for citizens, and established the franchise for black men regardless of race, color, or former slave status (previous conditions of servitude). National civil rights legislation was passed in the 1870s, but states continued to develop institutional practices that denied

TABLE 1.1 Major National Political Events Shaping the Modern Election Administration Environment

Year	Event
1791	Tenth Amendment reserved powers to states and the people
1819	National government has broad national powers over states (*McCulloch v. Maryland*)
1857	State slavery policies cannot be overturned by national government (*Scott v. Sanford*)
1861	Southern states formed Confederacy
1865	Slavery is abolished (Thirteenth Amendment)
1866	First federal civil rights bill is vetoed
1868	Federal civil rights are established for US citizens, including equal protection and due process (Fourteenth Amendment)
1870	States cannot use race, color, or slave status in qualifying voters (Fifteenth Amendment)
1875	Civil Rights Act protects against private discrimination
1883	Civil Rights Act of 1875 is invalidated (the Civil Rights Cases)
1896	Racial segregation upheld as "separate but equal" (*Plessy v. Ferguson*)
1913	US senators must be directly elected by popular vote (Seventeenth Amendment)
1920	Women now able to vote in all elections (Nineteenth Amendment)
1944	White-only primaries are declared illegal (*Smith v. Allright*)
1954	Segregated public schools are inherently unequal (*Brown v. Board of Education*)
1957	Civil Rights Act of 1957 created Civil Rights Commission
1962	Equal protection standards for state apportionment are established (*Baker v. Carr*)
1964	Poll taxes prohibited as qualification for federal elections (Twenty-Fourth Amendment); "one person, one vote" (*Reynolds v. Sims*); Civil Rights Act of 1964 prohibited discrimination based on race, color, religion, or national origin
1965	Voting Rights Act (VRA) of 1965 prohibited discrimination in registration and election practices, created federal oversight for specific jurisdictions
1966	Voting Rights Act upheld (*South Carolina v. Katzenbach*)
1970	Literacy and good character tests banned by VRA authorization, federal oversight continued
1971	Minimum voting age established as 18 for all elections (Twenty-Sixth Amendment)
1975	Minority language assistance required and federal oversight continued under VRA reauthorizations
1980	Intent to discriminate required to demonstrate VRA violation (*Mobile v. Bolden*)
1982	VRA reauthorization requires voting assistance for voters with disabilities, continued federal oversight and overrules *Mobile v. Bolden*

(continued)

TABLE 1.1 (*continued*)

Year	Event
1984	Access to polling places for voters age 60 and over and voters with disabilities required under the Voting Accessibility for the Elderly and Handicapped Act
1986	States required to accept absentee registration and voting for military and overseas citizens established by the Uniformed and Overseas Citizens Absentee Voting Act of 1986
1993	Racial gerrymandering prohibited (*Shaw v. Reno*); the National Voter Registration Act establishes voter registration applications at motor vehicle offices and other public service offices and establishes the position of state chief executive officer

these rights to racial and ethnic minorities, and these rights were eventually limited to protections only from national action.

It would be nearly a hundred years until national power was exerted to address state discrimination in voting. In the 1950s, the US Supreme Court order to desegregate public education (*Brown v. Board of Education*, 1954) paved the way for new federal involvement in voting rights. The Civil Rights Act of 1957 was signed into law by President Dwight D. Eisenhower as the first significant federal legislative action since Reconstruction. This act established the Civil Rights Division in the US Department of Justice and the US Commission on Civil Rights (USCCR) as critical administrative components of the federal government's involvement in election operations. The purpose of the USCCR was to investigate abuses that deprived citizens of the right to vote due to race, color, religion, or national origin.

The 1957 bill was diluted in response to political pressure from Southern states advocating state supremacy on voting questions, but the administrative institutions it established were nevertheless elemental in moving the voting rights issue forward on the national agenda. The USCCR and equivalent state commissions formed in many states held hearings to collect data about voter experiences, which in turn established evidence of state discrimination in voting. The USCCR's efforts were pivotal in providing support for the civil rights movement in general and for registering (or trying to register) voters in Southern states. It forged critical ground in documenting voting rights and other acts of discrimination that fostered the Civil Rights Act of 1964 (CRA) and the Voting Rights Act of 1965 (VRA). The testimony taken in USCCR hearings provided support for the CRA and for the VRA and all its subsequent reauthorizations. The VRA's requirements to preserve voting records, for example, responded directly to state-approved destruction of voting records. Most sweeping of all, the VRA established federal oversight for states and local jurisdictions with a history of discrimination. The DOJ's

Civil Rights Division would become the cornerstone of federal enforcement of the VRA.

It would nearly fifty years before states were able to remove this federal oversight, but in 2013 the case was successfully made in *Shelby County v. Holder* that it was inappropriate that all states did not have the same degree of independence in establishing voting practices on the basis of data and evidence that was nearly half a century old. States quickly used their newly restored power to implement policies that had been held at bay by federal oversight. Also, recent judicial decisions suggest that the states remain quite powerful in their ability to establish methods of voter identification, including photo identification and documentary proof of citizenship (although the latter only in nonfederal elections).

Recent decisions also indicate that states remain the arbiters of redistricting practices. In *Rucho v. Common Cause* (2019), the Supreme Court determined that partisan gerrymandering was a political matter for the states to resolve. The political remedy is for voters who do not agree with the redistricting decisions of current legislatures to vote in new representation; this option, however, remains constrained by the legislative district maps drawn under hyperpartisan conditions on both sides of the aisle. A political divide exacerbates the effects of districting processes; concentrations of voters with similar views have created landslide districts in at least two-thirds of the country, in which the winner prevails by a large and seemingly unshakeable margin (e.g., more than 20 percent). Relatedly, the method by which people are counted for purposes of districting has also come under attack. An initiative by the US Department of Commerce under the Trump administration to include a question about citizenship status in the 2020 US Census was turned back by the Supreme Court with a decision stating that the information provided by the agency in support of the need to add the question (to identify voting rights violations) was disingenuous (*Department of Commerce v. New York*, 2019).

The study of innovation in election administration also reflects on the distribution of power in the American federal system. As much as the federal system itself has been shaped by political views about racial equality and immigration, these views continue to shape election administration policy. Lieberman (1998) makes the case that the distribution of power in the federal system bends to accommodate political will. In studying social welfare policies, he argues that different strains of national policy were crafted to accommodate state interests intertwined with race and class. As in other policy areas, election administration issues engage tensions between national and state authority, and between tendencies to include or exclude.

Theories of the federal system of government suggest that the absence of national policy controls can produce individualized state responses, which are driven by unique political and cultural dispositions. Since the advent of devolution in the 1970s, research also argues that local control can lead to broader information seeking and sharing, because administrators and policymakers seek information beyond state borders and from national funding sources (e.g., Lieberman and Shaw 2000). The election administration field, barring candidate filing and finances, is not nationally regulated, except through the DOJ in the enforcement of federal election laws. Policy controls flow from judicial decisions as much as anything.

The interaction of these governing arrangements and political economy makes elections different than other policy areas. In most other policy areas where we saw expansions of national control and authority during the twentieth century, state authority rests simply on the Tenth Amendment, which provides that power not explicitly regulated by the national government is left to the states and to the people. Congress expanded the national role in areas such as welfare, education, and health (among others) rather significantly through the Elastic and the Commerce clauses of the Constitution, with significant expansions during the 1930s after the Great Depression and then again during the Great Society programs. Expansions in national control in these policy areas occurred because local and state governments lacked either the will or capacity or both to step in to help people who were struggling, and the national government was willing to provide resources to address state and local conditions, often tying the receipt of federal funding to the establishment of particular policies or practices.

Election policy and election administration are different. National control of policy and practice has not expanded in election administration in the way that we have seen the national presence expand in other, administrative areas. Through states, localities have remained powerful actors since the nation's founding, with constitutional authority flowing both from the US Constitution and from their own state governing documents. National election administration infrastructure remains essentially nascent in comparison with other policy arenas, although the US Constitution establishes a small platform for national action. National authority has been exercised primarily through the judiciary and the DOJ's enforcement actions rather than through an administrative bureaucracy and funding streams, though the national presence began to expand with the designation of elections as critical infrastructure in 2016.

The innovations explored in this book exhibit tendencies to both centralize in response to national conditions (e.g., cybersecurity) as well as to decentralize to reflect state conditions and norms (e.g., voter identification rules). We explore the "why" throughout. In both cases, the balance of power between and among the levels of government in various areas helps to explain many of the conditions that either encourage or discourage innovation. But these institutional arrangements only explain part of the story.

INTERGOVERNMENTAL RELATIONSHIPS

A defining characteristic of intergovernmental relationships in the American federal system is the national government's limited ability to control subnational governments. Election administration policy is not a matter of simply having the federal government tell states and localities what to do—constitutional imperatives structure this differently. Each of the three layers of US government—local, state, and national—plays important roles in the complex dynamics that govern and conduct US elections. Figure 1.1 illustrates these layers of government, along with other influences from the media, third-party groups, vendors, and other governments. The federal system of American election administration is shaped by divided national constitutional authority for elections vested primarily in the states, strong state policy influence, limited federal administrative oversight, and strong judicial influence.

Today, at the subnational level, the second-order federal system of election administration is characterized by historically strong local administration and rising state authority. The US Election Assistance Commission is the lead agency, and it is supported by the DOJ, the Department of Defense, and, most recently, the Department of Homeland Security (DHS). At the state level, legislatures promulgate rules and policies, which

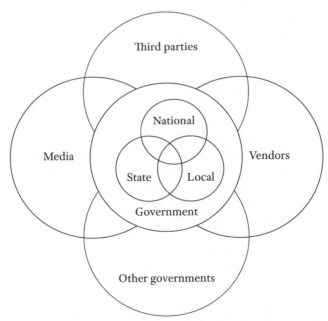

FIGURE 1.1 The American Federal System of Election Administration

are then implemented by state chief election officials (CEOs). Many state CEOs serve as secretaries of state (SOS), and most are elected to office. At the local level, local election officials are responsible for implementation, and county commissioners are the most common source of funding—and, in some cases, are responsible for creating the political geography of districts and precincts.

However, limiting the focus to government agencies truncates our understanding of the nuances necessary to truly appreciate the complexity and points of vulnerability in American election administration. The US political system is characterized by pluralism, which fuels advocacy and interest groups and private foundations, and by an intrinsic private-sector role, which is fueled by devolution. Election administration sits in the center of local, state, and federal mandates, subject to the influence of state legislatures and state professional associations, interacting with election technology provided by vendors and commercial components, and fielding initiatives and pressures driven by advocacy groups and foundations. Increasingly, its functions and outputs are subject to intense analysis and media scrutiny, either or both of which may (or may not) portray system elements or issues accurately. This increased visibility and attendant interactions add to the complex array of actors that influence the design and delivery of this public service.

Figure 1.1 provides a holistic illustration of the current election administration environment, and the actors that interact to foster or frustrate innovative efforts of election administrators. These arrangements are depicted as a collection of interlocking and overlapping circles, which demonstrates the systems approach to mapping election administration in the United States (Hale and Brown 2016; Hale, Montjoy, and Brown 2015). The locally driven, decentralized, and sometimes fragmented nature of the environment is compounded by myriad relationships with both nonprofit and for-profit organizations that have become essential to the conduct of elections, as well as the forces of media and other governments. Each of these components structures the activity of election administrators and affects their ability to respond within the American political system.

Collectively, these actors constitute a system. Here, we work with a straightforward definition: "A system is a set of separate but related elements that form a whole. A systems approach to election administration seeks to examine a *whole* system and the *relationships* among its parts (subsystems). The parts are important because all are necessary, and a change in one can affect the performance of others" (Hale, Montjoy, and Brown 2015, xxiii; emphasis in the original).

The interactions among the elements of these subsystems and systems are influenced by laws, authority, traditions, and relationships. Historically, election administration has been primarily the purview of local governments, subject to policymaking authority at the state level. Guided by themes of equity, citizens' rights, equal protection, and integrity, the national government plays an evolving and growing role in all aspects of US elections. Tension between system components is clearly articulated in the study of innovation; pressures and issues generated in one part of the system lead to solutions and responses in other parts.

In the subsections that follow, we set forth the major components of the governmental roles in election administration today and identify the roles of other actors outside government that are essential to understanding the election administration system and to setting the stage for our study of innovation. Intergovernmental relationships are fundamental to the election administration environment. We begin with the local election office because this is where voters meet the administrators of elections.

Local Governments

Local governments run elections—all types of elections, from national presidential elections to elections to select federal and state representatives to local elections for county council, school board, and in some cases even coroner. American elections have always been highly localized and decentralized: this localization predates the states themselves (Ewald 2009; Keyssar 2000). Across the United States, there are roughly 8,000 local election jurisdictions.[2] Usually, the unit of local government involved in election administration is the county, though this varies and includes parishes (i.e., county-equivalent jurisdictions in Louisiana), townships, and combined cities/counties, among others. In some localities, a stand-alone office is in charge of elections. In others, one office runs elections as well as other functions of government. In still others, more than one local office is responsible for different components of an election. Election officials are chosen according to the laws of their states, and they are most commonly selected by election. Local offices can be responsible for voter registration only, for election administration only, for both, or for one or both, along with other functions of local government such as licensing and permitting. No census has been taken of these local variations; Hale, Montjoy, and Brown (2015) present the foundational framework that identifies fundamental dimensions of variation.

Across all types of institutional configurations, however, there are some common functions. Before an election, local governments are engaged in registering voters, informing voters about upcoming elections and where and how to vote, identifying and training poll officials and workers, identifying and securing polling locations for nonmail ballot localities, designing and printing ballots, and obtaining and ensuring the functionality of voting technology. For some period leading up to Election Day, local governments provide ballots to, receive ballots from, and begin to count ballots marked by eligible voters. After an election, these same offices audit and certify the election results, and conduct recounts when necessary. Even within states, there is variation in the offices that are involved, the roles people play, and the equipment that is used.

Local election practices are tied to political geography—including counties, cities, and other substate jurisdictions, such as legislative districts, school districts, and other special purpose districts established for various services, including water and sewer delivery, and in some cases the arts and environmental concerns. The influence of political geography significantly expands the complexity of the election administration environment and the range of considerations that run throughout the innovation network.

Historically, local offices have conducted elections based on sublocal geographic units that are politically constructed and are most commonly known as precincts. Precincts are established for the purpose of casting ballots and either stand alone or in combination with one or more other precincts; voters are assigned to precincts based on their home address. Depending on state election law requirements, precincts stand alone, are combined with other precincts, or in some cases are combined with all other precincts into vote centers. Precincts may also be divided to accommodate different arrays of special districts, including taxing districts and school systems.

For each election, unique combinations of candidate races, issues, voting locations, and state ballot propositions (i.e., referenda or initiatives) represent unique ballot styles.[3] Each ballot style reflects the choices about candidates and issues that voters can make, depending on where they live. Ballot styles are unique to each election. Each ballot style appears in English, and it may also appear in one or more other languages, depending on local, state, and federal legal requirements. Figure 1.2 illustrates the generic architecture of the political geography that is embedded in elections at the local level: a local election system.

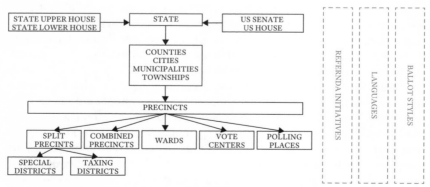

FIGURE 1.2 Subnational Election Administration Systems

State Governments

The state role in election administration can take several forms. State authority to determine the time, manner, and place of nonfederal elections is entrenched in the US Constitution, which vests authority in the states to determine the time, manner, and place of all nonfederal elections.[4] State legislatures are the source of most election policy, including politically divisive requirements for stringent methods of voter identification—such as proof of citizenship on one hand—and alternative methods of voting such as vote centers, vote-by-mail, and periods of early voting on the other hand. In most states, legislatures are also highly engaged in creating and redistricting state and federal election districts. State policy establishes the context for local operations, including the methods for conducting elections and the requirements for participation, as well as requirements for presenting results.

State policy also affects local practice by defining the structure and functions of state and local election offices, and by determining how key administrators will be selected. Each state has a designated CEO; however, the position responsible for performing this role varies across the states as a matter of state public policy, as does the method of selection (elected or appointed) (Kimball and Kropf 2006). In most states, the CEO is the SOS, and most of these are chosen by election. States vary widely on a number of dimensions, including the number of offices that work together to run elections (from one to five), whether these offices are administrative only or political, whether the leaders of the office are appointed or elected, and if appointed, whether the state plays a role in those appointments. State CEOs exercise different degrees of control over local election operations. State administrative centralization varies (Alvarez and Hall 2008), and the state role has expanded as a result of the Help America Vote Act (HAVA) (Montjoy 2008). Today, state administrative responsibilities focus primarily on statewide electronic voter registration databases, purchasing decisions, and, in some cases, election security.

The Federal Government

The federal government's role in election administration is also circumscribed by the US Constitution, which sets up a two-part authority structure under which responsibility rests first and foremost with state legislatures. The Constitution is, however, the source of sweeping principles that have expanded voter participation and have protected it in the face of discriminatory state policy decisions. In addition to the requirements about the Electoral College, the amendments to the Constitution address issues of voter access, notably by categories of race (Fifteenth Amendment), gender (Nineteenth Amendment), class (Twenty-Fourth Amendment, barring the poll tax), and age

(Twenty-Sixth Amendment). The Constitution also now limits the power of state legislators to choose US senators (Seventeenth Amendment).

The earliest systematic studies of US election administration showed the systems and subsystems to be inherently heterogeneous from their inception, evolving from path-dependent processes that were tied in many places to culture related to either colonization or the expansion and creation of new states (Harris 1928, 1934; Keyssar 2000). In some places, these differences were also related to the denial of suffrage rights of citizens. As a result of these differences, the federal government began taking a closer look at election practices through various civil rights commissions, which led, ultimately, to legislation. Beginning in 1965, with the Voting Rights Act, the federal role evolved in two powerful directions that affected modern operating practices but did not prescribe them. Through Congress, laws were passed to protect voting rights to access and participation and to prohibit discriminatory infringements by state and local officials. Through the federal courts, lines of authority and the boundaries of equitable treatment were interpreted and refined.

Under the Voting Rights Act of 1965 and its subsequent reauthorizations, federal intervention was targeted at political jurisdictions with low African American registration and voting rates through a process known as federal preclearance. In this, prior federal review and approval were required in order for covered jurisdictions (counties or whole states) to make changes in election law or practice. This continued for nearly half a century, until the Supreme Court's 2013 ruling in *Shelby County v. Holder* declared the approach unconstitutional. The VRA further expanded access by creating express provisions and protections for language minorities, voters with disabilities, and other groups facing discrimination related to voting.

Federal legislation has also defined the role of states and has expanded this role incrementally. States have always had a role in election administration, and individual states' focus on election policy has waxed and waned with certain issues; however, a more systematic role for states was nationally defined by the passage of the National Voter Registration Act (NVRA) in 1993. In particular, the NVRA required that states identify a CEO for reporting, transparency, and accountability. Although this had little or no effect in states with centralized election administration systems, in states with decentralized election administration structures the NVRA shifted authority and made some offices, usually the Office of the Secretary of State, more powerful, at least as it pertained to election administration. The NVRA also required motor vehicle and human service agencies to provide opportunities for voter registration, with the hope of expanding citizen access to voting. Importantly, the NVRA also required state registration list maintenance for federal elections, and left implementation to the states.

After the 2000 election, which called attention to voting equipment problems, HAVA was passed in 2002 with the purpose of modernizing voter registration processes and equipment, mandating statewide centralized electronic voter files, establishing standards for election administration, and establishing the US Election Assistance Commission (EAC). The voting equipment and software standards established through the EAC's Voluntary Voting System Guidelines had the effect of limiting the number of businesses and inventors interested in developing election equipment to just a few who could financially weather the certification process (for more discussion, see Hale and Brown 2013). Finally, the other major role developed at the federal level comes through the Uniformed and Overseas Citizen Absentee Voting Act, and later the 2009 Military and Overseas Voter Empowerment (known as MOVE) Act, both of which expanded earlier efforts, such as the 1942 Soldiers Voting Act, to ensure that members of the armed forces and other citizens living abroad have access to voter registration and voting.

The federal administrative role has expanded recently with respect to election cybersecurity. Through an executive branch decision made in 2016 and reaffirmed in 2017, election systems are now considered one of twenty-one sectors of the United States' "critical infrastructure"; this designation recognizes vital assets that, if incapacitated or destroyed, would have a significantly deleterious effect on the nation's security, economy, or public health or safety.[5] To foster cross-functional and cross-jurisdictional communication and information sharing, analysis centers have been established for critical infrastructure subsectors; these now include the election administration infrastructure. The interactions with election jurisdictions are voluntary, and the federal role is advisory. How this expanded national role will affect the intergovernmental balance in the election environment remains to be seen.

This array of federal agencies may suggest that the federal government is intricately involved in the administration of elections, but that is not the case. The EAC, established in 2002 under HAVA, is the lead agency on election administration issues; however, its role is purely advisory and does not include regulatory authority. The EAC's role is limited primarily to information clearinghouse functions and grant administration. The information clearinghouse function was originally housed in the Federal Election Commission; today, that commission focuses on campaign finance issues. The EAC built its clearinghouse role around a new national survey of election administration practices known as the Election Administration and Voting Survey, and an extensive library of research reports and analyses. Grantmaking has been somewhat limited. The EAC administered funds ($3.8 billion) allocated by Congress to aid the states in making the transition to electronic voting systems; states have largely spent these funds, although a small allocation ($380 million) that was released by Congress in 2018 to address election security planning has not been spent. When possible, the EAC made grant funds available for research on a variety of administrative topics, including ways to improve access for voters with disabilities and practical differences between conditions facing urban and rural voters, and how to understand the included topics.

The DOJ enforces major federal election laws that protect access to registration and voting. These include the VRA, NVRA, and HAVA, as well as the Americans with Disabilities Act and the Uniformed and Overseas Citizens Absentee Voting Act. From 1965 until 2013, VRA enforcement also included prior federal review and approval of state and local election practices in some locations; this review was declared unconstitutional in 2013 and discontinued. The Department of Defense administers voting practices for military and overseas citizens. Most recently, DHS has assumed a role in providing information and technical assistance to election offices on election security matters; this role is also advisory.

Vendors

The intergovernmental configuration of election administration responsibility has created significant space for nongovernmental actors, including vendors. The role of vendors in election systems has not been the subject of systematic research (Hale and Brown 2013) and has not been explored in the context of election innovation. Indeed, the first national study of election equipment as an industry was not published until 2016 (Hitt et al. 2016). The contribution of vendors to the work of public managers and to innovation in elections is nonetheless critical. Vendors of election equipment and voting systems contract with local election offices and state jurisdictions to provide essential elements of the election system.[6] Some vendors provide end-to-end hardware, software, and technical support that encompasses the election process, from voter registration through ballot counts; others provide equipment, software, supplies, and training for specific purposes.

Vendors touch every aspect of election systems across all election jurisdictions. Vendors provide forms, hardware, and software for voter registration and for local and statewide electronic voter registration databases. In some jurisdictions, vendors may be significantly involved in reconciling data inconsistencies, such as voter registration information that arrives from multiple sources. Vendors design and print ballots in some cases, and they distribute ballots in some states that conduct elections by mail for all or some voters. Vendors print pollbooks and provide hardware and software used to sign voters in at poll sites. Vendors also provide hardware and software for casting ballots, counting ballots, tracking activity, certification, and auditing. Vendors support their products and services by providing maintenance and training. Additionally, in some areas vendors provide people to operate voting equipment at particular points in the process; as a consequence, these people become part of the election administration workforce. It is particularly important to note in the current environment that vendors are central to election security—in the design of their products, in their certifications, in the information that they make available, and in the support they provide to election administrators.

Advocacy and Nonprofit Groups

The American political system is pluralist in nature. For the public managers of elections, this means that the election policy process is influenced not only by politicians but also by organized interests that band together when properly motivated to push for change (Dahl 1961). Often, this happens through organized interest or nonprofit groups.

The roles of nonprofit groups in elections vary. The earliest efforts began during the late 1800s to promote election reforms and the women's suffrage movement. After the passage of the Nineteenth Amendment, which institutionalized women's right to vote, the primary nonprofit group advocating for women's suffrage turned to encouraging turnout through the newly formed League of Women Voters. This group and other organizations, most notably the National Association for the Advancement of Colored People, were important in expanding the participation of underrepresented and persecuted groups during the civil rights movement and were critical to the passage of the VRA (Hamilton 1977). Since the passage of the VRA, third-party groups have played a significant role in voter registration, outreach efforts, and "get out the vote" activities (e.g., Stevens and Bishin 2011). Third-party groups became national news again during the presidential election in 2008, with the subsequent *Citizens United v. Federal Election Commission* (2010) Supreme Court ruling that has effectively removed limitations on campaign finance contributions from corporations.

In the election administration arena, these entities include identity groups, professional associations, philanthropic research organizations, and academic institutions. Organizations engage in a wide range of activities associated with the nonprofit sector—including education, training, and outreach for the general public and for members—and also participate in issue advocacy.[7] Identity groups are most commonly associated with advocacy activities. They exist to advance opportunities for access, to champion fair treatment, and to serve as watchdogs. Professional associations are commonly linked with professional development activities for members, including training and outreach. Philanthropic organizations fund research and other activities in pursuit of particular normative objectives defined by the funders, and in some cases establish internal programs to conduct this work. Academic institutions house education programs and research centers or institutes, in addition to the research efforts of individual faculty.

In our work with election officials, we asked a variety of them about the roles that these groups play in local election administration.[8] The most common roles reported to us include advocating for electoral integrity, protecting

and promoting the rights of underrepresented groups, and advancing particular political parties or issues. Most election administrators noted that the
main purpose of such groups is public education, followed by reaching out
to voters and assisting voters in registration. The problems that these groups
create for local election administration revolve around the approaches that
these groups take regarding both voter registration and voter participation.
In terms of voter registration, third-party advocacy groups can create problems by submitting incomplete registration forms, providing incorrect information, not following deadlines and other rules, and submitting forms for
people who do not exist (Hale and Brown 2016). Although electioneering
activities by political parties and other third-party groups have been studied
from a variety of perspectives (e.g., Berry 1999; Herrnson 2009; and Rozell,
Wilcox, and Franz 2011), this aspect of election activity was not reported in
our research. In terms of voter participation, monitoring and litigation activities typically focus on requests for information that can create administrative
burdens that strain the capacity of local and state offices.

State and national professional associations of government officials are
quite active in the election administration environment. These associations
design and deliver the bulk of training for election administrators and voter
registrars, and they provide venues for information exchange and the development of trusted information on both policy and practice. As with the
training function, this aspect of the election administration field is changing
rapidly.

Private foundations, including the Pew Charitable Trust and the Democracy Fund, are also involved in the election administration environment. In
the years after the 2000 election and the passage of HAVA, Pew maintained
and promoted a robust array of research and public education initiatives
directed at clarifying and tracking HAVA's implementation, encouraging
electronic formats for implementation and reporting, and increasing opportunities for participation through improvements in voter registration. Consistent with their mission, the research that they conducted and funded was
aligned with efforts to advance particular views about how elections should
be operated. The Democracy Fund is a relatively new actor engaged with
election practices and has begun supporting a number of initiatives across
the election administration network. Its approach includes engaging directly
with practitioners to support election activities; increasing the knowledge
that the media have about election administration to improve the accuracy of
reporting; and supporting an expanded role in academic research for focusing on election administration specifically, as opposed to the more traditional
studies that have focused solely on outcomes like registration and turnout.

Finally, the election administration environment is also influenced by
academic institutions. University centers and individual faculty researchers
provide institutional support for the field by generating questions, data, and

analyses. Funding for academic research and/or these centers comes primarily from private foundations, but has also come from the National Science Foundation, the EAC, other nonprofit groups, and state and local governments. In many cases, dedicated researchers interested in this area conduct research without external funding through their singular roles as faculty members. These researchers come from a variety of disciplines, including political science and public administration, law, computer science, sociology, and, more recently, information technology and security. Together, the group of scholars active in this area is larger today than it has ever been in history.

THE CONTEMPORARY POLITICAL CONTEXT AND THE ROLE OF THE JUDICIARY

Election administration has always been circumscribed by the judiciary. Over the two decades since the 2000 election, federal laws and judicial interpretations have shaped our understanding of the questions that can be asked about election administration. During this period, judicial interpretations have addressed some of the most fundamental questions that can be posed. Among these are questions about the separation of powers in deciding who can determine the results of an election, the limits of political activity in campaigns and redistricting, and the role of the states in the American federal system in setting specific requirements for electoral participation.

Given the constitutional authority vested in the states, the federal judiciary has been, on balance, supportive of state policy preferences on administrative matters, as long as fundamental rights are not violated. The concept of fundamental rights has been defined differently over time, as illustrated earlier in this chapter. Since the VRA's enactment, these questions of access and participation have, to a large extent, been evaluated under VRA requirements and have been considered in the context of enforcing it as the landmark legislation that protects voting rights.

In the modern, post-HAVA era of election administration, challenges to state practices have primarily centered on administrative reforms that address the mechanics of election operations. As new national policy was established after the 2000 election, the states set about the business of implementing new federal law and considering other reforms. State policy reforms have addressed issues such as the type of equipment used, the number of days that offices are open for in-person registration and voting, the adoption of measures to address voter convenience such as voting by mail and registering to vote online, and the methods that voters can (or must) use to identify themselves at various stages in the process; state choices have been upheld in the courts, for the most part. Redistricting decisions and identification policies bear the marks of political influence, and the results have been very evident.

The intergovernmental interactions during the modern era of election administration have supercharged the differences between the two major political parties. At the extremes, their views are diametrically opposed. Generally, Republicans at the national and state levels have favored administrative methods that arguably enhance the security of the election process but also have the effect of restricting access. In contrast, Democrats have favored administrative methods that facilitate greater access and participation but may also expose election operations to increased risks to system integrity, including voter fraud. Judicial interpretations always occur within the broader framework of national politics, and in the realm of election administration, they reflect distinct differences in operating practices across the states.

In the implementation process for HAVA, questions of discriminatory treatment covered by the VRA were typically referred to the DOJ or challenged in the courts. States had wide latitude in the implementation of the NVRA and HAVA; in time, state practices also raised questions about the limits of state power in establishing particular administrative requirements, and questions about these aspects of election administration became more common. These questions include thinking about the limits of voter identification, the procedures that are used to maintain voter registration lists, how to disqualify (or qualify) voters with criminal records, and whether past discriminatory practices have been sufficiently remediated. Across this period, questions persisted about whether state and local choices about election practices had run afoul of national requirements for equity in access and participation. Table 1.2 depicts the major laws, national political leadership, and US Supreme Court's decisions on a timeline from 2000 to early 2020.

The modern era begins with *Bush v. Gore* (2000), in which the US Supreme Court determined that Florida county election practices were so diverse that voters were not treated equally. The remedy was to call the Florida election based on the results in hand, and the result was that George W. Bush (R) won the state with a margin of 537 votes. HAVA was a direct result of the 2000 election, and its widespread media and public observations of the challenges of determining voter intent from punch card ballots. HAVA set the stage for expanded federal influence by establishing the EAC as a clearinghouse, funding a mandatory transition to electronic voting machines, and establishing voting system standards. HAVA required states to issue provisional ballots as a fail-safe for circumstances where a voter's eligibility was in question. HAVA also raised the profile of state election offices by requiring states to develop statewide electronic voter registration databases.

The states pushed back, and the pendulum of policy tensions between the states and the national government swung toward state authority in a number of areas. Arizona's Proposition 200 (passed in 2004) was forestalled by the courts; among other things, it required voters to demonstrate additional documentary proof of citizenship in order to be able to register and vote.

TABLE 1.2 Major National Legislative and Judicial Events in the Modern Era of Election Administration

Year	Event
2000	US Supreme Court stops Florida recount as a violation of equal protection requirements (*Bush v. Gore*)
2002	Help America Vote Act establishes provisional ballots as voter fail-safe, mandates electronic voting systems, and establishes Election Assistance Commission
2003	Redistricting does not require maximizing minority districts (*Georgia v. Ashcroft*)
2004	State criminal justice system declared racist but does not violate Voting Rights Act (VRA) (*Locke v. Farrakhan*)
2006	Federal oversight continued under VRA reauthorization
2008	States can impose photo voter identification requirements (*Crawford v. Marion County Board of Elections*)
2009	Political subdivisions in VRA-covered states can be removed from federal oversight (*NAMUDNO v. Holder*)
2010	Corporations can contribute to political campaigns without limitation (*Citizens United v. Federal Election Commission*)
2012	State voter registration list maintenance must not systematically remove names within ninety days of federal election (*Arcia v. Detzner*)
2013	Federal oversight provisions of VRA are no longer constitutional (*Shelby v. Holder*); states can require documentary proof of citizenship in nonfederal elections (*Arizona v. ITCA*)
2018	Voters can be removed from voter rolls for failure to respond to mailed notice (*Husted v. Randolph*)
2019	For the People Act (HR 1) introduced; partisan gerrymandering remains state issue with no requirement for federal intervention; Congress increasingly focuses on election security

The Ninth Circuit Court of Appeals declared the Washington State criminal justice system to be racist per se, but ultimately ruled that the state's felon disenfranchisement law did not violate the VRA's blanket prohibition on discriminatory election practices; the Supreme Court did take up the case (*Locke v. Farrakhan*, 2004). And yet, in 2006, Congress reauthorized the VRA for another twenty-five years by an overwhelming vote in the House of Representatives and a unanimous vote in the Senate, with no changes to its framework for federal oversight of state election practices in states that had histories of discrimination.

In 2008, the Supreme Court upheld Indiana's requirement for government-issued photo identification for voting in the face of evidence that a requirement for this form of identification was discriminatory for certain groups (*Crawford v. Marion County Board of Elections*, 2008). The next year, the Court found that a political jurisdiction in Texas with no history of discrimination could request permission to be removed from the federal review requirements of Section 5 of the VRA (*NAMUDNO v. Holder*, 2009). In *NAMUDNO*, the Court upheld the right of a local utility district run by an elected board to apply for a so-called bail-out from federal Section 5 oversight, even though Texas itself was covered by Section 5 and was subject to prior federal review and approval of changes in election practices. The Court did not strike down the federal review provision until 2013, when the question was again presented in *Shelby County v. Holder* (2013). The effect of declaring Section 5 unconstitutional was that states that were covered by prior review could now enact or implement voter identification laws and other election practices that had been held in abeyance by nearly fifty years of judicial interpretation.

Examining one of the many cases that came from Arizona Proposition 200, the Supreme Court ruled that the federal government could prescribe the form that voters use in registering by mail to vote, effectively meaning that states wanting to impose additional documentary requirements for proof of citizenship could do so for state and local elections, but not for federal elections (*Arizona v. ITCA*, 2013). Some states (e.g., Kansas) chose to run dual sets of elections for federal and state offices. States that intended to impose these additional proof-of-citizenship requirements continued to press their cases, but they were not successful in obtaining an interpretation that extended these requirements to federal elections. The Court did uphold one state's approach to voter registration list maintenance, allowing Ohio to remove voters from its role for failing, over a period of time, to respond to its notifications (*Husted et al. v. Randolph*, 2018).

In 2016, Donald Trump (R) was elected in the first presidential election since the *Shelby County* decision. The election season was rife with media reports of cybersecurity concerns, and this issue began to rise on the national agenda, where it remains. Trump won the Electoral College vote but did not win the popular vote, and he declared the election process "rigged." By 2017, DHS began working with election officials in developing a cybersecurity architecture to assist election jurisdictions on a voluntary basis.

Through the 2016 and 2018 election cycles, several state redistricting cases based on the 2010 census were addressed in state supreme courts, and some finally reached the Supreme Court. Key cases include legislative districting in Maryland, where redistricting plans advantaged Democrats (*Benisek v. Lamone*, 2018), and in Wisconsin and North Carolina, where the advantage went to Republicans (respectively, *Whitford v. Gill*, 2018; and *Rucho v. Common Cause*, 2019). At issue was the extent to which states could engage in partisan gerrymandering—that is, partisanship in making redistricting decisions. In some states, the effects of partisanship on drawing district lines has been to all but guarantee representation that disproportionately favors the majority party. The popular expression of the complex legal questions of these cases is whether voters are entitled to choose their legislators, or whether legislatures are entitled to choose their voters. These questions about redistricting are exactly the sorts of questions that the Supreme Court has traditionally refused to hear, on the grounds that the questions are inherently political and should be left to state legislatures. In contrast to the extensive records of judicial interpretation of the VRA, for example, judicial decisions about redistricting have been comparatively rare. The seminal opinions in *Baker v. Carr* (1961) and *Reynolds v. Sims* (1964), which had been decided more than fifty years earlier, forced states to address the population shifts brought on by broad urbanization, with the effect of requiring districts to be of relatively equal population and of establishing the proposition of "one person, one vote."

In these cases, the threshold questions were whether redistricting was a question that belonged in the Supreme Court at all; whether standards existed that the Court could use in giving direction; and, if so, what these standards were. The High Court entertained the questions and found plans to be unconstitutional in Maryland and Wisconsin, for example, only to return the cases to the states to reconstruct the district lines. Other such plans were struck down by state courts, including those in North Carolina and Pennsylvania, and were also returned to the legislatures. On a perplexing note, the 2018 election proceeded in North Carolina using districts that had been found unconstitutional. Suffice it to say that these districting plans would likely not have survived prior federal review by the DOJ, as would likely have been the case for least some of the voter identification laws enacted or implemented after 2013.

In its 2019 resolution of its pending state partisan gerrymandering cases, the Supreme Court defaulted to the right of states to determine the political parameters of districting (*Rucho v. Common Cause*, 2019). The 5-4 majority relied on arguments noted above; the issue is a political matter for the states, no clear standard exists by which to determine a violation, even if nominally egregious, and no method exists by which to develop such a standard. This decision essentially declares that the federal courts will not provide a remedy in this area; the federal courts have no authority to reallocate state political power. The political method by which district boundaries can be changed is through the ballot box, although the results are in many cases predetermined by the district lines that the plaintiffs in Maryland, North Carolina, and Wisconsin sought to change. Although this would appear to be a blow to Democratic interests, state courts are exercising their authority to examine motivations behind these decisions. In North Carolina, subsequent to the federal decision, a three-judge panel of the North Carolina Supreme Court struck down that redistricting plan, finding that partisan intent dominated all other redistricting criteria.

These enactments and pronouncements have occurred within an overarching national political context that is sharply divided along partisan lines about the ability of the national government to intervene in state policy decisions (see, e.g., Alvarez and Grofman 2014). Since 2000, the modern era of election administration has seen three presidents, and during this time, Republicans have held the edge in terms of years in that office (twelve years).[9] Republicans have also held the edge in terms of judicial appointments at the highest level, with four appointments to the Supreme Court confirmed by the Senate, compared with two for the Democrats.[10] More broadly, the High Court overall has experienced exceptional change since 2000; the majority of the Supreme Court has been appointed since 2005. Partisanship aside, this turnover has created a relatively uncertain environment for predicting judicial interpretations.

As the modern era of election administration continues to unfold, HAVA remains the last federal bipartisan policy effort to address election administration, as the access/security dichotomy continues. In January 2019, the new Democratic majority in the 116th Congress (2019–20) introduced the For the People Act (HR 1) as its opening policy proposal. HR 1 addressed voting rights expansion along with government ethics and campaign finance reform. With regard to voting rights, HR 1 would create an opt-out system of automatic voter registration; promote early voting, same-day registration, and online voter registration; create a federal holiday for Election Day; establish colleges and universities as voter registration sites; require notice of poll site relocations; increase support for poll worker recruitment and training; prohibit voter roll purges; prohibit the use of nonforwardable mail as a method of removing voters from voter rolls; and enhance support for electronic security. The Republican response was expressed by Senate majority leader Mitch McConnell (R-KY) in partisan terms. He argued in late January on the floor of the US Senate that creating an Election Day holiday was tantamount to paying federal workers to work on Democratic Party campaigns.[11] Interestingly, the Election Day holiday was already quite popular across the country; more than half the states require private employers to provide some form of time off on Election Day, and still others prohibit penalizing employees for taking time off to vote.

GOVERNANCE AND INNOVATION

The interaction of political ideology, intergovernmental structures, constitutional requirements, federal laws, and state authority has created several dilemmas for election administrators at the local level and within state offices for which there are no prescriptive solutions. In broad terms, these include how to maintain a voter registration list that is as accurate as possible; how to make voting more convenient; how to reach voters who may be excluded from the process; how to ensure an accurate and transparent process; how to protect the security of the election system; and how to demonstrate that processes are worthy of public trust and confidence in the results.

The governance mandates that support all American intergovernmental organizational arrangements are important because they indicate the types of communication needed to produce alignment with common goals and to create solutions and resolve problems. Government hierarchies rely relatively efficiently on command-and-control structures, which entail centralized authority and rules promulgated in a particular direction with a relatively particular result (e.g., Goggin et al. 1990; O'Toole 1988; Montjoy and O'Toole 1979). In the highly networked election administration environment, command-and-control relationships are rather loosely arranged and are widely and unevenly distributed across individual offices and jurisdictions.

The story of American elections today is largely a story of success. It is also a story of how election administrators and other election stakeholders have developed new approaches to address pressures from voters as well as state and federal policymakers. In election administration, national policies have been designed to leave many of the details of implementation to local and state offices. These details include how to implement particular provisions (e.g., what process is required for issuing a provisional ballot?), how to integrate federal requirements under various laws (e.g., exactly how should voter registration lists be maintained?) and how to respond to legitimate public concerns (e.g., I don't speak or read English. I don't trust my voting machine. Will my ballot be lost in the mail?). Command-and-control strategies are less useful in this context. To answer these and other questions, election administrators rely significantly on voluntary organizational relationships, and they treat information as currency. Information exchanges and methods of generating, vetting, synthesizing, and disseminating information across organizations and offices are essential steps in developing and testing solutions to the issues that they face.

In chapter 2, we take up these themes to discuss how innovation does—or does not—take place in such a complex intergovernmental environment. We lay out an innovation theory of change that considers factors that influence the creation and adoption of new approaches and methods in the election administration environment. Together, chapters 1 and 2 set the stage for our examination of innovation across election administration subsystems in chapters 3 through 8.

NOTES

1. Indiana was not admitted to the United States until December 1816; however, its votes were counted after challenge.

2. Through the EAVS, the EAC (2016) reports roughly 8,000 local election juris-dictions at the county and subcounty levels in states where election responsibil-ities devolve from the county to municipalities and/or townships. If the county is considered the relevant local election unit in states that share responsibility between the county and subcounty units (Michigan, Minnesota, and Wisconsin), the number of election jurisdictions is about 4,600 (EAVS 2016; Kimball and Bay-beck 2013).

3. The total number of ballot styles used across the country has not been recorded but is quite high and varies widely across jurisdictions and by election; a county in Iowa might use 35 ballot styles, whereas more than 3,000 might be required in Sacramento County, California.

4. Article I, Section 4, of the Constitution states that "the times, places, and man-ner of holding elections for Senators and Representatives shall be prescribed in each State by the Legislatures thereof; but the Congress may at any time by law make or alter such regulations, except as the place of choosing Senators." In prac-tical terms, states determine the time, manner, and place of all elections because the infrastructure supports holding consolidated elections for local, state, and national offices.

5. See *NIPP 2013: Partnering for Critical Infrastructure Security and Resilience* (DHS 2013).

6. We distinguish a voting system as hardware and software used end-to-end across registration, balloting, and counting. Election equipment simply refers to any one or more component parts of an election system.

7. We define issue advocacy as efforts directed at public and member education and outreach and did not identify or consider lobbying in our research.

8. An array of nonprofit groups active in election administration environment is dis-played in table C.14 in appendix C.

9. George W. Bush and Donald Trump held the office from 2000 to 2008, and from 2016 to the present; Barack Obama held the office from 2008 to 2016.

10. Republican presidential appointments confirmed by the Senate include John Roberts (chief justice), Samuel Alito (now deceased), Neil Gorsuch, and Brett Kavanaugh. Democratic appointments confirmed included Sonia Sotomayor and Elena Kagan; the nomination of Merrick Garland was blocked by the Senate from receiving a hearing.

11. "Just what America needs, another paid holiday and a bunch of government workers being paid to go out and work, I assume (for) our colleagues on the other side—on their campaigns. . . . This is the Democrat plan to restore democracy? . . . A power grab."

2

An Innovation Theory of Change: Professionalism, Politics, Resources, and Needs

Through all the structural and political changes across time, the goal of the American election system has remained, in large part, the same: to measure democratic participation in a manner that is fair, accurate, and transparent. In spite of the challenges posed by the US federal system, intergovernmental relationships, and policy—and perhaps because of them—election officials have developed innovative approaches for dealing with uncertainty, technological change, and politically charged circumstances. Even as complexities have increased, election administrators have made strides in addressing many of the pressing questions in the field. The innovations that we consider in this volume represent changes in orientation that have fundamentally affected the way in which election officials conceptualize and manage elections now and likely in the near future. To set the stage for analysis, in this chapter we examine the concept of innovation in public service, and the contemporary public management environment, which is dominated by networked arrangements of organizations within and across the public and private sectors and supported by growing professionalism. These networked arrangements suggest that public-sector innovation be conceptualized to explicitly acknowledge the intractable characteristics and challenges of networks, which include complexity and interdependence, political forces, and pressures for accountability practices that address concerns about democratic functioning as well as program management. These networked arrangements also suggest fresh consideration of the role of measurement and how we define success—or failure.

To articulate this context, we propose a model of network innovation as a theory of change. In this theory of change, we consider factors that may influence the adoption of new methods or approaches, and we extend our analysis beyond adoption to examine changes in process and governance. Chief among these is the professionalism that has evolved in response to networks as information-rich environments. Other factors include the political context, available resources, and the needs of voters and stakeholders, as well as the opinions of election administrators themselves.

INNOVATION IN THE PUBLIC SECTOR

Innovation is classically defined in the private-sector sense as something that is new to a given organization (Rogers 1995). Private firms develop new products or processes in pursuit of profit or to advance market position. The market rewards decisions in various ways, based on consumer behavior, individual transactions, and the value created for shareholders.

Public-sector innovation, by contrast, is more nuanced. Public-sector innovation occurs within the larger normative context of public-sector rules, structure, and activity generally. Public-sector motivations, legal constraints, and normative orientations are unique. Thus, government innovation is more than an efficiency calculus or the adoption of different management practices but also adheres to the imperative to serve the public interest and advance the public good. Innovation in public service is an honorable endeavor. Herbert Simon (1947, 106) notes that the power to innovate is perhaps the principal power of the bureaucracy in the realms of value and policy (Osborne and Brown 2013, 31).

In the broadest sense, the "reward" for government action is responsive and timely public service. Thus, motivation for government innovation stems from an intention to create public value. Lynn (1997, 96) argues that government innovation challenges the status quo, as "an original, disruptive act" that is transformative. Public service innovation tackles dominant public service paradigms. By definition, government innovation requires deviation from standard operating procedures; this can also mean thinking differently about the role of government, as is sometimes encouraged during periods of reform (Gore 1993; Kettl 2002; Kettl and DiIulio 1995; Osborne and Gaebler 1992; Simon 1947). At the most fundamental level, public service innovation challenges the prevailing wisdom about what is (or is not) considered to be a public problem, how public problems are defined, and how public solutions are configured.

Legal constraints also operate differently on organizational action in the public sector. In the private sector, organizational action is essentially unconstrained unless prohibited by law or regulated in some other way. Private firms are free to adopt (or not) the new ideas that they choose, unless law or regulation determines otherwise. In important contrast, government action is created by law and the exercise of administrative discretion, and, in most areas, is also subject to particular constraints. Put another way, under the American ideal of limited government, government organizations have no ability to act unless authorized by law. Public service innovation always occurs within the prescribed set of activities that government is permitted to undertake; public managers must take into account the reach of the mandate that their office is permitted to exercise.

Innovation in public service comes in at least two forms (Osborne and Brown 2013; Walker 2013). One is process innovation that responds incrementally to a changing environment. The other is innovation in governance, whereby a new organizational architecture is created. Both forms can be imposed through government mandates or can be approached voluntarily. New processes and new organizational arrangements are also characteristic outcomes of network arrangements. New processes within existing policy regimes can expand the reach of a policy to affect new groups or can evolve along a path with a consistent target group. Innovation in governance involves changing the architecture of organizational arrangements (Lynn 2013; Osborne and Brown 2013; Rhodes 2013; Walker 2013). These classifications are not necessarily discrete, but they do capture the spirit of public service at it seeks to evolve in serving the public good. These classifications take a holistic approach and subsume organizational characteristics and personal attributes, and we associate them with networks.

NETWORK INFRASTRUCTURE AND THE INNOVATION THEORY OF CHANGE

The concept of government innovation is undergoing a transformation as a result of our changed understanding of the context of government operations. Over the past two decades, our understanding of the organizational arrangements that support government action has shifted. Networks are now featured prominently in the scholarship that studies methods of organizing public service activities (Agranoff 2007, 2012, 2017; Agranoff and McGuire 1998, 2004; Hale 2011; O'Toole 1988; Provan and Milward 2001; Torfing et al. 2012; Torfing 2016). These networks are understood broadly to include a wide array of participants from government agencies at all levels: from nonprofit organizations, as service providers, funders, and advocates, and from private, for-profit firms.

To acknowledge this networked public service environment, we propose an innovation theory of change, in the form of an activity-based framework. The innovation theory-of-change framework for the contemporary public service environment is presented in figure 2.1. The dimensions of this theory of change incorporate interaction and synergy across the fundamental concepts of public service networks—cooperation, collaboration, and

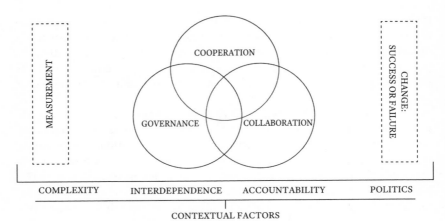

FIGURE 2.1 Innovation Theory of Change

governance. Networks require cooperation and collaboration across intergovernmental, cross-sectoral and interjurisdictional pathways. Governance bridges organizational arrangements, as organizations share authority both formally and informally, and new forms of governance emerge to reflect new collaborations and cooperative interactions (see Torfing et al. 2012; Torfing 2016). The network innovation framework reflects these concepts within the larger context of constraints that bear on networks generally, including complexity in both problem definition and organizational interactivity, organizational interdependence, how to demonstrate accountability and to whom, and the overarching influences of the American political system. Across all these dimensions is the enduring and powerful draw to measure activities and behaviors and to label change as either a success or failure.

The model of innovation as a theory of change considers public managers in government agencies alongside nonprofit and other private-sector actors. Considerable attention has been directed at the ability of nonprofit organizations to drive innovation (Light 1998; Rogers 1995). Government agencies, by contrast, must meet a broader mandate and fill an organizing and governance role that is both essential and more central to administrative and democratic functioning (Kettl 2002; Lynn 2013; Provan and Milward 2001).

The evolution of the literature that describes networks supports a holistic view of innovation. The idea of a "network" dominates the literature, but the term is used somewhat indiscriminately in generally referring to nonhierarchical organizational arrangements. Some usages refer to why an arrangement evolved (e.g., grassroots pressures, convenience, and policy responses to disaster, to name a few); some focus on how the arrangement is structured (degrees of centralization, role of government, degrees of formality); still others focus on the roles of actors outside government proper (roles for nonprofits, and the roles of private, for-profit actors). As we examined the innovations reported in this book, various organizational arrangements appeared, and the innovation context encompasses the arrangements that we encountered.

CHALLENGES AND GOVERNANCE, COLLABORATION, AND COOPERATION

In considering innovation in a network context, public managers accommodate governing arrangements that bridge various sectors. The innovations that they may consider must navigate multiple governing arrangements and both formal and informal relationships that cross organizational, jurisdictional, and political boundaries. Public managers also face the constraints of interdependency and complexity that characterize the institutional context of public service. The ability of any one organization to accomplish change is limited, so accountability is diffused in comparison with a standard or prototypical bureaucratic hierarchy. Accountability for change is necessary, and may require the creation of new governance structures. Public managers must navigate accountability questions about "to whom?" and "for what?" through the various and competing ideas, values, goals, and resource differences that exist across a network.

Our innovation theory of change also draws upon competing forces that have been identified in the collaboration literature, including the voluntariness of network relationships and the levels of trust within these. Within the election administration environment, some collaborations and cooperative arrangements are relatively more or less mandated, and some are entirely voluntary. Primarily, where federal mandates exist, they focus on outputs and outcomes rather than specifying particular implementation processes, methods of interaction, or institutional relationships; state autonomy and flexibility are supported, relatively speaking. In the election administration network, following the prompt of federal legislation, election jurisdictions have met requirements in a host of different ways.

In addition, a perceived national supremacy may exhibit informal influence. The prestige or cachet of national departments or offices may generate interactions in which the national government has more relative weight than is dictated by formal policy. Subnational actors and nongovernmental actors may be motivated to align with national goals for political reasons. In the absence of national enforcement authority, a national government may also hold the ability to punish deviations from informal policy. Grant awards are one example. Appointments to boards or commissions is another. Key stakeholders may also position the national government as "superior" in the absence of formal authority to the contrary (Emerson and Nabatchi 2015; Parsons 1960; Xu 2011). Barriers created by conflict can be overcome by a demonstration of credible commitments among participants (e.g., Feiock 2004, 2013; Feiock and Scholz 2010) and by the development of new institutional forms of governance (North 1990). Self-organizing groups may also emerge, along with the development of trust (Berardo 2009; Scholz, Berardo, and Kile 2008; Shrestha, Barardo, and Feiock 2014). Collaborations reflect the inherent tensions between competing public values and exhibit unintended consequences along with varying degrees of capacity; in some circumstances, the formation of a collaboration may be an end in and of itself (Bryson, Crosby, and Bloomberg 2014, 2015; Moore 1995; Torfing et al. 2012; Torfing 2016).

THE CHALLENGES OF MEASURING CHANGE

The networked environment also affects how change is operationalized, how it is characterized as either a success or failure (or a bit of both), and how measurement is involved. Multiple and competing perspectives, values, and missions are always implicated when defining public service initiatives generally, and these concepts are well understood in the public policy environment—including the administration of public programs (Brown 2008; Radin 1998, 2000, 2006; Stone 2011). The public service network infrastructure dictates that these considerations will be more complex and interdependent, and that partisan political support is always a factor. Innovation in this context means that multiple constituencies must reach some level of common agreement on a concept for change. It also means that multiple constituencies will be affected; some of these effects will be positive, some negative, and some a bit of both.

And yet, agreement on a concept for change is not enough. Public managers need to be able to communicate, and these layers of interactivity present an impediment. At the most fundamental level, definitions and terminology vary widely across network organizations. This variation is particularly acute when laws that define specific requirements for government action vary across network participants, as is the case for election administration. It is not unusual for American public policy mandates to range across different levels of government; in election administration, the degree of local and state variation is exceptional. Conversations within the election administration system often begin with discussions about terms and practices, and about how to align terminology and concepts in order to have "apples to apples" discussions.

Networks also pose challenges to the concept of measurement in public service. Values vary from organization to organization and across networks, and these differences can coalesce, align, diverge, or multiply. Measurement is an innate reflection of our ideas about accountability, and yet it is not a goal in and of itself and is not a panacea for misguided policy approaches. The reinvention movement (Osborne and Gaebler 1992), the National Performance Review (Gore 1993), and related efforts fostered a wave of trying to think differently about how government does its work. And yet, looking back over the past several decades of public management effort to reform government processes, the practice appears stymied. Risk-averse public managers are cited as one of several key factors, along with the most recent recession and the inability of bureaucrats to influence legislative policy trends (see, e.g., National Performance Management Advisory Commission 2010). Although public managers may be adept at driving internal budget reforms or building bridges with other management functions, systemic relationships with state legislatures are rare and necessary for cultural change. These relationships appear to be an important component of the networks of relationships that support innovation.

Another challenge is posed by measures that have been traditionally used to reflect election activity. A substantial volume of election-related research focuses on election law and policy through the related lenses of political outcomes and legality. These inquiries are concerned with whether particular changes in election law or practice pass constitutional muster and enhance or impede participation, both in broad terms and with respect to particular demographic groups. For example, does a particular method of voter identification depress turnout among voters who are older, poorer, or members of minority groups? Do text message reminders or Facebook posts increase the likelihood that voters will actually cast ballots? Does automatic voter registration favor one political party or another? Can party membership or race be considered when drawing lines to create the districts from which representatives will be elected—and if so, how? What is the importance, if any, of public opinion on various issues in particular electoral contests?

These lines of inquiry are important. We care about who participates, and why. We care about election results. We care about who wins, and we care about whether voters want initiatives and referenda to pass. It is important to understand whether and how law and policy affect participation and election results. A more subtle dimension of these inquiries, and equally important, is that data on voter turnout and participation, and election outcomes, are all readily available. Across the country, all the roughly 8,000 election jurisdictions generate data about participation and outcomes. Examples include how many people register, how many vote, how many ineligible prospective voters are turned away, who won, and vote totals for every candidate and every ballot question.

By measuring what is available, valuable insights have been gained about many aspects of American elections. As interest in election administration began, considerable research gathered new data to tackle a litany of questions about voter registration; poll worker attitudes, precincts, and polling place locations; ballot length and layout; voting technology; methods of alternative voting; counting ballots; voters' experiences, including voters with disabilities and in need of language assistance; and the effects of various methods of identification and registration.[1] The most consistent theme in these topics is the search for the effects of policy change on voter behavior; for example, does a particular policy cause an increase in voter registration or voter turnout, and are particular demographic groups affected differently? With a focus on voter turnout and results, researchers tend to treat the election operation as a uniform, opaque box. Election administration research that focuses on administrative issues of implementation, process, and governance may be considered something of an innovation by way of comparison.

More recent research has begun to explore performance measurement concepts in election administration (e.g., Alvarez, Atkeson, and Hall 2013; Burden and Stewart 2014; Gerken 2009; Hale, Montjoy, and Brown 2015; Moynihan and Silva 2008). Emerging research also examines the dimensions of system capacity, including the cost and funding of elections (Creek and Karnes 2010; Damschroeder 2013; Hale and Brown 2019; Hall, Atkeson, and Alvarez 2012; Hill 2011; Kimball and Baybeck 2013; Mohr et al. 2019; Montjoy 2010); waiting times and precinct resources (Herron and Smith 2016; Stewart 2013); and the capacity of election administration arrangements more broadly (Brown, Hale, and King 2019; Hale and Slaton 2008; Montjoy 2010; Moynihan 2004; Stein, Mann, and Stewart 2019).

The innovation theory of change model argues that the question of measurement—both what to measure about election operations and how to measure it—is a consideration for the front end of the process rather than the back end, and that measurement approaches have implications that run throughout the innovation process. The nature of complex public service systems generally, and election administration systems specifically, suggests that data will be defined differently and captured differently across organizations. This suggests, in turn, that it is critical to gain a common understanding of terms and processes in order for jurisdictions to compare and learn. In the election administration environment, this commonality has proven to be a significant challenge, and has no doubt stymied research about capacity building in the field.

Common comparison and understanding, however, are essential for innovation to diffuse. In a self-reinforcing cycle, these common elements support network collaboration and cooperation that can support the development of new external relationships, which then increase with experience and interaction (Austin 2000; Light 2004). These relationships are valuable in their own right, but also as a means of building capacity to address further change.

Innovation is both context- and path-dependent. Early choices about how to administer elections set localities and states on different paths about how to run elections. These early choices, determined by local resources and needs as well as traditions and customs of settling communities, and combined with the language in the Tenth Amendment to the US Constitution, meant that over time differences across the states became entrenched by law, tradition, and practice. Today's extensive heterogeneity in election administration is the result of those early choices, which make it more and more difficult over time to make other choices, even if they are more rational (Pierson 2000). Consequently, actors within a system lock onto particular methods of operation due to environmental conditions or interactions that occur early in the process.

FOSTERING INNOVATION AND BUILDING CAPACITY

Most broadly, innovation requires personal and organizational capacity. Defined as the ability to do what is intended (Burgess 1975; Gargan 1981; Honadle 1981), capacity has a reciprocal relationship with innovation. Capacity is a necessary ingredient for normal operation as well as for innovation; innovation can, in turn, increase capacity. When new organizational structures and routines are established in order to facilitate and support innovation, these same structures and routines are available to public managers to enable them to respond to new conditions or initiate changes (Hale 2011). The reciprocal nature of the relationship between capacity and innovation exists in part because of the essence of organizational capacity and sustainability, an outcome supported through innovation (Brown 2012). All three require resources (Hayes and Bryant 2002; Schorr, Sylvester, and Dunkle 1999; Staggenborg 1988), networked arrangements (Hale 2011; Kubisch et al. 2002, 2010; Wolff, n.d.), and collaboration (Torfing 2016).

Various descriptions have been used to identify the internal organizational context in which innovation occurs and the conditions and characteristics that support it. Some observers focus on personal attributes, while others focus on organizational methods for coping with uncertainty. There is no uniform or universal standard; however, there are commonalities. Across organizations, interoperability is the desired state (Agranoff 2017), and interactive governance has been observed in some organizational arrangements (Torfing 2016). Inside organizations, these include personal and organizational vision, communication skills, durability to pursue change over time and in the face of failure, a culture of learning from experiences that includes a willingness to make mistakes, and various leadership characteristics that support or intertwine with these dimensions (Eggers and Singh 2009; Light 2004; Mintrom 1997; Rainey and Steinbauer 1999). The growing study of managing in and with complex networked arrangements emphasizes the personal attributes that public managers value in generating and sustaining relationships, both with individuals and with organizations (Agranoff 2007, 2012, 2017; Brown 2012; Gray 1973; Hale 2011; Light 2004; Rogers 1995; Taylor 2016; Torfing 2016; Walker 1969).

Innovation also requires resilience and the ability to withstand the inevitable turbulence and exogenous shocks.[2] Organizations employ a wide range of management strategies to cope with environmental uncertainty that may shed light on how innovation happens.[3] Among the most classic, and not subsumed in more recent scholarship about networks, are boundary spanning, cooptation, and resource dependency. Although this list is not exhaustive, it does suggest a variety of formal and informal methods upon which public managers may draw in navigating network innovation. These different approaches also illustrate the enduring concerns that public managers have about how to create and sustain improvements. Each approach provides a lens through which to view the innovations we consider in this book, and the strategies and tactics that public managers deploy. These theories predate the current literature on interorganizational networks; however, the activities associated with each are part and parcel of the processes of collaboration, cooperation, and governance that are central to our understanding of contemporary public management.

Through boundary spanning, organizations act intentionally, working as brokers or intermediaries to engage with actors in other organizations in order to create relationships that enhance the stability of the home organization by creating patterns of coordination and interdependence (Thompson 1967). Cooptation refers to "the process of absorbing new elements into the leadership or policy-determining structure of an organization as a means of averting threats to its stability or existence (Selznick 1949, 13). Cooptation reflects an adaptive social structure that acts and reacts according to various goal sets that include, but are not limited to, the goals of the organization.[4] Goal displacement is an inherent tension in cooptation; outcomes can occur that are neither intended nor desired. Resource dependency addresses the notion that the primary governance responsibility is to acquire and preserve the resources necessary for organizational survival. Resource sufficiency reduces environmental uncertainty. Importantly, resources include not only financial wealth but also connections with other organizations and individuals through personal and professional relationships (Kreutzer 2009; Miller 2002; Miller-Millesen 2003). More recently, Torfing (2016) has argued that collaboration can be used intentionally as an innovation strategy in the public sector.

No single theoretical framework will explain all the approaches that public managers employ in pursuing innovation in a networked environment. There is overlap between these theories in terms of concepts and how we might operationalize and measure them. It is also the case that local organizations may react differently than national groups (Renz 2016). However, the factors described above suggest that collaboration, cooperation, and new models of governance are central to innovation.

THE RISE AND INFLUENCE OF PROFESSIONALISM
IN ELECTION ADMINISTRATION

Professional associations are central to the concept of innovation. Professional associations convene conferences and other similar gatherings at which information is exchanged and synthesized. Professional associations and the synthesized information that they generate and support are central to the link between professionalism and innovation (Hale 2011). Through professionalism, public managers are able to navigate the complexities of their networked environments and the demands of constituents, the available resources, and the political forces that favor or oppose change.

When the National Association of Election Officials (also known nationally as the Election Center) began its training efforts to professionalize the contemporary field of election administration in the mid-1990s, the field of election administration was largely an aside in public administration generally.[5] Election administrators were already entrenched in county and township governments across the nation. They typically arrived in those positions because a job became available and because they happened to fit the hiring specifications of the jurisdiction, which were typically related to politics. No formal training existed; there was no course of study or degree to pursue in order to "become an election administrator." In fact, the term "election administrator" is actually a recent development in the professionalization of the field, reflecting the efforts of the Election Center and its national certification program.

Today, the election administrators who take part in the professionalization training given by the Election Center and other professional associations that offer election-related training opportunities reflect a wide range of education and experience, running the gamut from high school education to postgraduate and law degrees. Some have intentionally pursued formal education in public administration or public policy to enhance their knowledge of the field. Most recently, some have sought advanced education specifically in election administration, as that has become available. This change has occurred in a comparatively short period in the study of American elections as a whole, and the most significant increase has been in the period since the 2000 presidential election.

Election administration as a field began its track toward professionalization in the 1970s. Professionalization of government service more generally began significantly earlier, and traces with the evolution of government administration, the civil service, and public management. Election administration lagged well behind the other aspects of public service, whether generic (e.g., general administration, public budgeting, and public-sector labor relations) or specific (e.g., education, social work, and emergency management).

Throughout the balance of its history, election administration has been a relative backwater of civil service, with most election administrators functioning as county generalists who often received their positions from established political spoils systems and machine politics. Professionalization efforts gained significant speed after the 2000 election (Fischer and Coleman 2008; Hale and Brown 2016; Hale, Montjoy, and Brown 2015).

Harris (1928, 1929, 1934) wrote the first and groundbreaking chronicles and studies of voter registration and election administration across the country. He noted specifically that election administration, as a function of the civil service, operated wholly differently than other fields: "In no other phase of public administration do the statutes bulk so large an administrative control and supervision so little. Ordinarily there is no office exercising any real control over elections throughout the state, and usually the local city or county officers in charge have only slight powers of control, supervision, and inspection of the work of the precinct officers" (Harris 1934, 7–8).

Against this backdrop, professionalism became an important tool to assist those working in the field. Professional, nonpartisan skills were necessary tools that had to combine with an understanding of the volume of election law, the nuances of practice, the obligation of openness, and the ability to limit fraud. Indeed, today there are reports in other countries about the effects of corruption on elections when election officials are not yet professionalized (see, e.g., the discussion of elections and corruption in Ukraine by Herron, Boyko, and Thunberg 2016).

The rise of professionalism brought a greater focus on the technical aspects of the day-to-day acts of governing and practice, a move away from administration based on "moral reasoning," which consequently necessitated a specific focus in professionalism on ethical training generally and the development of ethical codes (Adams, Tashchian, and Shore 1993). Supporting this observation, Harris (1934, 95) wrote that "no substantial improvement in elections can be made without improving the character of the election officers, without divorcing the whole machinery from politics."

The professionalization of a field may start with standardized (or increased) training. And this professionalization also brings with it a set of core values (some ideologically based) as well as defined skills, competencies, expected technical knowledge, and a path of education and training to achieve these (Berman 2006; Hale and Brown 2016; Hale, Montjoy, and Brown 2015). A natural outgrowth of professionalization is the development of formal educational programs.

The evolution of professionalization in election administration has not been categorized neatly into stages that can be defined by bright lines. However, some broad patterns are discernable. Figure 2.2 presents an estimation of the evolution of the profession of election administration and the evolution of public administration as a profession.

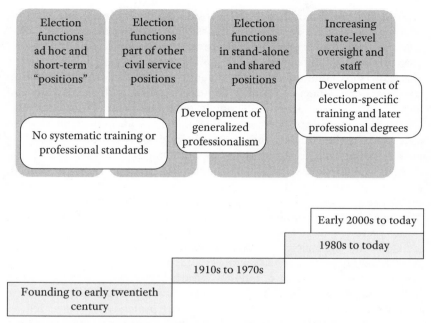

FIGURE 2.2. Evolution of the Profession of Election Administration

Four stages of election administration professionalization reflect general personnel-based descriptions of election administration workers over time from the nation's founding to the present. These four categories are positioned against four overlapping periods, arrayed to reflect the approximate times during which the various personnel types can be observed. The evolution of election administration professionalization begins with the early years of the nation through the early twentieth century, when election administration was without professional standards and systematic training, then follow the development of generalized professionalism, and the development of election-specific training and professional degrees in the field. The field began with ad hoc and short-term administrators (from the nation's founding through the early 1900s). Aspects of the job came under the purview of other local offices (from the late 1800s through the 1970s), and also evolved as stand-alone functions (from the 1940s to the present).[6] Although progress has notably lagged that of other areas of public administration (Harris 1928, 1929, 1934), election administration has certainly become more professionalized over time.

Systematic training started in the 1990s through the efforts of non-profit organizations established for that purpose, namely, the Election Center (Hawkins 2019; Saltman 2006). The Election Center offers the nation's professional certification for the election community, including election administrators, voter registrars, vendors, and monitors, known as CERA (certified election/registration administrator).[7] The curriculum reflects the core principles of public administration (e.g., systems design, management and leadership, communications and public relations, information technology, budgeting, strategic planning, and ethics), along with election law and history, voter participation, and public policy decisions (Mattice 2019).[8] CERA focuses on cross-cutting themes that have an impact on election offices across the country, and it engages in differences between states as well as national trends. Some state-based training programs were available at the time, although sporadically. After the 2000 election, public scrutiny of election operations expanded dramatically. State-specific training initiatives developed to respond to new requirements imposed on state chief election officials (CEOs) and state offices through the Help America Vote Act; state offices grew, as did the availability of state-based training.

Currently, the majority of states (more than 65 percent) offer training of some type for election officials with respect to their unique legal and policy environments. The source of training and whether it is required in order to hold employment in the field varies. State training models differ; some are conducted through a state election office, state professional association, or contracts between one of those with outside training providers. In at least sixteen states, training also confers certification; whether training is required is not necessarily an indication of program depth or rigor.[9] Many of the states without formal training are currently considering requiring it, while most of the states with training programs have to invest in regular updates to both content and delivery.

The secretary of state in Washington State is an example of state office involvement. Both Secretary Kim Wyman and the state election director working for her were local election officials before moving to the state office, and they took their understanding of local election operations to the SOS office to develop a state training program focused on local perspectives and building unity rather than adversity in the local–state relationship. Director Augino (2019, 112), in discussing the statewide training program, notes that its certification credentials "are earned through initial and ongoing training, with a Washington State component to ensure that election administrators are well-versed in what happens across the state. This helps build consistency in how elections are conducted throughout Washington." She describes the process as "interactive" (2019, 113), in which the state office works regularly with local offices on policy matters as well as training needs. In this process, the state office learns from counties about their training needs and then builds training that includes state delivery along with peer-to-peer training.

An example of a rigorous and voluntary program is offered in Florida, through the Florida Supervisors of Elections (FSE).[10] Florida supervisors are elected at the county level, and their association is designed to uphold election integrity using high standards of ethics and professionalism. The FSE is committed to continuing education and certification, as well as best practices, to provide the state's citizens with information that they need to vote and engage in the electoral process (FSE 2018). The FSE delivers a state-level certification program centered on voter confidence and consistent practices across the state. The Florida Certified Election Professional curriculum is organized into topical areas, including election process and law, administrative skills, and technology. Courses are arranged in three tiers. Election officials who complete advanced courses earn the status of master Florida certified election professional (MFCEP). In 2018, the FSE website listed more than 150 FCEP and MFCEP graduates, including elected supervisors, staff, and vendors. The FSE certification program has been recognized for excellence by other organizations that provide training and professional development for election officials, including the Election Center's Professional Practice Award and the Eagle Award from the International Association of Government Organizations.

Another example is the training program offered by the Colorado County Clerks Association (CCCA), whose members are the elected officials who lead the county clerk and recorder's offices, and their designees. The Colorado county clerks are responsible for voter registration and election administration as well as a broad range of other responsibilities typical of general purpose county offices that count elections within their portfolio.[11] This broad range of responsibilities is reflected in the CCCA's robust training program, one track of which focuses on election operations; other tracks focus on motor vehicle issues and recording responsibilities.

The Michigan training model illustrates the essential intergovernmental nature of training for election administrators. Michigan is one of several states that operate elections at the subcounty level. Michigan has slightly more than 1,600 election jurisdictions, including its 83 counties and 1,520 cities and townships. Township populations range from 10 to more than 100,000, according to census data. Voting jurisdiction size ranges from more than 40,000 (in 28 jurisdictions) to fewer than 2,000 voters (in 859 jurisdictions). Across this diversity and decentralization, the state office spearheads a training and accreditation effort for more than 3,400 local election officials and staff, as well as about 30,000 inspectors (poll workers). As Michigan Bureau of Elections training director Virginia Vander Roest notes, the state's online training platform provides an important supplement to the on-site visits that occur on a two-year cycle (Vander Roest 2019, 120–22). The site visits are essential for face-to-face conversations and problem solving that are critical to foster understanding, learning, and increased professionalization.

State associations such as the FSE and the CCCA design and deliver conferences for their professional associations twice each year or more frequently. Agendas provide members with information about the state of the field both within their states and beyond. National and state election officials are scheduled as speakers, as are representatives from university research programs and other third-party groups engaged in the field. New ideas and pilot programs are often on the agenda at these and other state association meetings. These ideas inform training for association members; for example, FSE recently (2018) instituted a training track in election cybersecurity.

Training for Alabama registrars of voters is an example of the use of outside training providers; the Alabama secretary of state John Merrill (the state's chief election officer) contracts with Auburn University to provide mandatory training for voter registrars. This program provides training through a nine-course curriculum offering three courses per year on a three-year cycle to every county in the state. Counties meet regionally in seven locations around the state, and the curriculum is specific to Alabama election law and practice. Training may be available for the other three local elected offices that are statutorily responsible for some part of election operations (probate judge, circuit clerk, and sheriff), but that effort is not conducted by the Alabama SOS.

Finally, only recently have formalized education programs been developed for the specific study of election administration as a field—notably, at Auburn University and the University of Minnesota, both of which offer graduate certificates. The University of Minnesota recently introduced (July 2017) an undergraduate certificate in the field. As programs offered in accredited curricula, these may foster the development of other programs. Because it is rare to find a concentration of faculty in the field in any one college or university location, accredited graduate programs in public affairs have formed a consortium to offer a pool of election administration courses that can be accessed by graduate students and working professionals.[12]

All these positive attributes associated with professionalism are salient for election administrators. Professionalism, especially accreditation, brings organizations greater credibility (McCabe, Ponomariov, and Estrada 2017). Broadly, professionalism confers expertise and is seen as an indication of neutral competence. This neutrality is a critical counterpoint to Harris's observations of nearly a century ago, in a public service domain where the majority of county and township leaders are directly elected, and the others are appointed by elected officials. Although CEOs and local election officials remain largely independent of national authorities, two-thirds of the state CEOs are directly elected, and in half the remaining states they are appointed directly by partisan election officials (Hale, Montjoy, and Brown 2015).

As scholars have noted, professionalism is not entirely benign (Friedson 1960; Radin 2006; Wilson 1989). Professionalism may generate ideological adherence to rules and duties of the broader profession as opposed to the norms and practices that guide the specific offices in which people work, or the larger jurisdictional framework within which they are accountable. Uninformed service departments such as police and fire are examples, as are professions such as accounting and law. Beyond healthy discussion of professional norms, rules, and operating options, the principles of a profession may collide with administrative or political preferences; and this is actually quite common. Divided loyalties may lead to corruption and decreased communication. Decreased communication and diminished ability to reach agreement are especially likely when seeking to reach across functions; difficulties can be expected to increase as activities span offices and jurisdictions. When professional norms and public office values collide, networks of information and practice can mediate differences and produce common ground.

The professionalization of a sector also leads to outcomes outside particular offices or organizations. Often, new interest groups of professional members are formed, designed to advocate for the interests of the members and for new policy approaches. Professional organizations can have tremendous influence on policy and practice change (e.g., Mintrom and Vergari 1998; Torfing 2016). Gamson and Wolfsfeld (1993, 121) found that "the greater the resources, organization, professionalism, coordination, and strategic planning of a movement, the greater its media standing and the more prominent its preferred frame will be in media coverage of relevant events and issues." Professional associations can also reinforce the status and standing of a field as a profession, and effectively create professional identity.[13] Given the potential benefits (and pitfalls) of the professionalization of a field generally, the professionalization of election administration should be expected to produce specific consequences. In the case of voluntary federal guidelines for voting systems, higher levels of professionalism give election officials greater capacity and therefore greater flexibility in deciding how to proceed (Hale and Brown 2013). The professionalization of election administration, as reflected by a range of professional association activities, has been recently linked to higher performance on some administrative and outcome indicators (Brown and Hale 2019; Hale and Brown 2016).[14] We discuss these further in chapter 8; findings from this emerging research suggest a self-reinforcing effect, in which professionalism leads to enhanced performance, which then generates interest in enhancing the professionalism of others within the system, leading to more and better training and national attention, and so on.

THE INFLUENCE OF POLITICS, RESOURCES, AND THE PUBLIC DEMAND FOR CHANGE

This book is a study of innovation in election administration that occurs within a system of networks of public and private actors. In addition to identifying and describing innovations in the field, the book also examines why

- Politics
- Demand   State context
- Resources
- Professionalism

FIGURE 2.3. Innovation, Implementation, and State Context

these innovations have taken hold and have spread from one jurisdiction to another. We add professionalism to the diffusion literature to consider how external environments shape innovation along with political factors, resources, needs, and public demand, and to examine the implementation of innovation in a state context. Figure 2.3 presents the innovation theory of change and implementation of innovation against these factors.

Diffusion research about the spread of policy innovation across policy areas and across American states demonstrates that a collection of factors come in to play (Gray 1973; Walker 1969). Resources, politics, and the needs or demands of the public all interact to shape a climate in which new ideas can take hold and spread from one jurisdiction to another (Berry and Berry 1990, 1999). Wealthier jurisdictions are thought to have "slack," or additional resources to pursue new ideas, whether in the form of additional staff members, additional staff time, or the ability to acquire new equipment or technology. The election administration itself also has slack. Slack in the system, or the fluidity of public spaces (Dahl 1961) within the election administration system, accommodates a variety of actors and organizations as different issues arise. In examining diffusion of various policies across time in the American states, Eyestone (1977) finds that diffusion patterns vary by policy area and argues that a focus on early adopters will yield fruitful insights about factors that initiate change.

Raw political calculations reflected in the balance of power between the major parties indicate whether an idea will have the traction and support necessary to advance through the one or more policy agendas necessary across branches of government in order to finally be adopted and implemented. Some innovations are linked to highly charged social issues, and carry an ideological valence that further affects the climate and whether an innovation will take hold (Mooney and Lee 1995). Innovations directed at particular demographic groups (i.e., some criminal justice policy changes and some welfare reforms) have been linked to increased demographic diversity and theories of social control (Soss, Fording, and Schram 2008; Soss et al. 2010). When innovations are perceived to address challenging issues, we should expect to see different and strongly held views. In the election administration arena, accessibility, security, inclusion, and integrity are valence issues. Voter identification methods could be perceived to be a policy choice within these broader concepts, as could state laws that impose additional requirements for documentary proof of citizenship for certain categories of voters when registering to vote, or a mandate for paper ballots to address election system security issues. The methods whereby election administrators are selected to hold office—by direct election or appointment—can also affect their policy priorities (e.g., for a study of election administrators in Wisconsin, see Burden et al. 2013). More broadly, partisanship appears to color voter perceptions and voter confidence about the election process, which is not itself a partisan activity (Atkeson and Saunders 2007, 658).

Adoption and implementation of new ideas also depends upon systematic methods for exchanging synthesized information across the intergovernmental system (Hale 2011). This type of information matters in the intergovernmental and intersectoral environment that encompasses American public policy, and that is particularly evident in the election administration arena. Information-rich (high-information) environments demonstrate significantly higher levels of policy adoption and more extensive implementation than otherwise (Hale 2011; Mossberger and Hale 2002).

Election resources that might be available for innovation are affected by a number of factors. Among these are reimbursements provided by state election offices, funds appropriated by the state legislature directly to local offices, and, most commonly, funds appropriated by local offices such as county commissioners. Significant population disparities exist across local election jurisdictions, and dramatic differences occur across counties in order to serve fewer than 400 voters and more than 4 million (Montjoy 2008; Tokaji 2009).

Most election jurisdictions are comparatively small in population. Kimball and Baybeck (2013) report that, for the 2008 election, about 30 percent of registered voters and 30 percent of total ballots occur in jurisdictions with fewer than 50,000 voters. Resources available in larger election jurisdictions may encourage innovation; that said, there is a huge discrepancy between the upper and lower bounds of this definition of "large." These disparities in size are often accompanied by a significant disparity in resources, which is important given the highly localized nature of American elections. Disparities in technology infrastructure—such as broadband and wireless services— also persist, in spite of its obvious, widespread expansion across the country

(Mossberger, Tolbert, and Franko 2012). These disparities may limit the ability to innovate, even in the face of desire to do so.

Although the responsibility for actually running an election lies solely with local government, local public managers are influenced by outside factors. In a survey of election administrators, when asked what were the most important factors that influenced local administration, the plurality of respondents indicated that the state government and/or the state office of the CEO (typically, but not always, the SOS) were most important, followed by the state legislature (Hale and Brown 2016). Thus, state resources for technology and state reimbursement practices come into play in considering the innovation landscape.

THE PRESSURE OF RISK

Among the most significant challenges for the complicated networked arrangements in the field of election administration are the pressures, risks, and rewards associated with the different stakeholders involved. The array of stakeholders on any given issue may include election officials, whether elected, appointed, or career; other types of elected officials (e.g., governors, members of state legislatures, the courts, Department of Justice officials, et al.); political parties; vendors; third-party groups; and the research community, whether associated or not with academic institutions. The work of each of these stakeholders takes a different pace, and the related risks and rewards are different. What this means for innovation is not necessarily good news—the stakeholders involved may or may not be aligned with respect to motivation, purpose, and urgency.

We lay out these competing dynamics in table 2.1. The risks and rewards for all public officials, whether election officials or officials involved in some other capacity, are essentially the same by type of position. Elected officials work through election cycles. The major risks they face in engaging in innovative work are reputational, which may lead to the loss of their position. Their major motivation is reelection at the most basic level, but motivations may also include policy goals, "promotion" to a higher level of office, party support, fund-raising ability, and voter support at the polls. Appointed officials by definition are largely motivated by reappointment, policy goals, and potentially promotion, but their time horizon is fixed to the length of their appointment. Career officials in secure positions still face the potential for being fired, but that is significantly less of a threat than not being reelected or reappointed.

Government officials are not the only people involved in innovation. Political parties are tangentially involved when overarching policy and ideological goals align with election administration concerns. More important for

TABLE 2.1 Rewards, Risks, and Time Pressures for Election Administration Stakeholders

Stakeholders		Rewards	Reward and Risk	Other Risks	Time Pressures
		Primary	Other*			
Election officials / other government officials	Elected	Reelection	Policy goals Promotion Party support Fund-raising Vote support	Reputation	Lose position	Election cycle
	Appointed	Reappointment	Policy Promotion	Reputation	Lose position	Appointment horizon
	Career	Promotion	Policy goals Promotion	Reputation	Lose position	Fiscal year
Political parties	Elect members	Policy goals Fund-raising Vote share	Reputation	Loss of party strength	Election cycle Appointment cycle	
Vendors	Profit	Market share Premiere products	Reputation	Deficit Losing customers	Fiscal year	

(continued)

TABLE 2.1 (*continued*)

Stakeholders		Rewards			Other Risks	Time Pressures
		Primary	Other*	Reward and Risk		
Third-party groups	Advocacy	Policy goals	Membership Fundraising	Reputation	Loss of relevance	Fiscal year
	Professional	Practice goals	Membership Fundraising	Reputation	Loss of relevance	Fiscal year
	Funders	Policy and practice goals	Policy goals	Reputation	Wasted investment	Grant cycles
Research community	Academic	Tenure and promotion	Publications Fundraising Awards Course release	Reputation	Tenure denial Promotion denial	Tenure and promotion, 5–6 years Publication timelines
	Nonacademic	Fund-raising	Publications	Reputation	Deficit	Fiscal year

Note: These are listed in no particular order.

innovation are vendors and members of third-party groups, who are differently motivated but often face the same time horizon concerns related to fiscal years and internal program planning and budgeting. What motivates them is fundamentally different. Whereas vendors must be primarily motivated by profit and market share, third-party groups are motivated by less tangible policy, practice, and ideological goals. The research community is also involved in innovation, whether by assisting it or studying it, but the motivations and rewards are very different, depending upon whether researchers are tied to academic institutions or nonacademic research groups. In this way, nonacademic researchers look much more like vendors than anything else, whereas academic researchers are a category wholly unto themselves, with extremely long time horizons (most marked by two- to six-year periods) and rewards that are tied to publications.

All these groups have one thing in common: the combined risk and reward of their personal and professional reputations. This is important for understanding engagement in innovation (or lack thereof) at the individual level. Those who are ambitious, forward thinking, and risk takers are much more likely to engage in this type of work. This should be particularly true when the risks associated with failure are limited. Thus, a small group of people, career government officials, third-party groups, and researchers (to an extent) ought to be the people most likely to push innovation at all levels.

The consequence of all this is that any innovation that is or must be cross-sectoral faces constraints that are not necessarily obvious or intuitive. For those actively interested in determining how to engage others in a new or innovative policy or practice change, it means thinking expansively about the different ways to engage partners and how to plan work. Further, the ability to work on long-range innovations is a luxury afforded only to a very few groups, which creates a strong potential for partners to drop out when success is not immediate.

HOW ELECTION ADMINISTRATORS ENVISION ELECTION INNOVATIONS

Innovation in public service is influence by visions of what the future might look like. The conditions that the future is believed to hold—both positive and not—will shape the ways in which public managers think about the information that they receive, and how they assess its value. Perhaps the people best able to predict the future are election administrators themselves. Thus, innovations are likely to be shaped in very real ways by the beliefs of election administrators about the future of elections—what they imagine to be their responses to the particular demands of the public, vendors, and other election community stakeholders, and how they see these responses fitting in to the political context of their state election laws and practices.

Election administrators are, as a group, optimistic about the public's future engagement with American democracy. They expect voter turnout to increase in the coming years, not least because voting will become increasingly convenient in comparison with traditional place-bound Election Day voting. However, election officials have no expectation of federal funding to support any of the changes that they anticipate.

When election administrators were asked at various times (2014, 2016, and 2017) about their perceptions about how election administration will change in the coming decades, they responded with a variety of answers both about election administration generally and about particular topics such as voter registration, methods of casting ballots, and technology. Figure 2.4 presents their opinions and perceptions in these four areas.

Their responses reflect new policies or administrative practices that range from automatic registration when obtaining a driver's license to the use of mobile apps for registration. Among the most prominent belief was that election administration will become more reliant on technology across all areas of their work. Administrators unanimously believe that the election process will include more and more complex administrative demands. Almost all believe that ballot-on-demand systems will be commonplace within the next four election cycles (by 2032) and that there will be better equipment and more diversity in the types of technology that are used in elections. A few participants (2014) thought that the future would revolve exclusively

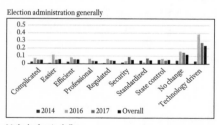

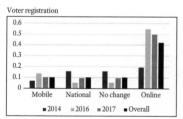

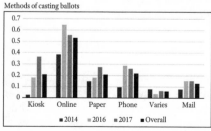

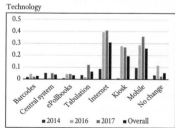

FIGURE 2.4. Proportion of Respondents Who Imagine These Changes in Election Administration by the 2032 Election

around commercial off-the-shelf (COTS) technology. On the surface, this could be interpreted to mean that they feel that there will be no place for traditional election equipment vendors in election administration. However, among more recent responses (2016), this view vanished; election officials noted that even if all voting systems were composed of COTS technology, vendors would necessarily remain involved to support software needs. Election administrators expressed an almost universal belief that the future holds a national voter registration database with portability, meaning that a voter's registration follows the voter as the voter moves within a state or around the country. However, almost no one believes that there will be federal funding to support these efforts, meaning that funding for elections and election technology will continue to come from state and local coffers.

Perhaps the most interesting prediction pertains to the actual future work that election administrators envision as a part of the responsibilities of their offices. Election officials envision myriad changes to aspects of election operations, ranging from constant, public recounts to the elimination of the EAC to voting kiosks.

Election administrators also believe that online voter registration will become ubiquitous, and that voter registration will occur through mobile apps. When thinking specifically about voter registration, election administrators again expressed the belief that the future will bring a national voter registration database. This national database would attach registration to the voter so that registration automatically follows the voter as the voter moves within a state (within-state portability) or around the country (fifty-state portability), and most believe that fifty-state portability will become a reality.

In 2016 and 2017, the election administrators with whom we worked expected that ballots would be cast online by 2032. Election rules that require that voters provide excuses in order to cast absentee ballots are expected to decline in popularity. Across the election administration system, including registration and balloting, election administrators expect app platforms to develop ballot-on-demand systems. It is perhaps noteworthy, when comparing 2016 and 2017, that the popularity of an online option declined relatively slightly and the use of paper ballots and kiosks increased.

Of course, there is no universal agreement on any of these predictions. The election arena has always been fraught with tensions between security, transparency, and voter convenience. The current election environment is no exception, as mistrust in government runs high, and as the integrity of election processes have been called into question in highly public ways, both during and since the 2016 election. Problems of trust may suggest that paper ballots will remain popular, and perhaps will be required. As one election official noted, "Paper ballots are most reliable in case of a recount or audit. We need that record to demonstrate the integrity of the process. Regarding online voting, we will either not have the ability to verify the integrity of the vote, or voters will lose their privacy. It really is a question of upholding all our current ideals more than a purely technical one."

Election administrators believe that new election technology is imminent. Future elections will focus on Internet and mobile options and the use of kiosks (which involve technological interfaces, to a greater or lesser extent depending on design). Interestingly, the popularity of these options among respondents did not decrease after the wave of publicity surrounding the 2016 presidential election, which continued in 2017, raising questions about the security of election technology that continue today.

In imagining technology for the elections of the future, a minority of respondents also mentioned electronic pollbooks and state-centric systems for vote tabulation and other aspects of election operations. We examine electronic pollbooks as an innovation in this book, and thus can perhaps interpret responses specific to that technology as an indication of further diffusion. Election officials also foresee greater diversity in combinations of election-specific technology, including increased use of COTS technology. They also believe that increased COTS options will not displace vendors. Not least, election officials believe that financial support for any technological changes and ongoing technological support will need to come from local jurisdictions.

Three themes persist across these opinions about the future. The first is the belief that national standardization will occur across voter registration records, and perhaps other areas of the election administration system. The second is the belief in the proliferations of options for methods of registration and casting ballots. And the third is the fact that predictions and preferences related to technology dominate the self-reported responses of election administrators. Of course, these opinions about the future are highly responsive to the climate at the time. Within these broad themes, we would expect to see the opinions of election administrators continue to respond to new public conversations, new information from vendors, and new pressures and opinions from advocacy groups, perhaps most specifically with respect to the pros and cons of various forms of paperless voting.

Public managers in the field believe that the force of technological change will change election operations and will further complicate their roles and responsibilities. One election administrator commented that "if you cannot understand or use technology, you will fail in your job." In a slightly different iteration of this sentiment, another noted that election administration will be "very IT [information technology] based—understanding cybersecurity and IT processes will be critical for anyone in the profession." Another predicted an Orwellian future of elections, in which there will be "very little face-to-face interaction" between election officials and voters. These views about the future of American elections help us understand the challenges that public managers can expect to face.

Predicting this future with some accuracy is critical for everyone involved in election systems and for the political execution of democracy. Election administrators are interested in this so that they can plan their administrative activities and budgeting needs in order to conduct elections and so that they can strategize about the future. Political parties care so that they can plan campaign strategy. Elected officials (including those responsible for the conduct of elections) care because the answers can influence their own campaigns as well as influence policies and predictions about future budgetary needs (and the tax levels needed to support them). Vendors of election systems, election equipment, and election supplies care so that they can prepare a path for serving current customers and meeting future needs. Interest groups care to the extent that their constituents' needs are protected or can be advanced. Ordinary citizens (should) care because of the influence this has on their own ability to influence government through casting ballots. And researchers and faculty in the field care because the direction of election administration will potentially have an impact on both possible avenues for research (for many) and on their courses (for a small, but growing, number who teach in this field). Although relatively new as a profession, election administrators are indeed experts. They are the "gatekeepers of democracy," and their opinions foreshadow at least some part of the future of election operations.

CONCLUSION

This chapter has introduced innovation in election administration through the concept of an activity-based innovation theory of change. This approach specifically focuses on networks and their interaction with the new and rising professionalism that is evident in election administration. The external environment of election operations has been illustrated through a top-level view of the election environment and its intergovernmental and cross-sectoral character.

In selecting examples for this book, we focus on jurisdictions that demonstrate high levels of professionalism that are consistent with the concept of an innovation network, and illustrate these in the cases. The innovations examined in the following chapters draw broadly from local election jurisdictions around the country, as well as offices of state election officials and the federal government. The election jurisdictions included as examples are led and managed by elected and appointed officials who are highly visible in the election environment and highly engaged in generating and sharing information across the election administration environment at all levels of government and with multiple stakeholders outside government proper. These include jurisdictions that have been invited to local, state, and/or national events to share their practices; jurisdictions that are highly visible in the network in leadership positions, working groups, and task forces; and jurisdictions that are interested in coming to the various tables around the country to learn and share information.[15]

National professional associations of government officials are prominently featured throughout the book. In some cases, these organizational configurations depend heavily on interactions with nonprofit organizations and private-sector firms. Within each area, election administrators utilize different methods of cooperation, collaboration, governance, and measurement to address their challenges.

Throughout, we consider innovation in election administration through the lens of the federal system. Election administration is unique among policy domains both in its constitutional grounding at both the state and federal levels, and in its primary deployment through local election offices. Explaining responses to uncertainty where organizations are arranged in intergovernmental relationships implicates the concept of political power. In the American federal system, for example, states and the federal government are both sovereign, legitimate governments with constitutionally conferred powers both express and implied. Sovereignty imposes constraints on the ability of the national government to compel states to act in matters where the national Constitution allows for state discretion. Individual states are unlikely to persuade the national government to adopt particular policies or to adapt policies to fit unique state needs. Similarly, the federal government cannot implement policy in this arena without state cooperation and explicit state action.

Across the election administration landscape of the last two decades, the balance of power within the federal system has shifted. And the election administration landscape itself has grown, in response to federal mandates and, recently, with new considerations about election security. State roles have become more pronounced in relation to local operations. These changing power relationships have not slowed the notion of innovation in the field, as illustrated by the innovations presented in this book. However, configurations of political power are manifested differently across these innovations.

As the following chapters demonstrate, each innovation in election administration presents election officials with unique configurations of organizations and actors within this environment. The pressures on these organizations and actors—as well as the opportunities they have to reform, change, and innovate in their practices—produce the results that we do (or do not) see in innovation. Chapter 3 begins this investigation with an examination of the first step in the election process for voters: registration. The changes that have taken place across the states in registration and the landscape to come capture the critical dimensions of innovation set out in this chapter.

NOTES

1. See Hale, Montjoy, and Brown (2015, 19–21) for a catalog of research across elements of election systems, cross-cutting issues in election administration, and the capacity of election administration systems.
2. Innovation also requires the involvement of actors and institutions with the capacity to interpret and understand these. But in some instances, these shocks may spark innovation, which also has strong ties to capacity.
3. See Renz (2016) for a catalog of factors that reinforce innovation in the nonprofit sector, and see Selznick (1949) and Thompson (1967) for a description and analysis of some of the earliest public agency strategies to cope with environmental uncertainty.
4. Among these are security with respect to the social forces in the environment, stability in lines of authority communication, stability of informal relationships in the organization, continuity of policy and sources of policy formation, and homogeneity of outlook about the role and meaning of the organization (Selznick 1949).
5. The Election Center is the only national professional association dedicated solely to the professionalization of election officials (broadly defined as election administrators and voter registrars) as well as vendors and election monitors.
6. These time periods approximate the end of the industrialized work era before the Great Depression, the passage of the Hatch Act, and major civil service reform in 1978.
7. Certification is also offered for vendors (certified election and registration vendor—CERV) and monitors (certified election monitor—CEM).
8. This is available at www.electioncenter.org.
9. Formal state certification programs exist in Arizona, Colorado, Connecticut, Florida, Georgia, Iowa, Michigan, Minnesota, Mississippi, Montana, North Carolina, South Carolina, Virginia, Washington, and Wisconsin.
10. The Florida association was known until May 2019 as the Florida State Association of Supervisors of Elections.
11. These additional responsibilities include issuing and recording marriage licenses and liquor licenses and recording real estate transactions. Somewhat less typical of offices with election responsibilities, the Colorado Clerk and Recorders office also operates the motor vehicle divisions for titling vehicles and issuing license plates.
12. The Network of Schools of Public Policy, Affairs, and Administration has hosted this consortium, which is developed and led by faculty who formed its Election Administration and Leadership Section.
13. One example is the National Association of Drug Court Professionals (Hale 2011), which did not exist in 1985 but is now active across the country as the idea of drug court policy has become established.
14. One example of a state-level measure of state election operation performance is the Election Performance Index, which is discussed in detail in chapter 8.
15. The illustrations of innovation in this volume are not exhaustive and do not represent a sample; no doubt there are other exciting developments that will be fostered by the rapidly changing election environment.

3

Innovations in Administering Voter Registration: How Prospective Voters Qualify

In this chapter, we consider innovations in the American election administration system that involve voter registration processes. Innovation in voter registration is important, for several reasons. At the most basic level, voter registration is central to the election process and a precondition to casting a ballot in every state except North Dakota. Another important consideration is the historic use of voter registration practices to disenfranchise voters. Practices such as poll taxes and literacy tests were used to discriminate against blacks until the Voting Rights Act of 1965 (VRA) and the Twenty-Fourth Amendment to the Constitution. Early colonial and state registration practices also discriminated against members of religious groups and members of minority political parties and racial and ethnic minorities, and these practices continued long after Reconstruction, into the 1960s (Keyssar 2000; Valelly 2004).

Today, across every local election jurisdiction, issues are raised about the inability to register and about the inaccuracy of voter rolls. Some of these are specific claims about improper methods used to maintain the voter registration lists and, most recently, concerns about election security. Where valid, these claims prevent participation. Even if not valid, public attention directed toward these possibilities can have a negative influence on public confidence in election integrity and political efficacy.

Historic methods of voter discrimination have been eliminated altogether, we hope. The legacy of these practices, however, is that ideological preferences about access and participation remain embedded in public opinion about reform proposals and policy initiatives, if not the actual proposals themselves. In voter registration, these reforms run the gamut—from tools used to encourage voter convenience, such as online voter registration and automatic (or electronic or automated) voter registration, to identification methods that are couched in security concerns, to administrative tools that facilitate the integration of data from a wide range of public sources. Election administration reforms are guided generally by state and local political dynamics (Pallazollo and Moscardelli 2006), and partisanship has guided the adoption of some aspects of voter registration reform. Most particularly, studies over time of more restrictive methods of voter identification from the time of the National Voter Registration Act (NVRA) and the Help America Vote Act of 2002 (HAVA) find that these methods are related to the strength of Republican political influence at the state level (e.g., Aistrup et al. 2019; Hale and McNeal 2010). As the innovations described in this chapter demonstrate, political influence remains, but it is also clearly supported by collaborative networked relationships and greater degrees of professionalism.

Innovations in voter registration are also important because differences in voter registration persist across various demographic groups, and innovations have the potential to ameliorate these differences. Scholars continue to find that voter registration requirements remain a significant institutional barrier to voting (Gregorowicz and Hall 2016; Rosenstone and Wolfinger 1978) and are associated with other election policies that have the similar effect of reducing participation. Bowler and Donovan (2016), in one of the earliest studies of state election reforms post-HAVA, found that states with greater numbers of voting restrictions, including restrictive registration practices, had a lower turnout in the 2004 presidential election. Disparities continue; of the more than 235 million Americans of voting age, about 20 percent of those eligible to vote are not registered (Pew Charitable Trusts 2017). Among eligible voters, those who are younger, less educated, at the lower ends of the economic spectrum, and nonwhite continue to register at lower rates than their counterparts who are older, well educated, have a high income, and are white. As Gregorowicz and Hall (2016) summarize, there are differences between the groups whose members are registered and those who are not. Only about half the youngest, poorest, and least-educated citizens age eighteen years or older are registered to vote.

Innovation in voter registration has evolved in the context of a thicket of administrative processes for data acquisition, verification, and storage and against a patchwork backdrop of state election laws, myriad electronic databases, and paper records. Innovation aimed at systems integration has the potential to enhance administrative capacity and improve office operations. No national registration system exists, and there are no uniform administrative practices across the states. Federal laws set some overall parameters, and state election laws establish others. The process details are institutionalized in local election offices; this local variation has been the source of great conflict in the past, but in itself is not a bad thing.

In many ways, the story of innovation in voter registration is a system-wide one because all election offices have been required to participate. From the perspective of local and state election offices, the voter registration environment is characterized by participation in involuntary administrative networks, required technical upgrades, and changing technology generally. The NVRA initiated required coordination among disparate offices. HAVA amplified this effect by bringing voter registration documents into the electronic era, with its requirement for statewide electronic voter registration databases, and by providing a backstop method of registration for first-time voters who register by mail. Conceptually, establishing a statewide database of any kind is relatively easy to understand. In practice, however, the process has been expensive. Between 2003 and 2014, states and territories spent $223 million in federal HAVA funds on developing and maintaining electronic voter registration lists (EAC 2015). The average amount was $8.25 million per state; however, this average obscures significant variation across states, and expenditures are not related to population during this period.[1] In every state, keeping voter registration lists up to date is a never-ending process.

Innovation vis-à-vis voter registration is also the story of required cooperation and collaboration between local election jurisdictions and state election offices, and required cooperation with public offices outside the election arena—all pushed by federal mandates. Public–private partnerships have also played a significant role in voter registration innovation. Data management tools—including online voter registration practices, electronic pollbooks, and big data–matching services—improve the accuracy of voter registration lists and increase voter convenience. States have also experimented recently with forms of automatic registration that link voter registration activities across public offices. Systems used to track voter registration data have been modernized over the past fifteen years to comply with HAVA mandates and through technological advances generally; however, conversion to electronic systems has ushered in new issues.

This chapter first outlines the legislative environment that constrains voter registration activities, including federal legal requirements and consideration of the constitutional authority of state and local election officials. We then consider administrative innovations to enhance voter convenience, including online voter registration, electronic pollbooks, and state policy changes for automatic voter registration. Last, we consider innovative public–private partnerships that enhance the accuracy of voter registration lists.

THE ARCHITECTURE OF VOTER REGISTRATION

In the modern era of election administration, the management of voter registration and voter registration list issues rest on details of the National

Voter Registration Act of 1993 and the Help America Vote Act that govern voter registration list construction and maintenance. Well before HAVA, the NVRA, also known as "Motor Voter," expanded the sources from which voter registration information would flow into local offices. The NVRA established the opportunity to register to vote at driver's license bureaus and at public service offices, including offices that provide disability services. The NVRA applies to all but six states; those excluded did not have voter registration requirements and/or permitted registration on Election Day.[2] The NVRA also required the option to register to vote by mail, and prohibited removal from the rolls purely because someone did not vote.

It is worth noting that the NVRA was itself an innovation in voter access. Its purpose was to expand voter access through additional opportunities for registration in hopes of increasing voter participation across the system, including turnout. One of the prevailing ideas at the time was that voter turnout would increase if more people were registered to vote. It was thought that if registration systems were more accessible, the quality and quantity of democratic functioning would be enhanced by greater numbers of voters turning out at the polls.

The NVRA increased opportunities for voter registration and was expected to translate into an increase in voter turnout, which had been steadily declining since the 1970s.[3] However, increased registration has not translated into an increase in voter turnout or to greater rates of participation among lower socioeconomic groups (Martinez and Hill 1999). There is some evidence that registration has increased in some groups that are less likely to register (Brown and Wedeking 2006; Rugeley and Jackson 2009).

Of course, the successful implementation of new voter registration methods is essential for public policy to achieve its intended results. In the case of the NVRA, implementation has been complicated by the design of the legislation, which reaches outside traditional election offices for assistance in gathering registration applications. This creates an obvious need for additional coordination and cooperation, as well as the need for new methods of oversight to ensure that implementation is proceeding as required. Research suggests that these sorts of changes will affect the work of public administrators. In the case of election officials specifically, the addition of different methods of voter registration has affected their daily work. In particular, questions have been raised about the capacity of election offices to administer the complex intergovernmental web of voter registration requirements created by the NVRA. In election jurisdictions with fewer financial (and therefore administrative) resources, local election officials (LEOs) may be less able to implement the NVRA and other election registration requirements (Burden and Neiheisel 2013). One study recommends that the administrative burden on election officials for NVRA compliance could be eased if the ancillary public offices that process NVRA applications also actually registered voters, rather than collecting information and passing it along to election offices (Nickerson 2014).

This administrative burden is quite real. Election officials responsible for voter registration activities around the country comment that their work is much harder to accomplish, particularly in a timely way, given the NVRA's requirements for intergovernmental cooperative interaction with offices whose functions are not focused on elections. Tensions have occurred in relation to work routines and office norms. As an illustration, one election official in Texas noted that "the information comes in to our system in batches, which is fine; once we understand the timing of the batches we can integrate that into our processes and plan for it. What is not fine is that the information is incomplete and creates more work for us than if we had done it ourselves." Said another, "Wrong information from them [ancillary public offices] generates multiple steps on our side in order to figure out what information is actually correct." Election officials across the country note the need for greater care and accuracy on the part of ancillary offices to assist them in fulfilling their responsibilities under the NVRA. They also noted that ancillary offices often seem to have different interpretations of the NVRA requirements; some ancillary offices may believe that those receiving public services are required to register to vote in order to receive services, rather than simply being provided with an opportunity to register. It may also be the case that ancillary offices do not appear to take voter registration very seriously; in one local motor vehicle office that we visited, the chalkboard notice "Register to Vote Here" was located in relatively close proximity to the customer service counter but was also partially concealed behind a potted plant.

Tensions continue among local offices because election officials have no direct authority to compel compliance or enforce standards of performance. In more than one office, election officials report inconsistencies in basic processes related to integration with outside offices. Although responsibility for voter registration rests ultimately with election officials, they can be constrained in their ability to enforce standards and practices across offices that report to different state authorities with separate constitutional mandates. Practical administrative questions are common, including whether election offices conduct training for ancillary offices, or provide training materials, or establish implementation protocols; these common questions also raise constitutional concerns about authority and the allocation of resources. The disputes about constitutional authority engage fundamental questions about whether one statewide election official, such as a secretary of state, can compel actions by appointed executive branch officials who serve another statewide elected official, such as a governor (see, e.g., *Scott v. Schedler*, Louisiana, 2016). These governance questions about voter registration responsibilities permeate election administration systems across the country, in which about half of all state election officials and LEOs are themselves elected as constitutional officers.

Relatedly, across ancillary offices, and in comparison with election offices, different cultures and different missions impede clear communication in many instances. Early culture clashes about implementation design and execution are to be expected as any public offices attempt to work together on tasks, and perhaps particularly so when the task seems more clearly the responsibility of one office than of multiple offices. These conflicts are common in the emergency management and disaster response arena, and they include consideration of planning and response efforts in natural and intelligent disasters ranging from hurricanes and wildfires to terrorist attacks (Birkland 2006; Comfort 1999, 2002; Comfort and Kapucu 2006; Comfort and Resolihardjo 2013). That said, cultural differences appear to persist more than twenty-five years since the NVRA (and fifteen years since HAVA), at least in the views of LEOs. One official commented that personnel from other county offices, when asked to work on election registration matters, "didn't bring the same energy and work ethic as we expect from our staff." "Their commitment to accuracy was not there," another voter registrar noted, in commenting about the batches of application forms that were received in the election offices from the driver's license office in their county.

In some ways, the changes required by the NVRA and HAVA may seem to be typical matters of administrative practice. Election officials have always relied on information from other local and state administrative units, including bureaus of vital statistics and the criminal justice system. These units provide election offices with information that election administrators incorporate into their existing protocols. However, the NVRA requires new input from administrative agencies that is more detailed (i.e., completed voter registration applications) and HAVA effectively requires that this information be integrated into electronic state voter registration databases.

The result is a complex information system. Figure 3.1 illustrates a typical and very general schematic of sources of voter registration information that come into local and state election offices. Election offices receive applications from a host of sources. Each information source has a unique administrative process and a unique method of constructing and maintaining data; election offices bear the burden of integrating these data sets.

Voters initiate registration in various ways: in person, online, through third-party registration drives, and through a host of local offices that are grouped as NVRA agencies. Local offices screen applications for eligibility, process the results, and notify registrants. LEOs also receive information from offices of vital statistics and the criminal justice system. All this information is supplied by the LEO to the statewide voter registration database. In many states, the database is also updated through interaction with data provided by third parties, such as the Electronic Registration Information Center, the National Change of Address system operated by the US Postal Service, and the Interstate Voter Registration Crosscheck program. Voters

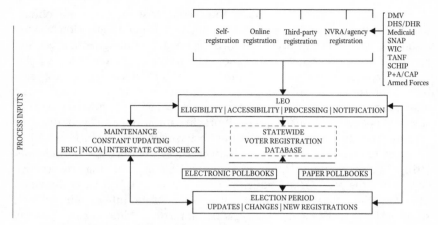

FIGURE 3.1 Statewide Voter Registration Process Model

interact with the registration database on Election Day (or days, or by mail) through a paper pollbook or an electronic pollbook. Election Day information is also used to update the voter registration system and to process new registrations according to state law.

Coordination is not limited to external offices. This generic voter registration architecture is also integrated with the local and state intergovernmental arrangements that make up each state's voter registration system. Roughly one-third (eighteen) of the states use more than one local office to conduct elections at the jurisdiction level and separate the voter registration function from Election Day operations (Hale, Montjoy, and Brown 2015). The Alabama local voter registration architecture is one example of the complex local voter registration networks that exist today. In Alabama, elections are administered by the coordinated operations of five county offices: an elected probate judge, circuit clerk, sheriff and county commissioners, and an appointed board of registrars. Each of the three members of the county board of registrars is appointed by a different statewide elected official; these statewide offices include the governor, auditor, and agricultural commissioner.[4] Registrars are responsible for maintaining accurate voter rolls in each county. With respect to voter registration alone, as only one activity within any election system, the network becomes more complicated as a result of required contacts and coordination with the Alabama Public Health Department, Human Resources Department (social services), Medicaid agency, and Rehabilitation Services Department, as well as the office of vital statistics and the criminal justice system. It is important to note that these offices in the network do not actually register voters, but they provide applications to voters and may assist in completing them, and they return completed applications to the registrars.

The activities necessary to gather and process voter registration information from multiple sources fall under the general HAVA requirement that states maintain electronic, statewide voter registration databases. Although an electronic format would seem to be an improvement over paper lists (or, more accurately, books of paper lists), this change has also created problems, for which election officials are developing innovative solutions.

Together, the NVRA and HAVA have established a typical network environment in which command-and-control authority structures are not effective across the entire voter registration process, and which requires electronic integration. In order to accomplish their responsibilities, election officials have looked outside the election structure proper to build new relationships and seek new resources. These resources have been found in existing government programs and have also been developed through new initiatives, including new technology and new organizations. Each represents a slightly different variation on innovation within the theory of change.

MAINTAINING ACCURATE VOTER REGISTRATION LISTS

The essential goal of federal voter registration requirements is that states maintain accurate and current lists, and that states avoid making changes, except in ways that are nondiscriminatory, uniform, and not conducted too close to an election.[5] The NVRA also specifies that registrants may not be removed solely because they fail to vote. This is especially relevant; before the NVRA, many state laws or practices used nonvoting alone as a reason for removing names from the voter rolls (Harris 1928, 1929).

Figure 3.2 gives a more comprehensive depiction of the list maintenance process for address changes.[6] As the figure illustrates, election administrators are faced with a wide range of circumstances and multiple decision points. The process varies depending on whether the voter responds, and, if the voter responds, the information that is contained in the response. Whether a voter's name is maintained on the rolls or dropped at some point depends on whether they respond, and whether their new address is within the same jurisdiction, in a different jurisdiction in the same state, or in a new state.

The complexity of this process is managed differently across election jurisdictions. What is the same across jurisdictions are the required interactions that engage LEOs and chief election officials (CEOs) with multiple offices outside their immediate purview. And what is significant about this illustration is its depiction of the interoffice cooperation that election officials must initiate and sustain.

State processes for list maintenance have been challenged as discriminatory against certain demographic groups, as illustrated by recent cases

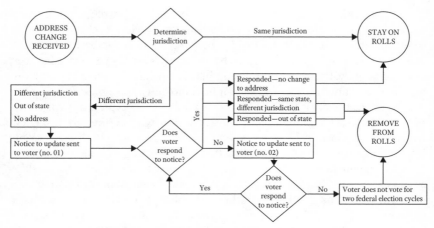

FIGURE 3.2 Model of Change of Address within
the Voter Registration Process

involving Florida and Ohio. Florida's list maintenance activities, which were directed by the Florida secretary of state (SOS) and conducted before the 2012 presidential election, were found to violate the so-called ninety-day-provision of the NVRA because they were conducted within ninety days of a federal election (*Arcia v. Detzner,* 2012).[7] The SOS program involved two distinct activities. The first was the use of a program that matched Florida voter rolls with a list of people who applied for a driver's license using a green card or a foreign passport. The conclusion was that these people were suspected noncitizens and could be removed, after further investigation by the Florida Supervisors of Elections (SOEs). The second was a list compiled by the Department of Homeland Security, generated by its Systematic Alien Verification for Entitlements (SAVE) program, which included names listed for similar reasons. The Florida SOS required that Florida SOEs investigate suspected noncitizens against the SAVE list and delete from their voter rolls the names of those individuals listed on the SAVE list. Interestingly, the Florida SOS did not contest the fact that names were removed during the ninety-day period, but rather argued that it was proper to remove the names of individuals who were never eligible to register in the first instance.

The practical administrative significance of list maintenance is illustrated by the recent US Supreme Court decision in *Husted v. A. Philip Randolph* (2018), which was brought by a voter who cast a ballot in the 2008 presidential election but found that his name had been removed when he appeared at the polls in 2015. The suit challenged Ohio's so-called use-it-or-lose-it method of removing names from the voter registration lists. Under this method, if a registered voter has no voter activity for a two-year period (including voting and signing candidate petitions), the local county election office sends the voter an address confirmation notice. This two-year period is used as a rough indicator that a registrant has moved. The voter can confirm their address through the mail using a prepaid envelope or can respond online. In either case, when the voter responds, the voter information is confirmed and updated as appropriate. Before the 2015 election cycle, Ohio removed more than 7,000 names of people who had not actually moved but had not voted in two years, did not respond to warning notices, and then did not vote for another four years; these voters were presumably eligible to vote, except for their failure to respond to the notification.

The *Husted* case illustrates the considerable challenges that election administrators face when integrating federal requirements with effective administrative practice and the general questions that public managers tackle in maintaining voter registration lists. In its opinion, the majority of the Supreme Court acknowledged these challenges, and the need for states to establish clear administrative processes. Ohio claimed that voter names were not removed for failure to vote, but for failure to respond to the address confirmation letter.[8] In June 2018, the Supreme Court ruled 5–4 in favor of Ohio's practice. The majority ruled that, although failing to vote cannot be the sole reason for removal, removal of registrants is proper if individuals have failed to vote and have failed to respond to a notice. The *Husted* case is expected to have an impact on election practices across the country as well as the administrative procedures that are used to maintain voter rolls.

Voter registration lists will always be inaccurate; the voter roll inaccuracy rate has been reported at one in eight entries, or 12.5 percent (Pew Center on the States 2012). However, achieving a level of accuracy in voter registration that will escape negative publicity is a challenging task. The responsibilities for election officials in this area are daunting, because voting is fundamentally tied to the political geography of voters; the interaction between a voter's address and the political jurisdictions attached to that address determines the offices and issues on which they can vote. This is obvious in the case of the precinct voting that is commonly used across the country. This is also the case even in states that have configured voting processes to encompass broader geographic areas (e.g., combined precincts, vote centers). The election system also uses a person's name as the personal identifier. Yet names and residences change throughout a lifetime, and sometimes in combination.

The US Postal Service estimates that more than 40 million people move from state to state each year. Of these, slightly fewer than 60 percent move within the same county, slightly fewer than 20 percent move to a different county in the same state, slightly fewer than 20 percent move to a different state, and the remaining roughly 3 percent move out of the country. In addition, more than 2 million people get married, more than 800,000 get divorced, and more than 2.5 million die.

Name and address establish eligibility for citizens age eighteen and over, but are not entirely dispositive. About 6 million people have been convicted of a felony that may disqualify them from voting, whether for a period of time or permanently. State laws on disenfranchisement and voting rights restoration vary widely; however, the disproportionate impact on African Americans is clear (see, e.g., King 2016; Ochs 2006; Pettus 2013). The state-level data on voting rights restoration are somewhat uneven; however, the acknowledged experts on the topic indicate that roughly 450,000 ex-offenders had voting rights restored from 1990 to 2015 (Mauer 1999; Love 2005; Uggen and Manza 2002, 2006; Uggen, Larson, and Shannon 2016; Uggen, Manza, and Thompson 2006). Further administrative changes are on the horizon in this area, although the results are far from clear.

In November 2018, Florida voters passed Florida Amendment 4 as an initiated state constitutional amendment to restore voting rights to felons automatically upon completion of their sentences (including postincarceration requirements). The initiative passed by a strong margin of 64.55 percent. This is a significant development; under previous law, felons never regained voting rights in Florida unless approved by an executive branch office (e.g., a state pardon board). Estimates at the time of the election placed the number of Floridians who were prohibited from voting at more than 1.6 million, nearly 10.5 percent of the state's voting population. Implementation squabbles ensued over questions about whether separate legislative procedures were required, and whether fines had to be repaid before rights were restored. At the time of writing, Florida SOEs are issuing voter identification cards to registration applicants who applied after the passage of Amendment 4. This initiative is certainly innovative in and of itself as an exercise of citizen preferences on a highly contentious issue and in direct opposition to the entrenched preferences of many established political leaders.

Relating to place, voter registration lists are now compiled and held electronically at the state level as a result of HAVA; however, moving from state to state always generates the need for a voter to reregister. And in nearly all states, moving within a state typically generates the need for updated voter registration. Election jurisdictions can, and have, mitigated the need for voters to take the initiative to update their registration information, depending on the method of voting that the state uses and the geographic units that are used to organize the voter registration end of the system. Thus, registration information may transfer across precincts, or it may encompass an entire county or an entire state without a need for independent voter action.

The innovation network for voter registration is quite diverse. Private-sector vendors and third-party organizations have been actively involved in promoting some aspects of new methods of voter registration and voter registration list maintenance. LEOs and state election officials have been leaders in these areas as well, which creates a rich environment for considering the influence of an innovation network on the work of public managers in the election administration field.

Promising developments revolve around technology and include online voter registration (OVR), electronic pollbooks (EPBs), automatic or automated voter registration (AVR), and third-party registration list maintenance tools. Some of these innovations have evolved and diffused more rapidly than others, and none of them have been universally adopted across all election jurisdictions. The effect of these efforts should be, and can be, an improvement in voter list accuracy, including the elimination of removals of eligible voters.

ONLINE VOTER REGISTRATION

OVR is now a relatively common aspect of election operations. It has been promoted as a way to encourage voter participation, and as a way to reduce the costs of registration in comparison with office staff members who interact directly with voters. The average cost per jurisdiction to develop and implement OVR across the country has been estimated at $250,000 and has produced considerable savings. Los Angeles County, California—with 4.5 million registered voters—reported a $1.8 million expense, and savings of $2.5 million, at an average savings of $2.34 per registration (Gregorowicz and Hall 2016).[9] Evidence suggests that OVR may be influential in boosting registration among younger citizens and those who have recently moved (Pellissier 2014). States that have implemented OVR have seen a small uptick in registration (1 percentage point), but there has been no reported effect on turnout (Gregorowicz and Hall 2016).

Although differences exist across states, the basic concept of OVR is that prospective voters can utilize an Internet site to access applications for new voter registration and for updates to their existing registration data. State requirements for signature verification are satisfied through methods of transferring signatures that have been stored electronically or by some form of electronic signature.

The first OVR was established in Arizona in 2002. The approach has diffused rapidly across many states, although not all. By 2012, fifteen states had adopted OVR; and by 2014, twenty states and the District of Columbia had adopted or implemented OVR (National Conference of State Legislatures 2015; Pew Center on the States 2015). By 2018, OVR was adopted or in use in an additional eleven states (Pew Center on the States 2018).

To examine the ways in which this innovation has been influenced by factors in the network innovation model, we examine OVR across the states through a lens that captures variation in the degree to which OVR applies and the differences in OVR system features. States may have adopted OVR across the state or in some jurisdictions, or not adopted the practice; in both cases, some adopter states have passed legislation, and some nonadopter states have laws that prohibit it. In addition to legislative adoption, different dimensions of OVR are considered, including voter access requirements, various dimensions of system development and maintenance, features of the OVR system, and system-processing characteristics; each dimension consists of multiple factors.

Across all these dimensions, we examined the influence of four factors that affect innovation and diffusion in our network innovation model. These include measures of politics, resources, and needs, as well as the influence of networks aided by professionalism.[10] Across the board, political factors and network interactions are related to some aspects of OVR adoption, and to some features of OVR systems.

Networks tend to influence states to use legislation to require the use of EPBs, rather than to simply permit the use; states with greater professionalism were more likely to require state legislation to adopt them. Greater professionalism also contributes to developing an OVR system through public–private collaboration, and to housing the system with a vendor rather than in a state office. This relationship may stem from a number of factors, but most likely suggests that as election administration is professionalized, the community of election officials is better prepared to advocate for innovation and reform.

Voters must provide various kinds of information as they access and interact with an OVR system. Across the states, the most prevalent access requirement is date of birth, with 58.8 percent of states requiring this, and the least prevalent is the full Social Security Number (SSN), with only 5.9 percent of states requiring this information for access. Political influence on the type of information required is slight. States with both Republican- and Democratic-controlled legislatures are equally as unlikely to require the full SSN.

How states develop and store OVR systems also varies. In a plurality of states, OVR systems are developed solely by state information technology staff. And for a majority of the states that use OVR, the system is housed in the CEO's office. In only one instance is the OVR housed with the Department of Motor Vehicles (DMV), and for a handful of states the system resides with a vendor. Regardless of the approach to system development, states are about evenly split over whether or not they run a pilot launch of the OVR system at introduction. Democratic-controlled states are twice as likely to have a pilot, and Republican-controlled states are twice as likely not to have one. Although very few states house their OVR systems with vendors, Democratic-controlled states are more likely to do so than Republican-controlled states.

In considering the confirmation features that could be used for OVR, most states utilize a confirmation screen, confirmation number, and confirmation email; a majority do not provide a confirmation email sent at activation. Of these, the use of one feature—a confirmation screen—is significantly related to politics. In this case, the significance reflects the underlying fact that Republican-controlled states are split between whether or not to use OVR, as compared with the Democratic-controlled states, which tend to use it; among states that use OVR, almost all have the option of a confirmation screen (in fact, only two do not).

Most states with OVR have mobile optimization but do not support multiple languages—both of which are significantly related to political influence. Proportionately, Republican-controlled states are more likely than Democratic-controlled states to have mobile optimization, while Democratic-controlled states are much more likely to have the systems optimized for multiple languages. Finally, although many states collect email addresses through their OVR systems, most do not make those email addresses a matter of public record.[11]

Not least, states process OVR in a variety of ways, including whether election officials review all applications or only those that are flagged for particular reasons. Systems also differ in their ability to differentiate between OVR and paper applications, to differentiate between new and updated applications, to process without a DMV record, and to process entirely electronically (without printing information). Most states that use OVR do not transmit the information in real time; nor do they notify the applicant in real time if they are submitting a duplicate application. Only one condition, the requirement for at least some manual data entry, was significantly related to the innovation variables. Although Republican-controlled states were less likely than Democratic-controlled states to have OVR systems that require manual entry, states with split legislatures were much more likely than the others to have it.

Despite the popularity of OVR, some research suggests that voters experience higher transaction costs when the process requires downloading forms (Bennion and Nickerson 2011). Only a handful of state OVR systems are electronically linked to DMV records and automatically update these records with new information. This disconnect—or rather, lack of automatic connection—illustrates the challenges that public managers face in meeting requirements to integrate information from multiple sources despite widespread use of electronic records across public services.

Election officials are also quick to point out that OVR is not a replacement for other strong administrative controls. In one office, top staff members noted that "remembering to have a manual backup is critical." In this particular office, manual processes are atypical; most processes are automated, and OVR is a key example. But as the administrators in this office noted, automation also brings risks of technology failure or hacking. "If the power grid goes out, or if there is a denial-of-service attack, or Internet access goes down, paper becomes—again—the basic way we get the job done." Thus, technological innovation does not eliminate the need for redundancy, and in fact emphasizes it.

ELECTRONIC POLLBOOKS

Another innovation in voter registration and election administration is the use of EPBs. An EPB is an electronic voter registration list housed in a laptop or tablet computer. The extent of the voter registration list varies with state law; in some states the list is statewide, and in others it is limited to a single county. One key advantage of EPBs is the time savings in looking up voter names and addresses at the check-in process. Because data encompass more than a single precinct or polling location, the EPB approach allows election administrators (typically, poll workers) to easily redirect voters to the correct voting location. Checking in through a scanned driver's license improves accuracy; voter convenience is enhanced through electronic signature capture. Other features can allow poll workers to determine whether the voter has already voted—for example, during an early voting period or by absentee ballot. EPBs also have the capability of using photography to verify voter identity. Data gathered through EPBs are also readily available after an election, including turnout data in various summary forms by location, and lists of those who voted.

Across the board, EPB adoption and system features are related to political factors. A slim majority of states (twenty-six of fifty-one, including the District of Columbia) allow EPBs. However, in most states they are not used statewide, and this is significantly related to politics. The ratio of statewide use to less than statewide use for Republican-controlled states is 1:6, and for Democratic-controlled states it is 1:4. The only split controlled legislative state to use EPBs does so statewide (Colorado). One-quarter of the states have passed legislation about EPBs, and a minority have state certification requirements.[12]

EPB systems, like OVR, were created in some cases by the state, in some by the vendor, and in some through cooperation between them. The most typical case is the use of systems designed and maintained by the vendor. In most cases, the software is proprietary to the vendor. And though some of the hardware used is commercial-off-the-shelf, software is also proprietary to the state or vendor.

The features of EPBs encompass, broadly, capabilities for voter check-in, including same-day registration, verification of cast ballots, testing, auditing, backup systems, and data transmission and security protocols. In a plurality of states, voters check in and the system verifies in real time whether a vote was cast. In a handful of states, different EPBs are used across the states with differences about whether ballots are produced, ballot totals are verified, and if same-day registration is allowed, whether the EPB allows for it. A plurality of states do not conduct testing done by the states in advance of the election, and instead this testing is left up to the local offices. This is also true for auditing the EPB systems. Most states do use backup paper rolls on Election Day for the EPBs as opposed to relying on backup EPB systems, though there is a great deal of variance for this both across and within states. In most states, data transmission occurs between EPBs within the counties, as opposed to data transmitted either directly from the local office to the state or between the local offices and the states. Finally, a majority of states that use EPBs use written security protocols to protect their systems. This is significantly related to politics, and is driven by Republican-controlled legislatures, which are more than four times more likely to require this, as opposed to Democratic legislatures, which are four times less likely to require this.

EPBs collect and hold various types of data about voters. In almost all states that use EPBs, almost all retain a voter's name and date of birth and whether a ballot was cast. Most do not record SSN information, either the last four digits or the full number. Among the states that use EPBs, most retain the driver's license or state identification (ID) number and the registrant's address, but not their phone number or email address. Most of the systems also retain information about absentee or early voting status, but not an electronic signature. Most systems retain information about the polling place, time of arrival, type of ballot issued, and voter eligibility. Finally, most do not hold voting history information. The only significant relationship between the factors that predict innovation and these EPB characteristics pertains to requiring and holding the full SSN of registrants. Only one state requires this (Colorado), and in states where there is variance in requiring this across counties, the variance is not related to politics.

The utility of EPBs has evolved rapidly in conjunction with the requirement for statewide electronic voter registration databases. The benefits are readily apparent in terms of voter convenience by preventing errors for both voters and election administrators, such as voting in the wrong location or providing duplicate ballots. As one election administrator noted, "Our EPB is really a piece of our voter registration system, and the statewide pollbooks are essential to the process. Our poll workers use EPBs to hit the system in real time with voters on Election Day, so there is no way [for a voter] to return a mail ballot and get another ballot at the polls." Election officials stress that EPBs require resources in order for the potential to be realized, regardless of the size of the jurisdiction. "As wonderful as the (product) is, it was labor intensive for our staff to configure them to the registration files of all the precincts. At ground zero, you need to have trained staff to do the work," commented one election official.

AUTOMATIC VOTER REGISTRATION

Automatic voter registration (AVR) options represent another method of innovation. By 2018, twelve states and the District of Columbia had approved the policy, and twenty states had introduced legislation to establish or improve existing AVR systems (Weiser and Bannon 2018).[13] AVR approaches share two common features: (1) eligible citizens who interact with motor vehicle licensing agencies are automatically registered to vote, or have their registration information updated unless they affirmatively decline or opt out; and (2) these offices transfer voter registration data electronically to the appropriate election office. The "opt out" aspect of the process is more convenient for citizens than a need to "opt in." This change should also be more efficient for motor vehicle agencies, by making the registration process a standard operating procedure rather than an exception. AVR should also result in cost savings and a reduction in errors through electronic records transferring.

Oregon was the first state to adopt AVR; the legislation passed in 2015, and the policy was implemented in 2016. Increases of about 230,000 new or updated registrations have followed. California adopted its AVR policy later in 2015 as a method of addressing its estimated 6.6 million eligible voters who were not registered. In other states the policy has been adopted with bipartisan support (West Virginia and Vermont), as well as through administrative procedures (Georgia). Alaska has taken a unique approach: voters directly approved the policy and are registered to vote or update existing registrations through the system that processes the state's Permanent Fund Dividend payment to all eligible residents.

In Washington State, a policy idea has been proposed that indicates what may be the outer limits of AVR: registration at birth. As an amendment to the AVR bill that was adopted (HB 2595), election administrators would reach out to newly born residents by mail every two years to confirm that these children are still in the state. At a minimum, local jurisdictions would need to address questions about privacy and consent, and procedures will be needed to obtain the voter's signature. Early commentary about this particular version of the bill may have evolved from consternation about citizenship. Washington does not participate in the federal Real ID program, so this policy approach was intended to address that aspect of state records. Not least, the results of registration at birth would need to be coordinated with existing frameworks within the state and local election systems, and with third-party vendor protocols for list maintenance through systems such as the National Change of Address (NCOA) system operated by the US Postal Service (USPS), the Electronic Registration Information Center (ERIC), and Interstate Crosscheck. As one LEO predicted, "This is going to cost us a ton of money over the lifetime of each new voter."

It is too early to measure the "success" of these AVR methods by a typical metric such as increased registration or cost savings. The administrative details of each approach are quite different and may generate different burdens for the election administration system in terms of data collection and list maintenance. However, AVR clearly addresses the needs of voters who move; it has long been observed that the personal opportunity costs of voting are highest for those who move, and that frequent movers are less likely to vote (Highton 2004; Wolfinger and Rosenstone 1980).

VOTER REGISTRATION LIST
MAINTENANCE ASSISTANCE

As the foregoing discussions about innovations in voter registration indicate, election administrators face a number of challenges in maintaining voter rolls and in using those data at the polls and throughout the election process. LEOs and CEOs depend on a variety of sources of information to identify people who have moved into or out of their state, and who have registered or not. They also must identify and resolve other inaccuracies, including voters who have died or who are otherwise ineligible, and entries on the rolls that contain incorrect or outdated information.

Major federal initiatives provide a variety of databases that election officials can use to maintain accurate voter rolls. The Social Security Administration (SSA), the USPS, and the Department of Homeland Security (DHS) all serve as sources of data that state election officials and LEOs can access to verify voter registration status. For example, state election offices can check the last four digits of SSNs against the SSA database; some state driver's license offices check SSNs as well. DHS records can be used to verify noncitizenship status through its SAVE Program.

In addition, third parties have entered this arena with various methods of data collection and management. These include established federal government programs, including the USPS and its NCOA program, and private list maintenance support programs such as Interstate Crosscheck and ERIC. Broadly speaking, these services are designed to assist LEOs and CEOs in improving the accuracy of their voter registration databases. Each represents a different method of innovation with a different combination of public and private actors, and all reflect the influence of networks and politics.

FEDERAL GOVERNMENT SUPPORT:
NATIONAL CHANGE OF ADDRESS

The NCOA system is operated by the USPS to provide new address information on forwarded mail when people move. It is a voluntary system; individuals—here, voters—choose to complete a change of address form through the local post office; the USPS forwards mail to the new address. More than 40 million people move in the United States each year, and the USPS uses

NCOA to correct addresses because incorrect addresses contribute significantly to undeliverable mail.

The NCOA database includes permanent address records that are captured by USPS change of address forms; USPS maintains change of address information obtained from these forms for forty-eight months. The NCOA database is made available to election offices and to private businesses. USPS grants access to NCOALink, a data-matching and -validation tool that is used to match business addresses against the NCOA database. NCOALink maintains roughly 160 million permanent change of address records. This tool provides the ability to update records into USPS format. The tool validates names and corrects addresses using address-cleansing software that fixes incorrect zip codes and resolves typographical errors in street names.

The challenges in data matching to obtain accurate records are evident, even with the support of federal agencies. One illustration is the data-matching requirement established by the SSA, an agency required to update its records using the NCOA database: "To be selected for an address update, there must be an *exact* match of the name, middle initial, and surname and also an *exact* match between the current address on our (SSA) records and the prior address on the USPS database" (emphasis in the original).[14]

USPS offers an address accuracy certification through its Coding Accuracy Support System (CASS). CASS is a self-test that a jurisdiction can use to evaluate the capabilities of their software in matching addresses and making corrections. CASS corrects misspellings of city names, street names, and street name suffixes (e.g., way, court, terrace, and place). By way of generic illustration, the fictitious mailing address 7333 Harvard NW, N. Olmstead, KS could be corrected to 7333 Harvard Blvd NW, North Olmstead, KS 45678-0912. NCOA and USPS have been leveraged by local and state election offices to expand their existing capacity to address voter registration implementation.

PRIVATE-SECTOR SUPPORT FOR LIST MAINTENANCE: INTERSTATE VOTER REGISTRATION CROSSCHECK AND THE ELECTRONIC REGISTRATION INFORMATION CENTER

States have also turned to one or more private programs that have appeared, which supplement the information available through federal and state agencies. In 2018, 80 percent of states and the District of Columbia participated in either Interstate Crosscheck or the Electronic Registration Information Center (ERIC). Only eleven states did not participate in either. Table 3.1 presents the array of states and their participation in these private-sector programs. The next sections discuss each program in greater detail.

The Interstate Voter Registration Crosscheck Program began in 2005 as a data-sharing arrangement among Iowa, Kansas, Missouri, and Nebraska state

TABLE 3.1. States' Choice of Third-Party Voter Registration List Maintenance Support, 2019

Third-Party Support	Number of States[a]
ERIC	30
Interstate Crosscheck	26
Both ERIC and Interstate Crosscheck	12
None	13

a. including the District of Columbia.

election offices, which was facilitated through software provided by a common vendor.[15] HAVA's requirement for statewide electronic voter registration databases was one impetus. Voter registration files were shared across these states to check whether voters were registered in multiple states; the results would facilitate the process of removing duplicate registrations from the rolls.

Interstate Crosscheck evolved from these four states in 2005 to twenty-seven participating states in 2018. Participating states provide election registration data annually to the Kansas SOS office for Interstate Crosscheck. This information includes the state's list of registered voters, complete with date of birth, last four SSNs where permitted by law, current registration address, voter history from the most recent general election, and date of registration. The Kansas SOS office matches this information across states, and provides each state with a report that lists voters who are registered in more than one participating state, along with applicable dates of activity to identify whether someone was moving into or out of a particular state. States then work together to further research possible matches and potential instances of double-voting and take appropriate action based on their particular state laws. Interstate Crosscheck reports screening nearly 100 million voting records in 2017, from twenty-eight states, that returned more than 7 million potential duplicate records. In Alabama, for example, data from Interstate Crosscheck led to the removal of 33,414 "surplus" voter registration entries as of January 2017.

Criticisms have been leveled at Interstate Crosscheck, both for the underlying political relationships of its leadership and for the performance of the program. Kansas secretary of state Kris Kobach, whose office administers the program, has been a lightning rod in his advocacy for a Kansas requirement that voters provide documentary proof of citizenship in addition to signing the oath of citizenship on the federal NVRA form. In his position as the state CEO, his policies have drawn national attention through the removal of tens of thousands of Kansans from voter rolls and have taken the state to the US Supreme Court (*Kobach v. EAC*, 2015). In addition, Interstate Crosscheck's matching criteria have been critiqued for a lack of rigor in comparison with other options and for generating a high number of false positive matches (e.g., Palmer,

Reimer, and Davis 2014). The results require considerable additional investigation by election officials to determine whether potential duplicates are actually
duplicates and to take further action when warranted. Interstate Crosscheck
reports suggest that the number of mismatches (errors) is much higher than
matching with other criteria will indicate. A number of election officials have
commented that publicity about these reports creates impressions that are significantly mistaken and that these undermine public confidence.

The other prominent private program that facilitates voter registration
list maintenance is the Electronic Registration Information Center. ERIC was
officially launched in 2012 as an initiative of the Pew Charitable Trusts' Center
on the States in response to an analysis of the 2008 general election. In the policy community, a long-standing lack of interstate cooperation in sharing data
was seen as a factor that exacerbated the inaccuracy of state voter rolls. Pew
brought together private-sector information technology experts (IBM and
others), election officials from around the country, and other election system
stakeholders to develop a format for states to share voter registration data and
the components needed to verify information across multiple sources.

Today, ERIC operates as an interstate cooperative under the association of
the Center for Election Innovation & Research, whose executive director David
Becker was integrally involved with ERIC while at Pew, and he assumed leadership of the project when Pew wound down its election initiatives (Becker 2019).
ERIC has brought new analytical tools and new governing relationships to the
election environment. To design and implement ERIC, it was necessary to
obtain legislative changes in charter member states; build an information technology and business process infrastructure for participants; navigate various
complex legal, policy, and technical issues for list maintenance; and negotiate
bylaws and a membership agreement for charter member states and beyond.[16]
ERIC member states securely share and compare their voter registration data,
voter history, and DMV data to increase the accuracy of their voter rolls. ERIC
includes activity dates for these elements. States upload anonymized voter
registration and DMV data on a recurring schedule throughout the year. Data-
matching software is used to issue reports back to the states identifying voters
who are deceased, have moved residence addresses within the state, or have
moved out of state. Moves out of state are also identified to the "receiving" state,
so that these states can contact eligible voters who have not registered to vote.

ERIC offers analytic tools to add voters as well as remove them. ERIC
provides state election offices with lists of eligible but unregistered voters.
Two years before federal general elections, ERIC member states alert these
unregistered voters of their status and provide information on how to register to vote. In 2016, for example, Alabama mailed a postcard notification to
1,252,444 potentially eligible voters; of that number, 53,468 people registered
to vote or updated their voter registration information. ERIC also provides a
degree of confidence in its matching information where records are shared.

For example, ERIC reports a 100 percent confidence match if two states share a record for an individual with the exact same name, date of birth, and last four digits of the SSN in DMV and voter registration data.

A comparison of the two programs illustrates the public policy values and ideologies at play in the election environment. On the surface, Interstate Crosscheck and ERIC are similar in concept; in both, states share voter registration data for purposes of matching, and both use many of the same data elements.[17] Differences begin when tracing activities against the purposes of these programs, which are different. Interstate Crosscheck is designed to identify potential duplicate registrations in keeping with a normative approach to combat voter fraud. The purpose of ERIC is to assist states in improving the accuracy of America's voter rolls and increasing access to voter registration for all eligible citizens. The normative approach here is increased access.

The move of states toward ERIC reflects this normative approach and its more comprehensive data-matching architecture, which incorporates DMV data, the Social Security Deceased Index for matching death records, and NCOA. Motor vehicle records are particularly valuable in this process because they are reported to be more complete than voter registration records (Presidential Commission on Election Administration 2014). ERIC requires member states to update records on a more frequent, regular schedule in comparison with the annual schedule used by Interstate Crosscheck. ERIC also produces reports of individuals that have moved from one member state to another and who have not registered to vote in the new state (nor, in many instances, cancelled their registration in their old state). ERIC member states can then send a mailing to these individuals informing them of their potential eligibility to register to vote in their new state.

In 2018, Interstate Crosscheck operated at no fee to participating states and was the slightly larger of the two programs, involving over half the states. It is also operated at no fee to participating states, although states do bear the internal administrative costs associated with implementation and operation. In the ERIC model, states share equally in the ownership of the program and pay for the service as members. ERIC program performance has been cited favorably by election experts in the latest national study of election administration (Presidential Commission on Election Administration 2014, 31–32).

The current climate for election security has perhaps changed the calculus of states considering whether to participate in Interstate Crosscheck. In early 2018, cybersecurity concerns prompted some states to question whether they will continue sharing voter registration data with Interstate Crosscheck, and whether they will suspend or withdraw their participation altogether. Election officials in Illinois, Idaho, and New Hampshire have expressed security concerns about the potential vulnerabilities of the system. The Kansas SOS office will delay uploading state voter registration data while security concerns are investigated and addressed (*Election Administration Reports* 2018b).

The increase in state membership in ERIC speaks to its perceived quality among election administrators. Through the efforts of ERIC, its number of participating states grew to twenty-eight in 2019, and the number continues to grow. The evolution of ERIC also speaks to the role of network relationships. Becker (2019) began his work with Pew, and when Pew wound down its election focus, he took up the mantle to continue ERIC, and to expand it, through private, nonprofit organizations.

DISCUSSION AND CONCLUSIONS

On matters related to voter registration, political forces emanate from multiple points in the federal system, but primarily from the states, within the constraints established by the national government under HAVA. The zero-sum game that pits security against access is well developed in the area of voter registration, and state policymakers have taken action in both directions. Voter identification methods, including government-issued photo IDs and requirements for additional documentary proof of citizenship, are politically divisive but are nonetheless on the rise in some states. Electronic innovations to handle a variety of voter services, including registration and Election Day check in, also carry ideological implications. New political challenges also continue to arise between citizen preferences and legislative actions with the implementation of Florida Amendment 4. Citizen initiatives that pertain to election administration are rare, although legislative opposition to citizen preferences is perhaps not. Thus, we argue that in terms of federal arrangements for election administration, each of these instances demonstrates both centralized and decentralized federalism. And though the national government is involved to the extent that it has set certain parameters around registration (i.e., restricting discrimination through the VRA and insisting on multiple points of access and statewide lists through the NVRA and HAVA), the states have set the stage for what else is possible.

The pressure of demand created by key technological changes has fueled the move to OVR and the use of EPBs, and by extension AVR in some cases. Third-party assistance in these innovations—through vendors and organizations such as ERIC—has been essential. It is worth noting that decisions about whether and how to engage in this type of assistance are made by election officials (most typically CEOs) and are embedded in whatever political calculus they choose to apply.

Of course, not all innovation produces positive results, and, as in any political policy environment, "positive" is in the eye of the beholder. Even after accounting for ideological differences and preferences, innovation may have unintended consequences. One such outcome is that the move to electronic options may leave some voters and potential voters behind. Broadband technology is not universal, and the digital divide disproportionately affects poorer communities, both urban and rural (Mossberger, Tolbert, and Franko 2012). Even in wealthy urban and suburban areas, where Wi-Fi would seem to be readily available, capacity is a problem; building density, population density, and high-rise construction continue to affect connectivity.

Another unintended consequence has occurred as increasing attention is focused on voter privacy and technological security. EBPs are viewed in a new light when considering the types of information that they collect and retain. Election transactions necessarily involve specific personal information, which is referred to by the technology security community as personally identifying information (PII). All voter registration systems rely on PII, which is defined in slightly different ways by the federal agencies that use this terminology, including the SSA. Figure 3.3 illustrates the range of PII in

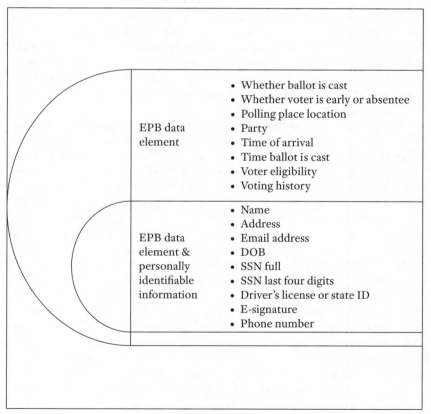

FIGURE 3.3. Intersection of Personally Identifiable Information and EPB Data

comparison with the range of data captured by EPBs and, by extension, most voter registration systems.

Another innovation in voter registration under discussion in some circles is the idea of a national voter registration database. Such a nationalized program has not come to pass. However, the concept may garner bipartisan support, although perhaps for very different reasons. Democrats see a national database as a method of increasing portability across local jurisdictions within states and across states. Republicans may see a national database as a method of tracking and reducing what some see as "voter fraud."

The Presidential Advisory Commission on Election Integrity (PACEI), which was established by President Donald Trump in May 2017, took steps that could be perceived as moving in the direction of such a national database of registered voters. The PACEI was established to investigate claims of voter fraud in the 2016 presidential election, including voters who were registered to vote in two states, were illegally in the United States, or had died. It is important to note that voter registration lists are always slightly inaccurate because systematic list maintenance practices are prohibited within ninety days of a federal election. In 2012, about 1.8 million voters remained on the rolls although deceased, and as many as 24 million voter records were inaccurate or invalid (Pew Center on the States 2012). Further, although voting more than once in the same election is prohibited, it is not illegal to be registered in more than one state.

The PACEI began its work by issuing a sweeping request for voter registration data from the states. The request included names, addresses, party affiliation, birth dates, felony conviction records, voting histories of the past decade, and the last four digits of SSNs for all registered voters. States declined to provide the information as requested, citing conflicts with state sovereignty in election administration, state public records laws, and the overly broad nature of the request, which included requests for SSNs and other personally identifying information. Some states (one-third) agreed to provide information, as long as it was limited to public information according to the specifics of their state laws (which vary). A smaller group (about 15 percent) agreed to provide public information for a fee consistent with their state public records laws. The majority of the states (54 percent) refused to provide information. Lawsuits ensued, filed by third-party groups, such as the American Civil Liberties Union and the National Association for the Advancement of Colored People. The PACEI did not survive to fulfill its charge and was disbanded in 2018, having collapsed under the weight of litigation and opposition mounted by state election officials and LEOs of both parties.

The back-and-forth of the PACEI is an excellent example of a new, emerging struggle for power in federal arrangements in the United States as they specifically pertain to election administration. Over the past hundred years, moves to expand national-level power in policy areas have been dominated by Democratic politics, with Republican political rhetoric holding fast that the states, not the national government, should make these decisions and control government programs writ large. And though the experience of the PACEI was a moment of federal schizophrenia for the parties, it is almost assuredly not the last attempt by either party to attempt to move power and control over election rules from localities and the states to the national level.

Private organizations also play a key role in the innovations that have occurred in voter registration methods. Private efforts have been essential in facilitating data matching from multiple sources and across jurisdictions in order for local and state offices to respond effectively to the federal mandates of the NVRA and HAVA to establish and maintain electronic databases. These efforts were made possible through other innovations in federal agencies that were designed to address other practical problems, such as forwarding mail through the USPS and communicating with military and overseas voters. EPBs and OVR initiatives are the result of vendor initiatives to offer options to local election offices that have independent discretion in this area, and to bring solutions to election officials both in anticipation of policy changes and during implementation. All these concepts have been diffused through the network of local, state, and national officials. Although voter registration portability is not widely practiced within entire states, the innovations to date have created an atmosphere of possibility for the development of some form of national voter registration system, given sufficient political will.

NOTES

1. Expenditure amounts per state range widely, from $24.4 million in Washington to $25 million and $161 million in Utah and Kentucky, respectively. Rhode Island, with a population of a bit more than 1 million, spent $10 million; and Indiana and Massachusetts spent $20 million and $7 million, respectively, on populations of roughly equal size (6.6 million and 6.9 million, respectively).
2. States not covered by the NVRA include Idaho, Minnesota, New Hampshire, North Dakota, Wisconsin, and Wyoming.
3. However, note McDonald (2014), who argues that the proportion of the population eligible to vote, and that votes, has remained relatively constant; instead, an increase in noncitizens and the effect of state felon disenfranchisement laws have increased the population of ineligible voters.
4. Jefferson County, Alabama, home to Birmingham, the state's largest city, is an exception; Jefferson County has a professional election administrator who administers voter registration.
5. Voters can be removed for a change of address, if they die, or if they are convicted of a disqualifying criminal offense. NVRA particularly addresses the removal of names for reason of a change of address, and requires a form of due process. A registrant can be removed from the rolls for change of address if the registrant either

(1) confirms change of address in writing, or (2) fails to return a preaddressed, postage-prepaid "return card" that contains statutory language and then fails to vote in any election during the period covered by the next two general federal elections.

6. Note that this process map is only an illustration; states differ, and processes within states differ as well.

7. NVRA Section 8(c)(2)(A) requires that "states complete, not later than 90 days prior to the date of a primary or general election for Federal office, any program the purpose of which is to systematically remove the names of ineligible voters from the official lists of eligible voters."

8. At the time of this case, specific procedures varied across Ohio's eighty-eight counties; in addition, in 2016, the percent of names removed from county voter registration lists through "use it or lose it" varied from 0 percent to more than 15 percent, without regard to population.

9. Savings cannot be compared across jurisdictions, for the reasons discussed in chapter 2.

10. Methodology and findings of the influence of networks, politics, resources, and needs across OVR system adoption, legislation, and features are presented in appendix C.

11. The states that make public the email addresses collected through OVR systems include Alabama, Arizona, Hawaii, Illinois, Iowa, Missouri, Nebraska, Oregon, Vermont, and Virginia.

12. EPBs were not included in the equipment covered by the federal voluntary voting system guidelines (VVSG).

13. States and jurisdictions that have adopted AVR include Alaska, California, Colorado, the District of Columbia, Georgia, Illinois, Maryland, New Jersey, Oregon, Rhode Island, Vermont, Washington, and West Virginia.

14. GN 02695.046 NCOA Processing (10/3013); see www.ssa.gov.

15. On December 11, 2005, Kansas secretary of state Ron Thornburgh signed a cooperative agreement (memorandum of understanding) with his counterparts in Iowa, Missouri, and Nebraska on the first day of the Midwest Election Officials Conference in Overland Park, Kansas (Kansas Secretary of State 2006).

16. In addition to Virginia, the charter members of ERIC were Colorado, Delaware, Maryland, Nevada, Utah, Virginia, and Washington.

17. These include first, middle, and last names; any name suffix; date of birth; registration address; locality of registration; registration status (active or inactive); last four digits of the Social Security number; date of registration; and voter history dates.

4

Catalysts for Convenience Voting: How Voting Has Become Easier

In all fifty US states and the District of Columbia, traditional, place-bound, in-person Election Day voting has given way to a variety of forms of convenience voting; the most notable are voting by mail (VBM) and related changes to absentee voting policies, and vote centers. Perhaps the simplest of conceptual changes to administrative practice, VBM involves using the US Postal Service (USPS) for mail delivery service of voter registration forms and ballots to and from voters. VBM exists in many variations, which include particular rules for absentee ballots and forms of precinct consolidation. In the cases of Oregon, Washington, and Colorado, VBM is used for all voters in all elections. Vote centers, by comparison, are a form of precinct consolidation.

This chapter explores developments in the policy and process of voting by mail and other forms of convenience voting such as absentee voting, vote centers, and their supporting infrastructures, including the USPS. In some jurisdictions, this infrastructure also includes private vendors—such as Pitney Bowes, in the case of Franklin County, Ohio—as well as many others. Taking this infrastructure into account across local jurisdictions and the ways in which they vary, we propose an original model of the VBM process that illustrates commonalities and differences. In the next sections of the chapter, we feature the problems, solutions, and innovations of several localities and states. These focus on collaborative efforts to establish and improve policy, process control methods, and the use of technology such as quick response codes and other tracking methods like intelligent barcodes. We conclude with a discussion of where and how innovation has arisen in these processes.

HISTORY

VBM is the most basic form of convenience voting. It has its roots as one of many methods of absentee balloting. Absentee voting has always been an allowable practice in at least some of the states since the country's earliest days; it became more widespread as a result of voting during the Civil War (for further discussion, see Keyssar 2000). Today, every US state and territory allows some form of absentee balloting. These approaches may require an excuse for being absent, and they may use lists of permanent or temporary absentee voters. VBM adoption is significantly related to region and population. The Mountain and West North Central states have been more likely to adopt this particular practice than other states (Hale, Montjoy, and Brown 2015).[1] Also, the relationship between VBM adoption in its various forms and region is statistically significant.[2] VBM is also related to population density; low-density states have been much more likely to adopt VBM measures.[3] Because of the variations in the evolution of these practices, and the variations in the administrative designs used to implement them, casting ballots in ways other than in person at polling locations in traditional precincts is now often referred to more generally as convenience voting.

Over time, absentee and mail balloting have morphed into three types of VBM practices across the United States. In the most common form, which is also the most simple, voters can return absentee ballots by mail if they cannot (or do not want to) cast a traditional precinct ballot on Election Day.[4] Less common, but popular in one-third of the states (seventeen states), VBM is available as an option only for some elections or for some types of jurisdictions, but it is not mandated. VBM is an option for a variety of reasons. Among these are very small precinct sizes; low expected turnout elections, such as state or local elections that do not coincide with a primary or general election; uncontested primaries; referenda-only elections; and, in some cases, the discretionary choice of the local election official (LEO) or governor (Hale, Montjoy, and Brown 2015). The most expansive form of VBM is found in three states: Oregon, Washington, and Colorado. These states no longer have traditional precinct-based voting, and voters instead receive and cast their ballots through the mail or at drop-off locations known as vote centers.

In 2000, Oregon became the first VBM-only state. These efforts began in the early 1980s with the approval for a test of this approach for local elections. A permanent allowance for local elections was established in 1987 and was championed primarily by Republicans in the state (Southwell and Burchett 1997). Through the 1990s, the use of VBM demonstrated increasingly higher levels of turnout for the same types of elections (Oregon Secretary of State, n.d.). Momentum and support for the approach grew throughout the decade, and in 1998 voters overwhelmingly decided by referendum to adopt VBM for primary and general elections.

The rising support for the approach was fueled in large part by its success in the 1995 primary and 1996 general elections for a replacement senator for Bob Packwood (R), who was forced to step down (Southwell 2004). In addition to the two major parties battling for the Senate seat, they also battled about the use of VBM for the elections. The members of each party had some evidence to believe that the technique might help their candidate, along with fears that they could be wrong. The League of Women Voters, a consistent forerunner in the advancement of reform over the past hundred years, was the primary driver behind the initiative petition to advance VBM, despite legislative gridlock in the state over the issue. The primary and general elections in 2000 were the first in the country to be decided by VBM across a state.

Amid early research on VBM, a concern was raised about "lost votes," which referred to ballots that were sent through the mail but were not accounted for because they were either never received or never returned. Stewart (2010) initiated a line of inquiry to fill the gap in knowledge about ballots that were mailed but not returned to the election office for counting, imputing the difference between ballots sent and received by local election offices as captured in data from the Election Administration and Voting Survey conducted by the US Election Assistance Commission. These data, however, do not parse the reasons that sent ballots were not returned. Any number of error possibilities exist. It is impossible to actually know which of these ballots never made it to the voter (for reasons including incorrect addresses and USPS error), which were intentionally (or unintentionally) not returned by the voter, and which went missing during the return process before they could be received by the local election office. Election officials in particular were dismayed by the implications of the early research on VBM, fearing that it would cast aspersions on the quality of their work through the unintentional implications of the research design and "lost ballot" moniker. Pushback from election officials about the possible intent, meaning, and implications of the lost ballot research was the impetus for our own work in this area.

One outgrowth of the lost votes study and the anecdotal experiences of LEOs about USPS rules and quirks was the formation of the Postal System Task Force by the Election Center. At its regional and national conferences held regularly around the country each year, the Election Center provides a forum for election officials to meet face to face with top USPS staff. These meetings take the form of a working group where members meet for several hours to learn of USPS updates and share their concerns. A number of new developments have sprung from these working group meetings, including a special election stamp, a USPS designation for "election mail," and the use of intelligent barcoding to track election mail. Some jurisdictions have taken these tools one step farther and have developed applications that allow the tracking of mailed ballots within the election office and, in some cases, by the voter.

Another form of convenience voting that election officials are particularly excited about is the vote center. Vote centers are a form of precinct consolidation, a move made by many LEOs because of problems in finding adequate polling locations. The lack of poll sites in general has become increasingly consequential. Public school sites may be available only with particular adaptations to accommodate students—using half a lunchroom, or half a gymnasium, for example. Poll sites must also meet accessibility requirements, and this can be very challenging in urban areas with older buildings (including schools).[5] LEOs are also interested in saving resources, and vote centers may facilitate this, although the studies are mixed and results depend on how resources are reallocated and to technology in particular (e.g., Pew Research Center 2012). Where precinct consolidation involves the use of modern spaces, it has enhanced accessibility for voters with a variety of forms of disabilities. Conversely, consolidation is related to short-term decreases in turnout because of voter confusion, along with the potential for longer lines and waiting times (for more discussion, see Hale, Montjoy, and Brown 2015).

Vote centers are an extension of precinct consolidation in the extreme. The idea behind them is that voters from anywhere in an election jurisdiction can go to one or any of a few locations to receive and cast their ballot. Vote centers have been significantly facilitated by the use of electronic pollbooks. With electronic pollbooks, all voters in an election jurisdiction are included in the available voter rolls, not just those connected to a particular precinct. The voter checks in at the vote center and is given the correct ballot for that address, either because all ballot styles are available or because the jurisdiction uses a ballot-on-demand system that prints the correct ballot when the voter checks in to verify their eligibility and the address linked to the correct ballot races and initiatives.

The first vote center was opened in 2003 in Larimer County, Colorado, as a pilot that consolidated all 143 precincts and opened 22 different vote centers across the county. This innovation was a response to a need—the Help America Vote Act mandated accessibility requirements for precincts, and Larimer County could not meet them in many of its old precinct locations (Larimer County 2014). Shortly thereafter, several other states began experimenting with vote centers through local pilots, some of which have been adopted statewide.

Like precinct consolidation, vote centers have many advantages, including the potential for cost savings, greater accessibility because they are widely understood, and in some cases greater turnout. Conversely, there is typically some voter confusion when vote centers are first implemented. The research on turnout related to the implementation of vote centers is mixed. Some studies find that turnout increases, some find increases for certain types of voters (i.e., infrequent voters), and some suggest that vote center placement matters a great deal in terms of the distance that voters travel (Lawson 2013; Scheele et al. 2009; Stein and Vonnahme 2008).

CONTEMPORARY ISSUES

Today, VBM is used in some form in every state when absentee balloting and military and overseas citizens ballot processes are included, although the method may not be termed VBM. States that intentionally choose to use VBM in place of precinct voting must administer their elections, by definition, differently than voting based on casting ballots in person by precinct areas.

A review of state election law demonstrates that local and state institutional arrangements of elected offices that administer VBM are statutorily prescribed and also differ across the states. A variety of local offices administer VBM, in keeping with the general diversity of local units of government that are responsible for elections. Local power for VBM elections usually resides with the LEO (i.e., the county or city clerk); the next most common arrangement is a local board of elections. Circuit clerks are involved in six states, and probate judges are involved in four states. Mayors do not appear to influence election administration practices, at least not according to statute. At the state level, secretaries of state (SOS) matter the most; governors and lieutenant governors largely have no influence on VBM processes. About a quarter of states have a board of elections, and in those states their influence on decisions about adopting and implementing VBM tends to trump that of the SOS. The local and state offices involved in VBM in addition to LEOs are summarized in figure 4.1.

Across the states, laws vary about when VBM ballots are sent out in advance of an election.[6] The outside of the range is sixty days before Election

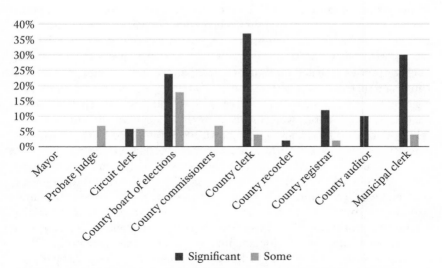

FIGURE 4.1 Proportion of Jurisdictions Reporting the Involvement of Local Government Offices in Mail Balloting in Addition to LEOs

Day, and it varies up to the day of the election.[7] The median advance mailing period is six days before Election Day, and the mean is eight days. These deadlines and advance mailing periods do not include the federal required timelines for voters under the Uniformed and Overseas Citizens Absentee Voting Act to return their ballots by mail, which LEOs must integrate with their state requirements.

Against this basic institutional and legal background, current concerns about VBM fall into three categories: how VBM is conducted, the effects of VBM, and the possibility of expanding VBM across the country. In the next sections, we present the state of knowledge, practice, and research related to mail ballots in these areas.

HOW VOTING BY MAIL IS IMPLEMENTED

Balloting by mail is done differently both across and within the states (Brown et al. 2017). To understand the range and depth of these differences, we collected a variety of types of information about mail ballots over a three-year period (see appendix C for a more detailed discussion).[8] The conclusions of this story were twofold: (1) there are important similarities both across and within the states; and (2) best practices in VBM should focus on requests, office processes, delivery, balloting, and data (Brown et al. 2017).

Perhaps the most important part of this work has been the analysis of mail ballot administrative processes. From this, we learned that there is tremendous variance in administrative processes for mail ballots, both across and within states. Because of the differences in state laws, cross-state variation was expected; however, the within-state differences were a surprise. To compare processes at the jurisdictional level across and within states, we relied on the reports of LEOs as local experts to learn how they process mail ballots. Their responses revealed four major steps that encompass interactions with voters and internal office administration: (1) receiving requests; (2) processing requests; (3) issuing ballots; and (4) receiving and counting ballots. Three major groups of actors were involved in this, including the voters themselves, election officials, and often the USPS. From these LEO reports, we constructed maps of the VBM process across jurisdictions, grouped by size according to the number of registered voters. We then compared processes across these maps, looking for convergences (similarities) and divergences (differences).[9] The synthesis of these process maps illuminates several similarities in the overarching processes that are intrinsic to voting and managing elections administration: (1) voters can request a mail ballot; (2) when valid requests are made, they are documented; (3) when requests are valid, ballots are issued; and (4) when valid ballots are returned within required periods, they are counted. This convergence is depicted in figure 4.2; given the wide

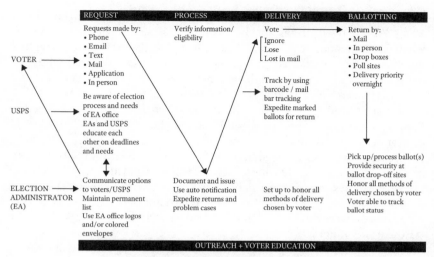

FIGURE 4.2 Mail Ballot Process Model

variation on so many aspects of election administration across the states, this convergence strongly suggests that the underlying mechanics of VBM are sound across the states.

The differences in how the VBM process is conducted at the jurisdiction level exist in two areas. First, for some states, the process significantly diverges from the start because they are mail-only states. Second, there are differences across all states in terms of who is responsible for handling this process; how and why the requests are handled; the timing of requests, delivery, and return; methods of delivery and return; and communication with voters. It was unclear from the information obtained how jurisdictions treat applications that are improperly filled out or improper as a matter of policy.

The role of vendors in these processes also varies across and within states, as well as across the processes themselves. In some cases, vendors receive voter registration lists and print and mail the ballots, and in some others they do not. But in every state and locality, vendors provide all the hardware and software that make any of this possible. Their role in all parts of the election process is intractable, but nowhere is this more clear than in VBM.

To date, VBM appears to have two major impacts. The first is on cost, and the second on turnout. Each of these is contingent on implementation and context. One of the hopes among election officials is that VBM will reduce costs. The logic goes that the costs associated with mailing ballots to all voters would be less than the cost of precinct-based voting, which includes some combination of rental fees, poll workers, transportation of equipment and ballots, and staff time for coordination. One early study of VBM in Oregon found that VBM decreased election costs by as much as 30 percent (Bradbury 2006). Alternatively, it has also been shown that savings are only obtained when implementation is accomplished in a specific way (i.e., correctly); implementation errors may in fact increase the costs associated with mail ballots and offset savings from those other areas (e.g., Flaxman et al. 2012).

Early research into widespread VBM found that turnout increased in elections that utilized VBM exclusively. The research was mixed as to whether this effect was just for off-year elections among likely voters and high socioeconomic voters (Banducci and Karp 2000; Kousser and Mullin 2006, 2007; Monroe and Sylvester 2011; Southwell 2010), or whether it was also for general elections and unlikely voters (Gerber, Huber, and Hill 2013). In some of the early studies, turnout was enhanced when the ballots themselves were simple (Monroe and Sylvester 2011). It was also not clear if increases in voter participation were due to the VBM method itself or to the effects of novelty (Gronke and Miller 2012).

Advocates point to VBM's potential to increase turnout among unlikely voters in particular (Edelman and Glastris 2018). Evidence from the Colorado 2014 election support this. An analysis of this election's voter files indicates that, when the state implemented VBM, turnout was significantly higher among low-likelihood voters than models would normally predict, and that this was particularly true for younger voters (Showalter 2017).

HOW VOTE CENTERS HAVE CHANGED

The use of vote centers across the states is far less ubiquitous than VBM, but vote centers have been used both alone and with great success in some places to support VBM. Their first use was in Colorado in 2003, and the approach has slowly expanded since then. By 2018, thirteen states had approved them for use on Election Day, and even more states allow them for early voting, combining that with precinct-only voting on Election Day. The trajectory of state adoption began in 2004 with Colorado, and the most recent state adoption occurred in California in 2017. The 2011 and 2012 state legislative sessions saw the biggest increase, with half the fourteen states adopting them during those sessions, including Arizona, Arkansas, Indiana, New Mexico, South Dakota, Tennessee, and Utah.

The story of vote centers is, at least in part, regional. It is also a story about need and necessity. Analysis across the fifty states and District of Columbia demonstrates that region is particularly important.[10] Vote centers emerged in the middle of the country, and they have been adopted more in the West than in any other region, particularly in states with vast swaths of land and smaller populations.[11] Vote centers are also more likely to be adopted when turnout is higher, suggesting that they are related to need.[12]

We visited some jurisdictions with vote centers used on Election Day and others with vote centers used for early voting but not on Election Day. Each center was similar—a large government building (for the most part) is utilized with well-coordinated and staffed lines that, though sometimes long, moved quickly and in an orderly fashion. One election official who uses them for early voting told us that "it hasn't been controversial at all. . . . We had over 100,000 people in early voting this year, and our turnout on Election Day [in the traditional precincts] was 62 percent. We close early voting on the Friday before the election—on the last day, the line wrapped all the way around the building, but the wait was only a little over an hour." Most election officials with whom we spoke noted that issues arose when they first used vote centers; in every case, they learned from these problems, improved their planning and processes, and solved them within one or two election cycles.

EXPANSION

The same advocates who espouse the potential for VBM and other forms of convenience voting to increase turnout rightly point out that this should provoke partisan anxiety both for and against the approach. Younger people and unlikely voters tend to vote with the Democratic Party and are also supporters of and responsive to convenience voting. If this continues to hold true, the disincentive to move to VBM in Republican-controlled states is clear. The obvious question, then, is whether there is a relationship between party control and state adoption (or lack thereof) of VBM.

We began this chapter by stating that VBM in the broadest sense exists all over the country, which it does. VBM is far less prevalent as a technique for collecting ballots from all voters—as opposed to precinct or vote center voting or some combination of these, along with VBM for absenteeism. Most states do not have explicit allowances for elections conducted *only* by VBM; and where VBM is allowed, it is usually permitted only for certain types of elections, certain types of jurisdictions, or some combination of the two. Figure 4.3 displays the array of state VBM approaches across types of jurisdictions (all, local, pilot, and small, or special) and types of elections (all, not certain types, local elections, referenda, special, uncontested, off-schedule) or during a state of emergency.[13] The most common approach across the states is to use VBM for any type of an election in a "very small" jurisdiction. Here, "very small" varies from as few as 100 to as many as 500 voters, based on either the last decennial census count or the previous general election. A few states permit VBM in all jurisdictions and in all types of elections (Colorado, Oregon, and Washington). A few states permit VBM only in off-cycle elections, emergencies, or for referenda, including bond issues.

Jurisdictions	Type of election	States
All	All	CO, HI,[a] OR, WA
	Referenda and bond issues	MO, NM
	State of emergency	FL
	Off-cycle or special	HI, KS, MD, MT
	Uncontested	AR
	Jurisdications can opt in	CA, NE, ND, UT
	Some elections or based on population	AK, AZ, FL, ID, KS, MD, MN, MO, MT, NV, NJ, NM, WY
Small or special purpose	All	AZ, CA, ID, MN, NV, NJ

Sources: Adapted from the National Conference of State Legislatures (Underhill 2019); independent of absentee ballot processes.
a. Hawaii begins with the 2020 primary.

FIGURE 4.3 State VBM Options by Type of
Jurisdiction and Type of Election

To test for political party effects as a way to explain the expansion of VBM, as well as the other factors related to innovation, we examine the relationship across all states between party dominance and the passage of VBM legislation in the year when the policy was adopted by the legislature. We looked for the effect of partisanship on the spread of VBM by analyzing the states according to two classifications. In the first, we grouped states according to the type of VBM (all elections and jurisdictions; particular types of elections in all jurisdictions; particular types of elections in specific jurisdictions; none). In the second, we collapsed the types of elections and jurisdictions and grouped states according to whether their policies allowed for any type of VBM.[14]

Our analyses indicate that partisanship is not a significant factor in the policy decisions to adopt VBM-only voting. In fact, the decisions to adopt VBM are significantly influenced by levels of professionalism, which we measure through network relationships in our innovation theory of change. States with ties to national and state professional associations of election officials and with more professionalized election workforces are more likely to move to various methods of VBM. Need also plays a role. As persons per square mile decrease, states are more likely to adopt VBM measures.

Determining the roles of politics, professionalism, need, and resources in state choices about VBM is challenging. And attempts to parse the influences of these factors on VBM are confounded by the different approaches that states have taken in combining VBM with other reforms. The recent case of election reform in New York illustrates this point. In early 2019, the New York legislature used its new Democratic majority to adopt a package of election reforms that established early voting days and eliminated excuse-based absentee voting. The shift to early voting includes a specified number of vote centers set up according to political and geographic units (i.e., election districts or precincts). Election officials will have difficulty finding early voting sites to use as consolidated voting locations for voters from multiple election districts in some parts of the state (particularly older urban areas, such as New York City). It is too early to predict the options that voters will choose, though one likely outcome is an increase in the use of vote centers. Another expected outcome is an increased use of no-excuse-based absentee voting; however, this change requires a constitutional amendment and has not yet been implemented. Although our quantitative models were not able to establish the influence of politics as a factor in VBM adoption across the country, it is worth mentioning that this package of election reforms was introduced in the New York State Assembly as its first initiative in 2019, after the 2018 midterm election put Democrats in firm control of the State Assembly.

The interrelationships between political factors, levels of professionalism, resources, and needs come through in the stories that election officials tell about their experiences with administrative innovation and policy change. Our research highlights the experiences of the Election Office of the City/County of Denver in creating a voter-centric model that interacts with various methods of convenience voting and that is supported by a culture of innovation, both in this office and within the broader context of state support.

CONVENIENCE VOTING IN COLORADO: THE CASE OF DENVER

When you walk into the Denver Election Division's office building, it seems like any other government office, but this belies what comes out in a behind-the-scenes tour of the division's offices. The office area begins with a customer service area that is spacious and open. Each room is dedicated to a different part of the mail ballot processing system and is designed to facilitate efficient processing, security and integrity, and public transparency. The rooms are thoughtfully laid out to facilitate public exchanges and to efficiently process mail ballots. Each room is clearly marked, so visitors instantly know the purpose of the room, and flowcharts on the walls illustrate the location and flow of the activity being undertaken inside. The division's twenty-two staff members are welcoming, professional, courteous, well trained, and genuinely excited about what they do and how they do it. But it was not always this way.

Colorado is the twenty-second-largest US state (in population), and Denver is its largest metropolitan area. Elections are administered at the local level through of the Office of County Clerks; the clerks are elected and the office is responsible for other governmental functions, including the issuance of motor vehicle licenses. The clerks have also established a state professional association, the Colorado County Clerks Association. The state election office is housed within the Office of the Secretary of State. State election laws are forward thinking, and the state as a whole has consistently been an early adopter of a number of innovations. Potential voters may register as early as sixteen years old, as long as they will be eighteen by Election Day; residency requirements are twenty-two days out from Election Day; the state has same-day registration (to receive a mail ballot, you must register at least eight days before Election Day); it was an early adopter of online registration; it was an early adopter of vote centers; the identification requirements permit a wide range of identification methods; and there is no felon disenfranchisement after prison release or conclusion of parole. In 2013 Colorado became the third state in the nation to move to all-VBM, a move that has been touted as one of the reasons for the state's comparatively high voter turnout rates. As of 2016, Colorado had six counties with coverage under Section 203 of the Voting Rights Act of 1965 (VRA), four with Spanish language and two with Native American languages (Ute).

Situated at the heart of the state, with its largest population, is the City/County of Denver. The Denver Elections Division runs elections for both the county and city of Denver, which had a combined population of almost 700,000 in 2016.[15] The City/County of Denver is rapidly growing, and has added almost 100,000 residents since the 2010 census. It ranks among the top 1 percent of jurisdictions (by count) in the number of registered voters. About 80 percent of Denver's population is over the age of eighteen, and thus potentially eligible to vote if they have citizenship. Denver County is covered by VRA Section 203, and about 17 percent of the people over five years of age in the county speak a language other than English in the home.

A decade ago, the Denver Elections Division did not have the same reputation that it does today. Its staff members believe that much of the shift has to do with a climate change that addresses four key areas: (1) orientation toward innovation; (2) treating voters as customers; (3) treating staff as experts; and (4) prioritizing the staff's professional development. One staff member with whom we spoke said that "what has changed over time is a commitment to a culture in which we listen to ideas and innovate, and then run with the idea and implement it to see what happens and correct later if things didn't work out. We have significantly changed the culture of the office, and it's had the effect of improving the climate and our ability to make changes."

The Denver Elections Division's staff members also noted the importance of a customer service orientation to enhancing their work. As one person explained: "A part of our success is that we have taken the idea of customer service seriously—elections should be more than the regulations, we should be serving our voters effectively. So we interpret regulations to better serve our voters. We have come to all of this as a customer service issue—you don't give people the law, you simplify the language and make the process accessible. We can save money, be efficient, have transparency, and make the process better while getting more people to vote."

Another critical aspect of the climate in the Denver elections office is the relationship between elected and appointed election officials. Staff members noted that they are seen and treated by other election officials as competent professionals, and consequently they are listened to and taken seriously. This atmosphere of professional respect has made all the difference in the energy staff members have for their work. They are motivated to develop and promote new ideas that increase efficiency and public responsiveness in order to improve the voter experience.

This professional attitude reinforces the development of additional expertise within the local office. The Denver Elections Division's staff members take part in professional certification programs like the Certified Election/Registration Administrator program, which is the national certification in the election field. Professional development also extends into operations management more broadly. Many of the executive staff members have participated in LEAN / Six Sigma training, which was initially introduced for city employees by Denver mayor Michael Hancock, and which focuses on process metrics and monitoring. Individual training and development are encouraged. During our site visit, one person noted that "in our performance plans, we encourage staff to research [training sessions] they want to attend, they give this to their managers, and we approve [training] once a year."

The Denver office also supports its mission and vision of customer-focused service by engaging the community. The office has an election advisory committee that includes any stakeholder, self-defined, who wants to be involved. Open meetings are held quarterly, and staff members lay out their ideas and plans and get community feedback. Although this is not uncommon at the local level across the country, these Denver staff members believe that they have developed strong, trusting relationships with community leaders and residents, and these people in turn believe it is worth their time and energy to bring issues to the staff members and engage in troubleshooting and problem solving together, which has further enhanced trust over time.

Organizational structure and staffing levels are also important aspects of the overall context, and both are related to resources. As noted above, the Denver Elections Division has twenty-two full-time-equivalent employees along with a thriving professional internship program, and it has cultivated good relationships with other county and city offices, including access to technology services. The division's strong capacity also attracts resources.

Denver County itself has been able to attract industry, technology, and grants in a culture of local innovation that reaches across both public and private sectors. This context provides fertile ground for staff members to observe and learn about what is happening in other sectors, and it has sparked ideas for additional changes and improvements for their own operations. A perfect example of this is Denver's mobile vote center, which is a trailer that folds out and looks like a small storefront when parked. The division's plan is to take the mobile vote center to areas where people may be receptive—such as park-and-ride areas for the commuter train at rush hour, areas with food trucks at lunchtime, school parking lots, grocery stores, and houses of worship.

The success of Denver County in elections administration has in turn raised the bar for other area counties. Between 2015 and 2017, the Denver Elections Division hosted over three hundred visitors from other election offices, including both from within Colorado and from other states around the country. The purpose of hosting these visits is to share ideas and demonstrate how Denver has set up its vote centers and mail ballot processing so others can take back ideas to their home jurisdictions. This philosophy of sharing information across jurisdictions is exemplified in this comment from the division's executive leader: "The best advice I can give to other jurisdictions wanting to innovate is to start small and test whether it's working. . . . So start small, talk to people who have done it well, find the expertise to do it, evaluate the organizational structure to see if you have the skills or leadership to help make the innovation happen."

The Colorado Mind-Set

A piece of Denver's success has to do with the State of Colorado's overall pro-innovation orientation. In an interview with staff from the Colorado SOS office, one staff member noted that "Colorado likes to be out there first. We were the first state to let women vote, we did that before anyone else, and we took Oregon's [VBM] model and made it user friendly. We started the vote center concept, and it is what makes our mail ballot system possible. With vote centers, we have the ability to make sure that movers haven't voted elsewhere. It took us a few years to sort it out because we had to first figure out the e-pollbooks." Although various states and localities might contest which one was first with various innovations, the fact remains that Colorado is an early adopter in many areas, and it is certainly a national leader in combining a variety of innovative approaches to make voting open, accessible, accurate, and efficient.

Moving to mail ballots for Colorado required vision from above, time, tenacity, and careful planning. The state's election officials began in small ways in the early 1990s, and they have been working at the margins since then to make a statewide policy shift in this area. As recently as 2010, there were disagreements about this between the SOS and the county clerks, all of whom are elected officials. Concerns centered largely on taking choices away from voters about how to cast ballots. Little by little, however, these political disagreements were overcome.

There were also logistical problems that had to be addressed. Colorado uses a formula to determine the number of election judges (i.e., poll workers) needed for the voting period, and as state processes shifted, this statutory formula had to be changed to accommodate the staffing needs dictated by new procedures. Cost concerns also had to be addressed. Although mail ballots are generally less costly, vote centers can be quite costly on days when the volume of voters is low, especially in larger urban centers.

The state election office has been able to address the problems created by these policy shifts through the use of data. The office captures real measures of staff assignments, the flow of voters and ballots over days. And it uses these data to build models to better capture when and where people are needed. Collectively, these data allow the office to plan to reduce waiting times and save taxpayers' money. These data also make it possible for the state election office to build models that inform statutory changes, and these models can provide solid information about costs.

The Colorado election office is able to collect these data and promote innovation for four main reasons: (1) institutional arrangements related to technology; (2) a forward-thinking SOS; (3) forward-thinking LEOs; and (4) a commitment to turn problems into opportunities. The state election office's use of technology is quite sophisticated compared with other states' offices. The Colorado office has a strong working relationship with the state's chief information officer. The office also has its own independent information technology team (with more than forty full-time-equivalent employees), and therefore it is not entirely reliant on the goodwill, time, and resources of the chief information officer's office to initiate and complete projects. The state election office is able to fund this level of support because of its funding relationship with other state agencies. This circumstance is the direct result of the leadership and vision of a past SOS. Moreover, the revenue generated within the office of the SOS stays there—business, finance, and licensing fees collected by the SOS remain within that office and are used in part to pay for an internal information technology department. Because the office generates revenue and is able to control its own expenditures without having to go to the legislature for spending approvals, it has a large measure of flexibility to determine how to support its priorities.

Election operations in Colorado also benefit from an important mind-set across counties and in the state office—thinking about the future in a forward-thinking way and being open-minded enough to turn problems into opportunities. Continuity in the state election staff's leadership and the respect that staff members have received from each SOS have encouraged them to use their expertise to effectively pursue their projects. In turn, state staff members respect the local county election offices, listen to local ideas and innovations, and work together with the local offices to enable them to innovate and disseminate their ideas to other counties throughout the state, and in turn to other jurisdictions.

The Colorado state election office is also orientated toward professional development. Its staff and leaders speak frequently at election conferences across the country to share their experiences about the new solutions that they are developing. Top executive staff members, including the state election director, are professionally certified and encourage their colleagues to participate in certification programs. In our theory-of-change model, this form of engagement with the national network of organizations that are perceived to be key stakeholders in election administration is associated with innovation.

The Colorado experience also illustrates the ability of its election community—both local county clerks and the state office—to assess challenges as opportunities to pursue policy change. One example of this is the response of Colorado election officials to a lawsuit filed in 2008 about state and local cancellation of voter registrations in violation of the National Voter Registration Act (*Common Cause v. Bruescher*, 2009). In 2004, Colorado began the move to its statewide voter registration database. This program, which was named the Statewide Colorado Voter Registration and Election system (SCORE), was implemented by the Colorado Department of State to comply with the Help America Vote Act. As with many such systems, SCORE was designed to establish a centralized system that also maintained the integrity of voter information, the integrity of the electoral process, and audit capability. While enabling LEOs to administer elections, SCORE was also intended to leverage the coordination inherent in a centralized system.

Although this particular initiative stalled temporarily, by 2008 Colorado had moved from a fully decentralized system to the SCORE system. The effort was challenging because the LEOs and the chief election official (CEO) discovered sixty-four different registration processes across sixty-four different counties. Yet this type of situation is actually quite common, due to the intensely localized, homegrown ways voter registration developed across the country. In an effort to achieve uniformity in processes, Colorado election officials used this knowledge combined with the lawsuit as an opportunity to continue to experiment, innovate, and improve processes for everyone. Numerous meetings and discussions of the Colorado County Clerks Association were devoted to analyzing, understanding, and honing processes. Over the next decade, SCORE transformed election operations in Colorado by facilitating the development of the state's centralized election management system and its associated technology, moving local offices away from legacy technology and reporting. Operated through the state election office, SCORE has become a central resource for LEOs for data extraction and reporting, process standardization, customer support, and training (including the use of the system). This is not to suggest that innovation pursued a straight-line path or that each attempted iteration toward improvement worked or that all innovations worked in each county because of the differences in local resources and capacity. However, with time and flexibility, LEOs have learned from one another and, with CEO/SOS support, they have been able to significantly improve these systems.

The capacity built through SCORE has been a resource in helping election officials inform policymakers about how policy changes will affect the election system and in helping election officials address policy changes. More recently, LEOs and the CEO have responded to a ballot measure passed in 2016 to grant unaffiliated voters (who do not declare party membership) the opportunity to vote in party primaries. Following the approach taken to address SCORE, how best to administer this process was discussed at numerous conference sessions of the Colorado County Clerks Association. Meetings between LEOs and the CEO were also devoted to administrative issues, and they resulted in a process through which independent voters will receive both Democratic and Republican ballots.

ANALYSIS

The innovation theory-of-change model rests upon four critical factors: politics, professionalism, resources, and need. Analysis of VBM and convenience voting suggests that each of these four factors is important, and in nuanced ways. And with respect to the federal system architecture, the institutions at the state level are able to set the conditions for innovation to thrive, in terms of both constraints and opportunities.

The primary drivers of innovation in mail balloting appear to be a combination of need and professionalism, along with the significant resource of strong, visionary leadership. Although some proponents of VBM in particular suggest that it may be more supported by Democrats, this is not revealed in any of our analyses. In fact, of the four elements that lead to innovation that we investigate, partisanship is perhaps the least important. Anecdotally, some of the election officials with whom we spoke felt that a nonpartisan or bipartisan orientation helped to drive adoption of these changes. We have not uncovered systematic evidence to support this. However, the Colorado partisan political context may be unique; in 2018 the electorate was aligned roughly one-third Republican, one-third Democratic, and the remainder unaffiliated. This overall mix suggests that political compromise is the norm in this state's environment rather than the exception, given that no one political group has a majority.

Professionalism is critical for innovation in this case, and it takes two forms through its role in networks and internal capacity. We believe this is endogenous. More highly professionalized election officials are, by definition, more likely to be part of national conversations about ways to make elections more effective, accurate, and cost-effective, and they are more likely to adapt other models to their own contexts. More highly professionalized election officials appear to have a greater capacity to experiment with possible innovations, as well as a greater capacity to advocate for legislative changes when they are warranted. And once they have achieved success, professionalized election officials are more likely to be open to talking about their experiences with their peers in other offices, both within their own state and across other states, and to take part in national conversations about what they accomplished and how they did it.

The importance of resources for achieving innovation did not come to the fore in the cross-state quantitative models. However, resources were critical in the Denver and Colorado case, and this is evident in several ways. Over time, money, leadership, and human resources were driving forces in bringing about all the changes identified in this chapter. It is true that Colorado is well financed today; however, even before the state's coffers grew after the legalization of marijuana sales, Colorado's state election office was, and remains, an entity independent of state politics because its revenue streams are independent of state legislative budgets. This circumstance is itself the product of the leadership and vision of the SOS office, and these funds allowed the SOS to hire sufficient staff members and to concurrently support their professional development as national leaders in the field.

The final driving component of innovation vis-à-vis VBM and related processes is need. In this case, need is also related to resources. Geographically large and less densely populated states are far more likely to adopt VBM approaches than smaller and more densely populated states. To the extent that mail balloting leads to cost savings, this must be particularly true for large, rural states. And to be clear, cost savings in these cases take two forms. Possible savings involved the cost to voters to get to the polls in terms of the time and financial resources related to travel, and the cost to election administration offices, which need to open low-density precincts. Mail balloting in these types of states can address multiple problems.

The role of politics in VBM and the adoption of other forms of convenience voting is less clear, and it is certainly mixed from the standpoint of which political party might champion or challenge the VBM approach. Western states, which tend to be thought of as progressive, adopted these convenience voting methods first. But many of the champions of these reforms were in fact Republican legislatures or SOS offices.

In addition, a different strain of political activity has been introduced into the VBM conversation. Progress toward VBM options (including no-excuse absentee balloting) has been halted in some places because of the threat of potential ballot manipulation by third-party groups. The 2018 ballot harvesting scandal in North Carolina's Ninth Congressional District seems to support this concern. In this instance, there does not seem to be a dispute that ballots were mailed in a timely manner by local election offices and were sent to the correct individuals. In one county in the district, however, a third party was hired to collect ("harvest") absentee ballots, which is against North Carolina state law. Further complications arose when, during the investigation of this harvesting, those working on behalf of the third party acknowledged that they had been paid to collect ballots and, in some cases, had signed the voters' names on ballots in place of the voters; indictments followed, and the election could not be certified. In the special election in September 2019 to fill the seat, a new Republican prevailed over the original Democratic candidate.

One irony, of course, is that though concerns about election fraud have been touted by Republicans since 2000 and have served as the basis for a presidential commission, the ballot-harvesting problem in North Carolina occurred on behalf of a Republican congressional candidate. Another irony is that the 2019 HR 1—which was introduced in the US House of Representatives by the new Democratic majority, and which proposes a sweeping overhaul of some aspects of election administration—does not include a provision to address absentee ballot issues. Mitch McConnell (R), the majority leader and president of the US Senate, noted this omission recently in remarks reported by NPR (March 12, 2019). In more than one-third of states, it is permissible for voters to give their absentee ballot to another person to turn in. These and other questions will continue to generate partisan controversy, given that one in five voters voted by mail in 2016, and that this proportion has doubled in the last two decades (Vote at Home 2019).

Another complicating factor that will hamper diffusion of VBM is the administrative dimension related to the functionality of the USPS. The move by the USPS to consolidate its operations using regional distribution centers means that mail within a town or county often leaves the area before it can be returned, making the de facto time frame for mailing and returning ballots longer than what a voter might logically believe. This will make legislation about counting based on postmarked dates as opposed to received dates an important battleground. VBM also adds a different kind of cost to voting, which some states have attempted to ameliorate by having county offices pay for postage. Additionally, proposals have been made at the national level to privatize the USPS, and these attempts are likely to continue. Vote at Home (VAH), an initiative launched in late 2018 by the nonprofit Vote at Home Institute, suggests that political factors and public opinion are in play regarding VBM. VAH has essentially relabeled the collection of various methods of VBM, and it appears to have modified the current terminology a bit, by referring to "mailed-in ballots" (see www.voteathome.org). The VAH label may be intended to personalize the practice of voting by mail and to distance it from any negative public connotation regarding the USPS and "mail" per se. The Vote at Home Institute indicates that one of the advantages of VAH is ballot security, in addition to voter security. These language and label changes indicate an attempt to create a new policy image to capitalize on public concerns about voting equipment security as well as public interest in greater convenience. This new policy image may also be intended to address political opposition or to build new coalitions around non-precinct-based voting practices (e.g., Stone 2011). Regardless, VAH also relies upon the USPS. The implications of all these factors, individually and collectively, is that though VBM is being pushed by some as the sine qua non of convenience voting reform for the country, it is in fact complicated and not as straightforward a solution as its advocates want people to believe.

CONCLUSIONS

Convenience voting takes various forms across the country today. Using the example of VBM, in some states, it is only possible in certain circumstances as a form of absentee balloting. In other states, it is allowed for very small jurisdictions or for certain types of low-turnout elections. In yet other states, it is is essentially the only way to vote. The process involves multiple actors—election administrators, the USPS, vendors, and voters. VBM shifts the burden on voters away from remembering that there is an election on a specific day and figuring out how to get to their precinct. VBM asks voters to remember where they put their ballot after bringing in the mail, and to remember to mark it and mail it back or go to an election office or drop-off site to return it. Early research suggests that VBM saves resources if done properly, and it may increase turnout.

VBM and vote centers seem innovative with respect to process and method—and, ironically, the use of the US Mail itself is essentially antiquated. Convenience voting methods do significantly change the voting experience for voters, but they remain unavailable in many states. The voter experience changes are only the surface of the innovation, however. The underlying, innovative component is essentially the elimination of in-person voting tied to precincts. Uncoupling voters from the need to vote at a physical voting location may also mean that other information important for political parties (and candidates) becomes unavailable as a result. It also means that election jurisdictions must have a method of generating ballots that are specific to races and issues. In this way, VBM has been a catalyst for innovation on multiple fronts. VBM has served as an important step toward more widespread convenience voting. Paradoxically, the outdated nature of paper-based mail in balloting, generally combined with greater calls for convenience voting, has led to and will continue to spur continued interest in Web-based voting methods, even in the face of strong and seemingly intractable concerns about election security. VBM is also a catalyst for additional technology to support ballots on demand. VBM may be one step forward and two steps back—or to the side—but it will likely be the catalyst for more change that supports voters' ability to cast their ballots in ways they find to be convenient.

NOTES

1. These include Arizona, Colorado, Idaho, Iowa, Kansas, Minnesota, Missouri, Montana, Nebraska, New Mexico, North Dakota, Nevada, South Dakota, Utah, and Wyoming.
2. Cramer's V = 0.745; p = 0.000.
3. Cramer's V = 0.429; p = 0.009.
4. We do not detail here the differences across the states between excuse-based and no-excuse absentee voting rules; our research indicates that these differences are often embedded in local administrative practice as well as in law. We find that the trend is toward no-excuse absentee voting—which is VBM by another name in some states.
5. Poll sites are public spaces required to meet the requirements of the Americans with Disabilities Act of 1990, which is automatically the case for spaces built after 1990.
6. Data reflect laws in effect in 2016; we do not observe changes in these.
7. One would imagine that, on the day of the election, a potential voter would just go to the election offices and obtain the ballot in person, fill it out, and turn it in, much like precinct voting.
8. This work was conducted in conjunction with Robert Montjoy and Mary Afton Day, along with election officials who are members of the Election Center through the joint Auburn University and Election Center Professional Measurement Project.
9. In some of the cases of multiple responses per jurisdiction, there were sometimes different answers about processes. Although this might suggest that our method of documenting these processes is flawed, anecdotal discussion suggests differences in perceptions and terminology depending upon who is "laying hands" on the requests and ballots at different times.
10. Significant at $p < .05$.
11. Significant at $p < .10$.
12. Significant at $p < .05$.
13. Here we analyze rules that apply to VBM separate from absentee ballot rules.
14. Data analysis is presented in table C.13 in appendix C.
15. County information was accessed on February 11, 2018, from www.census.gov /quickfacts/fact/table/CO,denvercountycolorado/PST045216.

5

Collaboration on Language Assistance: How Critical Voices Are Heard

Across the country today, voting assistance is provided throughout the registration and voting process to those who do not understand English well enough to be able to read and cast a ballot in some, but not all, jurisdictions. Federal assistance in this area of election administration is designed both to protect particular groups against potential discriminatory actions, and to facilitate voter participation by supporting those who do not understand English. Some states also provide assistance to voters who are not able to understand English well enough to vote, and who speak languages other than English not covered by federal policy. Local election offices have navigated policies from both the federal and state levels, along with pressure from citizens and stakeholders both in favor of and opposed to language assistance in adopting methods of meeting the needs of voters.

At the federal level, voting assistance is guided by the Voting Rights Act of 1965 (VRA) and requires generally that all election materials (including ballots) and all information about the election process be made available in Asian, Alaskan Native, Native American, and Hispanic languages when particular population thresholds are reached and where English language proficiency is lower than average. Historically, federal requirements for language assistance were determined after each decennial census. Determinations are now made more frequently—at the decennial census and at five-year midpoints based on estimates from the American Community Survey, which is conducted continuously by the US Bureau of the Census, with results published annually.

This chapter focuses on the challenges posed for language assistance activities and innovative steps that are being taken in several jurisdictions. We focus on the challenges of finding those voters who need assistance; of providing accurate assistance; and of how, where, and why this is working well in some places but not necessarily in others. Language coverage is an area that exemplifies innovation driven by public need but limited by resource constraints and embedded in a highly charged political atmosphere. Professionalism plays a significant role through the collaboration between stakeholders.

HISTORY

Modern policy about providing language assistance to voters and voter registrants has traveled a long arc that is reflective of the changing American political context. Today's language assistance requirements and language supports acknowledge that the Colonies and, later, the United States were populated by people who spoke many languages other than English. During the opening session of the Summit on Language Assistance—which was developed and sponsored by the US Election Assistance Commission and Democracy Fund and held June 3, 2016, in College Park, Maryland—Republican commissioner Christy McCormick noted for the audience that "the Founding Fathers had the Declaration of Independence translated into German. They recognized that there are people of different languages living in this country and we need to continue on what they started and provide the information that people need to participate in our elections across the country." Discussion of language issues at the summit ranged across commentary that identified the origins of language assistance, the exclusion of groups that need assistance, and conversations about current laws, needs, struggles, and outreach efforts.

Language assistance today seems to be fueled by recent immigration concerns. Since the 1990s, through ballot initiatives such as Arizona Proposition 200 (1996) and California Proposition 197 (1998), states with large immigrant populations have sought to require identification of and from immigrants in particular ways that are directed at the provision of public services. Either directly or indirectly, these provisions also affect the ability of some to register to vote and to cast ballots.

However, American concerns about languages and elections issues began to emerge systematically in the late nineteenth century. At that time, language concerns focused primarily on imposing English literacy tests in order to disenfranchise Irish and later black voters. Katharine Culliton-Gonzalez noted at the same summit that "the first known language access cases were actually about literacy tests. . . . The first known literacy tests were efforts to keep Irish Catholic immigrants from voting by Connecticut in 1855 and Massachusetts in 1887." In her comments, she goes on to detail use of the same means to disenfranchise African Americans after Reconstruction, particularly in the South. A year later, at the next language summit—held by the US

Election Assistance Commission in conjunction with the Democracy Fund held on June 6, 2017, at Northern Virginia Community College—Virginia state senator David Marsden (D) discussed previous uses of literacy tests and other attempts to disenfranchise voters and suppress votes; and he advocated making enhanced voter access the goal of election administrators.

The evolution of efforts to provide public support to those who do not understand English well enough to vote involves a combination of requirements for assistance and prohibitions of practices that discriminate against particular groups. Voters who do not understand English well enough to vote need various types of assistance, including help in learning where, how, and when to register to vote; how to read ballots and instructions; and how to cast a ballot. In this context, language assistance covers the use of interpreters in the voting process and the use of translated and multilanguage materials across all phases of election systems. It may also require outreach to particular groups in need of these services.

Federal requirements for language assistance began with the passage of the VRA in 1965 and its authorization of federal intervention to prevent discrimination against various groups. As one result of federal monitoring through the Commission on Civil Rights, testimonial evidence demonstrated that there was indeed discrimination against voters or prospective voters who were members of particular language subgroups, and as a result modern federal language assistance policy was created. Federal requirements have expanded and changed with the various VRA reauthorizations, and language assistance is also required by some states. Nationally, language assistance requirements are found in the VRA in several places. These include Section 203 of the VRA, which lays out the requirements for providing language assistance to four language groups (Spanish Heritage, Native American, Native Alaskan, and Asian) whose US population meets a 5 percent threshold for limited English proficiency. Other VRA provisions have been used to advocate for or require language assistance, including Section 208, which addresses voter assistance for disability or illiteracy, and Section 4, which details the criteria for invoking federal intervention for a variety of reasons.

The primary focus of federal enforcement of VRA language coverage requirements has been on the so-called Section 203 jurisdictions. In 2013, the Supreme Court decision in *Shelby County v. Holder* invalidated the formula used to require jurisdictions to submit their election law and practice changes to the federal government for review and approval before implementation. Since then, federal strategies for VRA compliance on language issues have drawn upon the many other areas of the VRA that provide a considerable number of avenues for investigating election practices.

Ballot offerings in languages other than English have a straightforward impact on democratic functioning. Language assistance has been shown to be associated with increased political participation by language minority groups. Increased rates of voter registration and voter turnout are reported consistently over time and across covered language minorities (Benson 2007). Nonuse of language assistance when needed by voters is associated with decreases in participation and increases in error. At the same time, since the enactment of VRA and the implementation of provisions for language assistance, language minority groups continue to participate at a rate lower than the rate of increase of these groups in the population as a whole (for more discussion, see de la Garza and DeSipio 1993).

Federal government requirements for the provision of language assistance for those seeking to register and vote is relatively more recent than federal prohibitions of racial discrimination in the electoral process. The VRA was originally enacted to remedy voting discrimination against African Americans in the South. It was crafted around prior federal civil rights acts passed in 1955, 1960, and 1964, whose provisions were not adequate to prevent widespread barriers to voting such as poll taxes, literacy tests, and voter registration procedures. Having been structured primarily to cure the deficiencies of these earlier attempts, the VRA did not contain broad provisions to facilitate access for those language minorities excluded from the election process. The notable exception was Section 4(e), which prohibited literacy tests for voters who completed the sixth grade in American-flag schools where the language of instruction was not English. The effect was to enfranchise a substantial portion of the Puerto Rican population of New York.

The VRA was amended in 1975 to clarify the reach of its application beyond black/white racial discrimination. Three basic approaches were established. One clarification pertained to Hispanics/Latinos, whose group racial/ethnic status under the 1965 provisions was unclear and who nonetheless experienced widespread discrimination. The "language minority" classification created voting rights protection for members of four groups who had historically experienced discrimination in the election process: (1) individuals of Spanish heritage; (2) Asian Americans; (3) Alaskan natives; and (4) Native Americans (American Indians). The 1975 amendments prohibited English-only elections and extended the permanent, general antidiscrimination provisions of Section 2 to add coverage for language minorities and brought language minorities within the preclearance requirements of Section 5.

The 1975 VRA amendments also extended the VRA's reach to cover limited English language proficiency as a result of educational inequality, which included widespread educational discrimination and resource disparities. Section 4(f) targets jurisdictions with a long history of discrimination by using a triggering formula. This section prohibits English-only materials and requires language assistance in states and political subdivisions where three factors exist: (1) more than 5 percent of the voting age citizens were members of a language minority group on November 1, 1972; (2) registration and election materials were provided only in English on that date; and (3) fewer than 50 percent of the voting age citizens were registered to vote or voted in the 1972 presidential election. Language assistance means that the covered jurisdiction must provide all election materials, including personal assistance and ballots, in the language of the minority group. The coverage extends to all political units that hold elections in the covered political subdivision.

Also enacted in the 1975 amendments, Section 203 applies to all election jurisdictions throughout the country and uses a similar triggering formula to require language assistance. Unlike Section 4(f), which focuses on the most egregious conditions of disenfranchisement for language minorities, Section 203 essentially creates a national language assistance program for language minorities. Section 203 mandates language assistance in states and political subdivisions where more than 5 percent of the voting age citizens are members of a language minority group and where the illiteracy rate for this group exceeds the national rate. In 1982, Section 203 was amended to require a language minority group to be limited in English proficiency, in order to trigger the language assistance requirement. The US Census Bureau defines as "limited English proficient" those citizens who speak a language other than English in their homes and who do not speak English "very well."[1] In 1992, Section 203 was amended to impose an additional test that focused only on the number of language minorities in a jurisdiction, in order to provide assistance to the members of large groups of language minorities who did not meet the 5 percent population threshold in many of the country's large urban areas. The 1992 amendment extended language assistance to jurisdictions with more than 10,000 voting age citizens in a language minority group with an illiteracy rate more than the national average.

Section 203 requires covered jurisdictions to also provide all voting and election materials that are provided in English in the minority language that triggered coverage. These include "registration or voting notices, forms, instructions, assistance or other material or information relating to the electoral process, including ballots." Where the language is oral, unspoken, or unwritten (as in the case of some American Indians and Alaskan Natives), written materials are not required. Materials must be clear, complete, and accurate, which may require consideration of multiple dialects. Covered jurisdictions must also conduct outreach to minority language groups to make known the availability of language assistance and materials to the affected groups. Assistance also includes bilingual voter registration, election administration, and voting processes. This assistance has become more complex as alternative methods of voting have become more popular—for example, extensive early voting periods, Election Day registration, and requirements for public assistance agencies to offer voter registration.

Assistance is also available to voters who are unable to read or write generally, without regard to their language of origin. VRA Section 208, which was enacted in 1982, also provides all voters with an assistant of their choice if they require assistance because of an inability to read or write; this section also provides the same assistance to those who are blind or otherwise disabled. As with previous amendments to the VRA, Section 208 was enacted to quell the prospect of intimidation and discrimination that some voters feared or experienced by allowing voters to bring into the voting booth someone whom they trust (with the exception of a voter's employer or agent, or an officer or agent of a voter's labor union).[2] Section 208 does not explicitly provide minority language voters with an assistant, and it may only give some voters with limited English proficiency the option of having a personal assistant at the polls. Some states have attempted to use Section 208 to provide such a right; however, the provision has not been uniformly interpreted in this manner (Barbas 2009).

Although designed to be temporary, the basic framework of language assistance has been in effect under the VRA for more than forty years, and Congress has continued to expand its reach. Today, the language assistance provisions target groups that have experienced significant discrimination in the conduct of elections and in the educational system, and groups of substantial size that justify government expense in providing assistance (e.g., Ancheta 2006). In 2006 the VRA's reauthorization extended language assistance provisions for twenty-five years, and added a mechanism to generate more frequent attention to language assistance. Previous language assistance trigger calculations were based on the decennial census; new trigger calculations will be made every five years based on the American Community Survey (ACS).

In spite of this array of federal protections, three distinct groups of potential voters present needs that are not addressed systematically by current policy requirements for language assistance. American citizens with limited English proficiency and who belong to language minorities other than the four groups for which language assistance is required do not receive the same benefit of government assistance. This issue is not particularly new, and it persists around the country (Abdelall 2004). For example, Barbas (2009) cites Dearborn, Michigan; the population of Dearborn is 30 percent Arab, but election materials in Arabic are not required under the VRA. New York City is also home to concentrations of considerable numbers of Russian and Haitian Creole speakers; however, state election policy authorizes materials only in the four VRA-required languages. In some recent elections, the New York City Mayor's Office has authorized interpreters for Russian and Haitian Creole speakers on a pilot basis at some polling sites. Although this assistance was hailed as a policy advance, the effort was criticized in some quarters because the sites of particular political contests were chosen for the pilot.

Another group of potential voters with language needs are American citizens with a limited ability to understand election materials, including ballots, but who speak English in their homes. These potential voters are essentially "defined out" of the equation because they speak English in their homes and thus are not captured by the US Census or ACS projections. This circumstance reflects the essentially passive nature of Section 203.

Of course, election jurisdictions can choose to provide language assistance. More than thirty states have enacted provisions that permit some form of assistance to voters with limited English proficiency (Barbas 2009; Benson 2007). The approaches, however, vary widely. For example, California and Colorado have enacted state laws that lower the threshold for language assistance to 3 percent of the population for any language minority, and Florida has adopted a statewide language accommodation. Texas allows all voters to receive assistance marking their ballots if they are unable to read the language of the ballot. Some states require voters to declare by oath the reason they need assistance, or to declare that they cannot read the English language. Finally, some states require assistance and bilingual materials beyond federal requirements, while others only make it permissible for election officials to provide such information.

VRA Section 203 coverage is determined by the Bureau of the Census. Coverage occurs if any one of the following conditions exists: (1) more than 5 percent of the voting age citizens are members of a single language minority and have limited English proficiency; (2) more than 10,000 voting age citizens are members of a single language minority and have limited English proficiency; and (3) in a political subdivision containing any part of an Indian reservation, more than 5 percent of the American Indian or Alaska Native voting age citizens are members of a single language minority and have limited English proficiency. This last condition is essentially an alternative coverage formula for Native American voters living on reservations; reservation boundaries typically do not conform to county boundaries, and the result is that these voters are distributed across counties and individual counties do not contain a critical mass of voters, although the reservation itself may include sufficient numbers to trigger coverage.

The number of jurisdictions covered by federal language assistance requirements has changed since their original enactment in 1975. These changes are due to several factors, including how the need for language assistance is defined, how population concentrations are determined, and how data are collected. In 1975, requirements counted all voting age citizens in a language minority. In 1982, the English-language proficiency requirement was added, so that the count would include only those voting age citizens in a language minority group who spoke English less than very well. The number of jurisdictions requiring language assistance declined as a result; the number of counties covered declined from 369 counties before 1982 to 197 counties by 1992 (Tucker 2006).

Through 2000, language proficiency data were collected through the long-form decennial census, which asks whether the respondent is able to speak English very well, well, not well, or not at all. According to Census Bureau reports, respondents tend to overestimate their English proficiency and, consequently, limited English proficiency includes those who respond in any way other than "very well" (Benson 2007). As a result of the VRA's 2006 reauthorization, the director of the US Census will determine language minority coverage on the basis of 2010 ACS data and will use the ACS data to make this determination in five-year increments. Thus, instead of using population data to make determinations about language minority coverage, the Census Bureau will rely on estimates from sampling. These estimates will change, depending upon the assumptions made in the computations that are not proscribed in the legislation.

However, the US population affected by language minority determinations is significant and steadily growing. The population in need of assistance as required by federal requirements more than doubled in recent decades. In 1980, 23 million people in the United States, or 11 percent of the population age five years and older, spoke a language other than English at home (Shin and Bruno 2003). Census data reported in 2002 and cited by Tucker (2006) indicate that in 2000, 47 million people, or 18 percent of the population age five and over, spoke a language other than English at home. In this group, nearly half (21.3 million) spoke English less than very well, and thus are defined as having limited English proficiency; Spanish speakers constituted nearly two-thirds of this group, and thus they are the largest language minority group overall (Tucker 2006, 195–96).

In spite of this increase in need across the overall population, a wide array of language minorities remain outside federal requirements. The ten languages most frequently spoken at home in addition to English and Spanish are Chinese, French, German, Tagalog, Vietnamese, Italian, Korean, Russian, Polish, and Arabic. But VRA coverage extends only to the Asian and Pacific Island languages among this group (Chinese, Tagalog, Vietnamese, and Korean). The states of Alaska, Arizona, California, New Mexico, and Texas are particularly affected, as are two hundred additional jurisdictions across sixteen additional states.[3] Across these states and jurisdictions, illiteracy far exceeds the national rate; the average for Spanish Heritage limited English proficiency citizens is more than fifteen times the national illiteracy rate, and more than half the covered political subdivisions have illiteracy rates of more than 20 percent (Tucker and Espino 2007).

CONTEMPORARY ISSUES

The landscape of language assistance today is increasingly complicated. More and more immigrants who speak languages other than English are naturalized citizens. The effects of more frequent measurement of language needs are not yet fully clear. However, these two factors suggest increasing need. Although some states and localities provide more than is required by the federal government, there remain documented instances in which even covered areas do not fully comply. As the immigration policy environment remains superheated going into the 2020 election cycle, third-party groups continue to be vigilant in their advocacy and in their interactions with local election officials (LEOs).

What Are the Challenges, and Who Helps?

In an open-ended survey of over one hundred election administrators from a variety of types of jurisdictions from around the country, we asked about local experiences and the challenges that LEOs face regarding language assistance.[4] Their challenges can be grouped into four categories: need, administrative concerns, language issues, and bias. Challenges related to need vary. Some felt that there were other language groups that have tremendous needs; but because they are not covered languages, their states or localities would not provide funds to meet these needs and therefore they did not or could not do so. Some felt that there is a real need for increased bilingual election outreach, but little time or resources to offer it. Alternatively, others felt that though they met the threshold coverage, there was not nearly as much need as the numbers indicated, forcing them to provide assistance that voters did not in fact need.

Three major administrative challenges were identified by election officials, and are likely familiar to any election administrator working in a jurisdiction that provides language assistance. First, election officials noted problems with finding interpreters who are actually fluent in the language(s) and dialect(s) that are needed. Second, election officials discussed the financial resources available for language assistance, which often are not adequate to meet legal requirements and/or needs. Third, election officials mentioned real problems with ballot design, and paper ballot design issues in particular. These include problems with ballot length when English and covered languages are required on the same ballot, typesetting issues when separate ballots are allowed, and even confusion by poll workers when handing out ballots in a precinct with multiple ballots in different languages.

Unwritten languages present a particular kind of need both for voters who need assistance and for election administrators. As the number of native speakers of unwritten languages dwindles, this challenge has become more acute. As with all languages, translators and interpreters are difficult to locate and employ; for unwritten languages, this difficulty is particularly significant.

Finally, the administrators' answers suggested that there are concerns related to bias against non–English speakers. This is two-pronged. Voters sometimes express opposition to resources being used to provide ballots in a language other than English. Other comments suggest that some election administrators are opposed to resources being used in this way, although language assistance is required. As an example of one such comment, an election administrator noted that "all voters should be able to communicate in English to vote." Although this type of response was extremely rare, its presence does underscore that both explicit and implicit bias remain in the language arena, despite the fact that the United States does not have an official language.

So who helps with this work? When asked, election administrators pointed to a variety of players from well-known, business-as-usual groups like the League of Women Voters to an array of homegrown, local advocates and their political party groups. The latter include local community-based organizations designed to support and advocate for minority ethnic groups, community leaders, media channels focused on language minority groups, and tribal councils. Others mentioned that the federal government played a significant role in helping. Enforcement action by the Department of Justice can motivate (or force) reluctant state or local governments to provide the resources to support this work. Finally, a few election administrators said that no one helps them, and that they must do all of the work internally. For those who struggle with providing language assistance, the universal response to what is needed is "staff for outreach," which is a resource problem.

VRA Section 203 Coverage and ACS Estimates

The demographic changes that have occurred since the 2000 census are evident.[5] The 2011 voting age citizen language minority population had increased 41 percent over the 2002 determination, and 2011 language coverage affected 31 percent of citizens of voting age. Use of the ACS data on a five-year schedule will generate a new, more frequent schedule of review and training language assistance needs; these are occurring more rapidly than the decennial census can capture.

Language diversity is increasing as well.[6] Across the country, in eleven states, there are thirty-six counties with multiple language groups covered. The county with the most requirements for VRA language coverage is Los Angeles County, which requires bilingual materials in seven Asian languages plus Spanish. Spanish Heritage language assistance is the most common requirement. Not surprisingly, Alaskan Native language assistance is required in Alaska, and American Indian language coverage includes Choctaw, Hopi, Kickapoo, Navajo, Pueblo, Tohono O'Odham, Yaqui, and Yuma. For Asian Americans, the leading language for coverage across the country is Chinese, followed by Filipino and Vietnamese; other Asian languages with county coverage include Asian Indian, Japanese, Korean, and Bangladeshi.

Several questions emerge from this evolutionary overview of government assurance of assistance in the election process to language minorities with limited English proficiency. One set of questions has to do with US Census parameters for using estimation in general. Broadly, how has the move to ACS estimates changed coverage, and, if so, for which jurisdictions and which language minorities? Another set of questions has to do with the census parameters for interpreting English language proficiency and literacy. Currently, particular administrative interpretations guide the understanding of who speaks English well enough to participate in elections without the government requirement of language assistance throughout the process, and literacy parameters are set at fifth-grade reading level. How do coverage requirements change if these parameters are adjusted to reflect higher or lower levels? And finally, what are the policy and normative implications of current practice and of these potential changes? Our discussion here about innovation relies on interviews with LEOs in both covered and noncovered jurisdictions.

Limited but significant research (Tucker 2006; Tucker and Espino 2007) suggests that the cost of language assistance is nominal in spite of its broad reach. However, LEOs continually comment that resources are limited for all aspects of election administration, and they cite the lack of resources for language assistance in particular. Anecdotally, LEOs note that certain forms of language assistance may be more effective than others, like radio coverage as opposed to translating and distributing printed materials. LEOs also note that certain forms of language assistance may be more expensive than others. Perhaps most salient, LEOs feel that, despite considerable effort, they continue to lack the ability to locate actual voters in need of assistance because the ACS estimates target geography areas too broadly.

Growth in language assistance seems assured. It is true that the overall number of covered jurisdictions declined between 2002 and 2011. However, between 2011 and 2016, the first year the ACS estimates were used to determine coverage, states gained far more than they lost; for every state where the number of covered jurisdictions declined, two states saw increases in the number of covered jurisdictions. States with the greatest variations in changes were Alaska, Colorado, Massachusetts, Nevada, South Dakota, and Texas. These changes, with the exception of those in Massachusetts and Texas, were driven primarily by changes in American Indian languages. This increase in coverage suggests two possible outcomes that are not mutually exclusive. First, the need for specific location information may fade as the purview of federal coverage broadens. Second, multilingual election materials may be the new normal.

Assistance Beyond Section 203 Requirements

Several states and localities have moved beyond federal requirements to expand language assistance, either by providing assistance to voters in languages other than the four required groups or by using lower thresholds for these or other languages. For example, California State Code (CSC) 14201 establishes a 3 percent state threshold and makes the language requirement a law for all languages in which citizens in an election jurisdiction meet the threshold, not just the four language groups. What this means practically for the state is that counties can be covered by federal requirements, state requirements, or both. That is, they can be covered by VRA 203 only, VRA 203, or CSC 14201, depending upon the size of the population, or by CSC 14201 only.[7]

In 2018, California added Panjabi (Punjabi), Hmong, Syriac, Armenian, Persian, and Arabic to the VRA-covered languages; the result is that voting materials are required to be provided in up to fourteen languages in addition to English, depending on the concentration of these languages in each county. California law also provides determinations as to which precincts must provide facsimile ballots, or post photocopies of ballots, in non-English languages. The practical effect is that nearly every county in the state must consider language assistance in its election administration efforts. Half the counties were covered by federal requirements, and 90 percent by state law; state requirements reached 100,000 precincts, and in 2016 only two counties were not covered by either federal or state requirements. State requirements for language assistance are not as extensive as federal requirements. Counties covered under CSC 14201 must post a translated ballot for each covered language group in the polling place. Voters do not necessarily vote on a translated ballot, but they can use it for reference as they vote on an English ballot. Local election offices must also attempt to recruit poll workers who speak the languages covered by state law. This represents a significant effort for election administrators, an expansive understanding for politicians about their duty to citizens at the polling place, and in the end an increased outlay of resources.

One method that states and localities have used to expand the quality of their language support is by establishing advisory committees. Again in California, the Office of the Secretary of State (SOS) has created the Language Accessibility Advisory Committee (LAAC) "to advise and assist the SOS with implementation of federal and state laws relating to access of the electoral process by low-English-proficiency (LEP) voters, so that all voters can understand the voting process. The LAAC also provides recommendations identifying and prioritizing activities, programs, and policies to ensure every voter has equal access to the ballot."[8]

The California SOS has also encouraged all local election jurisdictions across the state to form their own LAACs. Los Angeles County in particular is home to a significant number of LEP voters, and it exceeds state requirements for providing assistance to language groups not covered under Section 203. In addition, the county has a long history of local community outreach efforts and collaborations, which has been written about widely (e.g., Hall

2003; Ramchandani, Chisnell, and Quesenbery 2017). In another example, King County, Washington, formed a partnership with the Seattle Foundation to provide small grants to community-based organizations to help them expand registration and offer assistance in voting for LEP citizens who speak Chinese, Korean, Vietnamese, and Spanish.[9]

Efforts to Roll Back Language Coverage

The purpose of this book is to focus on innovation in election administration vis-à-vis voting and how it occurs. And yet, the importance of efforts to curtail such innovation cannot be ignored, and these efforts speak to the politics of innovation broadly understood. In the area of language assistance, the influence of politics is also clear. Despite the more expansive coverage in California than is present in much of the United States, several third-party groups have worked together to bring suit against California for the coverage it provides, alleging that it does not go far enough. These groups include Asian Americans Advancing Justice–Los Angeles; Asian Americans Advancing Justice–Asian Law Caucus; the American Civil Liberties Union Foundation of Northern California; and Wilson, Sonsini, Goodrich & Rosati—to name a few. Their claims are sophisticated and recognize the realities of combining the political geography of US Census data with individual-level data about the particular voters who are in need of assistance. These groups claim that by focusing on precincts for coverage, not entire counties, many LEP voters will be missed and their full access to voting will be curtailed.[10] These claims persist despite the fact that English is the official language of the State of California (see the California Constitution, Article III, Section 6b). In November 2019, a California Court of Appeals agreed and ruled—in *Asian Americans Advancing Justice v. Alex Padilla*—that the state's 2017 interpretation of its state language coverage law was too restrictive, at least for Asian language speakers with limited English proficiency. As a result, beginning with the 2020 elections, fourteen new languages will be covered for the entire state under state law, including eleven that have never been covered in California.[11]

Other states have also placed limitations on what can be done. These limitations range from laws that explicitly state that voting materials must be in English to states that require affirmative oaths of being an LEP voter before assistance is given (Ramchandani, Chisnell, and Quesenbery 2017). About half the states have adopted English as the official state language, and nearly all have done so since the 1980s. On a more expansive note, in April 2019 Florida governor Ron DeSantis initiated rulemaking to require all the state's sixty-seven counties to provide Spanish language ballots and voter assistance, although federal law would compel only about one-quarter of the counties to provide bilingual ballots and election materials.

REFLECTIONS FROM JURISDICTIONS
AND ELECTION ADMINISTRATORS

Minority language assistance is not possible without the extensive involvement of LEOs. Numerous studies document instances over the past thirty years when language assistance was required and was needed but was not provided by poll workers or permanent election staff. Accounts indicate a wide range of possible motivations, including a lack of knowledge, inattention, callous disregard, and intentional discrimination (e.g., Benson 2007; Weinberg and Utrecht 2002). To understand more clearly the challenges that LEOs face in the current environment, we interviewed a number of LEOs in jurisdictions that are covered by VRA Section 203 language requirements.

One exemplar county in California is home to about 1 million voting age–eligible citizens, roughly 70 percent of whom are registered voters. The county provides assistance in two languages required by the VRA (Spanish and Chinese) and four additional languages pursuant to the state's 3 percent threshold (Vietnamese, Tagolog, Japanese, and Korean). Spanish language assistance has been provided for more than almost twenty years; however, Chinese language assistance was required starting with the 2010 census determinations in 2011. Pursuant to state law, at the time the jurisdiction used optical scan equipment (for additional detail, see Lavine and Jarboe 2019).

At the time of our interviews, the jurisdiction had about 500 polling places to accommodate roughly 700,000 voters. The jurisdiction provided language assistance across the voting process, including assistance inside the election office, voter outreach, precinct-level translation, review of voter registration cards, interaction with the press and other media, and attendance at citizenship classes to teach prospective citizens about voting. Telephone banks on Election Day are staffed with speakers of Spanish, Mandarin, and Chinese. About 40 percent of polling locations are covered with a Spanish speaker, and the jurisdiction had roughly 20,000 registered voters who requested materials in Spanish.

The level of complexity for any election jurisdiction of this size is high, and it increases significantly with the addition of a newly covered group. Although this jurisdiction is larger than many, it is not unrepresentative. About 25 percent of the election jurisdictions in the country have 500,000 registered voters or more (Brace 2017). In addition, complexity in local election operations is affected by language needs and also by other state election law requirements.

One way that this complexity becomes obvious is in the ballot styles that are required. A ballot style represents a unique combination of political jurisdictions and contests at the lowest level possible. Language requirements apply at the level of the ballot style, and different combinations of school districts and municipal races expanded this number significantly. For example, in this jurisdiction described above, the 2012 primary election required twenty-seven versions of each ballot in order to have a ballot in each language for each of the then nine political parties entitled to appear on the ballot at the same time. For the 2012 general election, the jurisdiction provided a single ballot, which included all three languages—English, Spanish, and Chinese. The LEO reported to us that this single ballot format in three languages prompted some voters to express dissatisfaction at the cost of printing ballots in languages other than English. The LEO also described voting system limitations, including software difficulties, in accommodating multiple spoken dialects of the same written language (e.g., both Mandarin Chinese and Cantonese Chinese), multiple character-based languages on a single piece of equipment, and inadequate font capacity to support character-based (here, Asian) languages.

Overall, the LEO expressed frustration with the inability to accurately locate language minority voters in order to target voter outreach and pre-voting assistance. They also expressed frustration at the lack of resources to support language assistance, which was noted as critical to supporting these efforts, despite the narrative among some in the pro–language assistance community that the costs related to election materials in other languages is minimal (see, e.g., Ao 2007). The LEO noted that this jurisdiction received no federal or state financial support and very limited resources from a statewide association of LEOs. The cost of implementing Spanish language assistance was estimated at $200,000, and the cost to implement Chinese was about the same, though translation assistance for Chinese was more challenging than for Spanish. They reported that this stemmed from two factors: first, when they added Chinese, the newly required poll workers tended not to want to stay for an entire day (which is required of poll workers by state law in this and many states). Second, additional translators were needed in order to handle different dialects.

The LEO reported challenges in interpreting cultural differences and also translation difficulties; it takes time to learn these differences, and community groups can be of significant assistance. Hall (2003) reports similar findings from a small-scale study conducted in Los Angeles County in 2001 during the Los Angeles mayoral election. Perhaps foreshadowing the experience of other jurisdictions, in 2001 Los Angeles County worked with six different language minorities, including Spanish and five different Asian languages; and since that election, its coverage has steadily grown to include other language groups.

By the time of our visit to Los Angeles County in 2017, the county's LEO had engaged in a multiyear process to address language assistance among myriad other issues by collaborating with academic, community, government, and third-party partners to design a voting system that could seamlessly and more cost-effectively address these issues and generate a paper ballot for counting and auditing purposes. In relation to language assistance issues in particular, this election management system was developed to include a geographic information system platform that serves multiple purposes, including targeted geographic data to support greater precision in language minority outreach.

In Colorado, many jurisdictions have multiple languages covered by Section 203 and provide assistance to other significant language groups that are not covered. One bilingual staff member in a local election office we visited legally immigrated to the United States and noted a problem with local election jurisdictions' responses to VRA Section 203, which is that most of the assistance is accomplished through the translation of materials. There are still high illiteracy rates among some immigrant groups, which means that these translated materials are not accessible either. Reilly (2015) observes that illiteracy is common among nonnative English speakers, as are problems with the use of professional translators, who tend to speak more formally and can generate reduced readability.

Election system stakeholders also observe that understanding ballots' language is an issue in and of itself, and recent research chronicles the importance of bilingual ballots over time (Tucker 2016). The formal verbiage required by state election laws can be intimidating, even to those who are quite literate. Translation can lead to misinterpretation; basic illiteracy regardless of language only compounds this dynamic. In that vein, some stakeholders advocate the application of plain language in ballot layout and design and in the instructions and information provided to voters and registrants (Lausen 2007). Field guides have been developed for designing usable ballots and testing them and for writing instructions that voters understand (Chisnell 2013).

Also, although these translations are in fact required by law, jurisdictions may be deploying resources inefficiently or ineffectively. Money spent on print may be better deployed through investment in radio, at least with respect to the potential impact of resources used.

One of the cost-saving solutions adopted by election administrators in large jurisdictions with many language requirements is a system that incorporates translation information into a ballot on demand or an online ballot. This is the approach used to interact with uniformed and overseas citizens under the Uniformed and Overseas Citizens Absentee Voting Act: the translated ballot is online, and the voter downloads and prints it and mails the ballot in. Programming the multilanguage capability to generate ballots in multiple languages remains an essential expense, so this approach is not entirely cost free. The approach of the Uniformed and Overseas Citizens Absentee Voting Act illustrates how solutions to one issue may overlap into other areas. However, to the extent that jurisdictions choose to mediate concerns about security and integrity through audits of paper ballots, innovation in all online options will remain limited.

Private-sector electronic translation services commonly used by corporations and across other fields of government service may offer a relatively lower-cost option. LanguageLine, which is operated by the LanguageLine in Monterey, California, provides a range of translation services for voters that can be accessed via telephone and online videos. The District of Columbia, for example, uses LanguageLine to assist its voters. This solution can be particularly valuable in meeting voters' needs for translation when local needs are not reflected in national or state mandates for assistance.

These responses to LEP voters and to an expanding array of language needs foreshadow a growing trend in innovation in election administration across levels of government. At the federal level, the US Election Assistance Commission (EAC) has taken a leadership role in setting a tone of inclusion. In a conversation with EAC commissioner Christy McCormick, she noted that "the attitude of serving customers is a theme now—so language is a natural part of what jurisdictions are doing. And people are realizing we are a multilingual society." Then–commission chair Matt Masterson added that "with language and accessibility—technology has allowed election administrators to do more of this as customer service—which then lessens their call volume, and so on. If we provide the service, then they have fewer issues on the back end." Commissioner Thomas Hicks added, "I think that we can't just look at English to be the dominant language of providing information" (see also Hicks 2019).

In keeping with its clearinghouse role, the EAC provides election information in twelve languages, and it has generated resources for LEOs. The EAC has also convened two language summits, held in 2017 and 2018, which were described earlier in this chapter; these day-long meetings of seasoned practitioners and researchers are open to the public and highlight best practices and emerging issues. The conversations in these forums generate new ideas and foster relationships that provide support for LEOs as well as state offices. Together, the work of the EAC and the perspectives of its commissioners suggest that language assistance will continue to be an area to watch for reform, innovation, and expansion of the work done in election administration.

ANALYSIS

Our innovation model suggests that of the four overarching factors critical to explaining innovation in election administration—politics, professionalism, resources, and need—all are important in one way or another for explaining language assistance innovation and related failures. However, the relative importance of these factors and how they exercise influence depends on the level of government and timing. Influence may also depend on whether the type of assistance is mandated to prevent potential discrimination or is adopted voluntarily at the state level to provide administrative assistance.

At the start of the language assistance provision in the VRA's reauthorization of 1975, the purpose was to expand the VRA's reach in order to extend federal remedies already provided to African Americans to members of other groups who, at the time, had also experienced significant discrimination at the polls because of the languages they spoke and read. Some of this was related to long-standing discrimination and inequitable treatment (i.e., coverage for Native Americans, Alaskan natives, and some Spanish speakers), and some was related to both long-standing and more recent discrimination against immigrants (i.e., Spanish speakers and Asian Americans). Innovation in this area was initially driven by politics and remains largely a political problem, heightened by persistent concerns about rising Latino empowerment and the influence of Latino voters (Baker 1996; Cha and Kennedy 2014; Hopkins 2011).

Language battles in the states during the 1980s and 1990s, like their counterparts in the 1900s during other waves of immigration, appealed to patriotism and unity and often cast language minorities in the role of outsiders who deliberately chose not to learn English. Research about the waves of ballot initiatives during the 1980s and 1990s, which ran the gamut from English as the official language to various forms of English-only education initiatives, demonstrate ties to increased rates of immigration and increased public attention to immigration (e.g., Donovan and Bowler 1998; Hero and Tolbert 1996; Smith and Tolbert 2007; Tolbert and Hero 1996). More broadly, state policy decisions with adverse consequences for Latinx are linked to increasing Latinx population and increased populaton diversity generally, although mediated by Latinx political efficacy (Hero 1998). These links persisted as the nation overhauled welfare policy (e.g., Soss et al. 2010).

Over time, however, the national politics related to language assistance has changed. As detailed by Ao (2007), the fight over reauthorization of the Section 203 portions of the VRA in 2006 was largely political; numerous partisan attempts to amend it were proposed, but all these efforts failed. In the end, the reauthorization was unanimous. This could suggest that, today, there is little lasting political entrée to a discussion of substantive differences at the national level about public requirements for language assistance. Discussion is all but assured on House Bill No. 1, which was introduced in early 2019 in this chamber of Congress controlled by Democrats since the 2018 midterm elections. The legislation contains a considerable number of provisions for electoral reform; the pitched political climate for immigration reform may provoke additional discussion about public policy in this area.

Looking at innovation and reform across the states tells a more disjointed story. Although it is anecdotal and not systematic, there is evidence that some states actively work to support LEP voters, some do nothing, some do what is mandated by the federal government, and some choose to go beyond the federal mandate to do more. Explaining this array is more difficult. In another area of election administration policy—voluntary voting system standards— state responses were dependent in part on levels of election administration professionalism; states with higher levels of professionalism were more likely to choose a path that diverged from federal standards but was designed to produce the same result: a certified voting system (Hale and Brown 2013). Here, similar factors tested using multivariate quantitative models did not explain state variation in language assistance, including factors often used to explain state-level policy differences—for example, political culture (Elazar 1966).

At the local level, innovation and reform can be explained by all four interconnected factors: professionalization through collaboration, politics, resources, and need. Important work occurs at the jurisdiction level through voter education, outreach, and advisory boards to connect LEP voters, community members, activists, and organizers with LEOs and their staff members; these efforts are an important component of successful efforts to provide high-quality language assistance. This type of community–government collaboration has been documented to be a critical component of innovation in this area. More recently, election stakeholders that focus on improving the voter experience and on clarifying voters' intents have advocated for the use of plain language in ballot design and in the instructions and other information that are provided to registrants and voters. These initiatives can be expected to infiltrate election offices in more general terms, improving the fidelity of the voting experience across all voters. Networks and the professionalism necessary to navigate them are clearly important, as are the roles of community and third-party groups as drivers.

The second component is politics. On the surface, the political discussion is highly partisan, with Democrats preferring broad-based inclusion and access and Republicans preferring systems designed to ensure integrity. Beneath the surface, the political element at work in this aspect of election administration also revolves around the politics of immigration. The State of Arizona is a perfect example of the current divide about this. At the state and local levels, Arizona's practices comply with the federal laws regarding language assistance. However, the state legislature has instituted other methods of identifying voters with photo identification as well as birth certificate documentary proof of citizenship. Language assistance driven by the federal level with a focus on equity and access was met by state and local pushback. The language used in Proposition 200 in Arizona in 1996 was clear. Section 2 states that

> this state finds that illegal immigration is causing economic hardship
> to this state and that illegal immigration is encouraged by public agen-
> cies within this state that provide public benefits without verifying

immigration status. This state further finds that illegal immigrants have been given a safe haven in this state with the aid of identification cards that are issued without verifying immigration status, and that this conduct contradicts federal immigration policy, undermines the security of our borders and demeans the value of citizenship. Therefore, the people of this state declare that the public interest of this state requires all public agencies within this state to cooperate with federal immigration authorities to discourage illegal immigration.

Research on the relationship between immigration and politics suggests that increasing immigration has an impact specifically on white politics, driving white Americans to the political right over time and influencing political rhetoric toward more protectionist as opposed to expansionist policies (Abrajano and Hajnal 2015). Even as scholars find a decrease in the role of ethnic politics in elections internationally, they continue to show its prevalence and role in US elections (Jupp and Pietsch 2018). These politics indirectly influence seemingly neutral election practices and administration. The national immigration debates are likely to generate pressure for changes that are likely to affect election practices.

The third component is resources. Resources, as has been noted above, can take many forms. Most obviously, resources equate to money, and money has certainly helped in each of the cases we have documented of innovative responses to language assistance needs. This is particularly true in the resource-intensive efforts that have been dedicated to developing election systems that are capable of accommodating multiple languages, and that will be needed in the future. Vendors will be an essential part of these conversations as jurisdictions begin to replace aging voting systems; software updates that might facilitate expanded language assistance today have been observed to be limited by the parameters and capacity of existing equipment.

But resources involve far more than money, and in this case, innovation has been spurred by the resources of the will, vision, and inspiration of LEOs to take on language assistance. Some of the themes that bubbled up from our conversations were about customer service and efficiency orientations, and about the civic duty to serve all voters. These are hallmarks of professionalism and go hand in hand with collaboration and with leadership in particular.

The third component in the story of language assistance innovation is the influence of growing need, and in some areas this also equates to changing needs. This need takes on a couple of dimensions. First, new immigrant groups not encompassed by current federal requirements will create demand for language assistance. This will create the need for response by LEOs and perhaps state offices. Increased frequency of information will now require responses by local and state officials. Second, the move to the use of ACS estimates will likely increase the number of covered jurisdictions, and will also increase the likelihood that jurisdictions move back and forth between being covered or not. Both growing and changing need will put pressure on LEOs to continue to devise new approaches in this area.

Escalating need and escalating frequency of review for the application of federal requirements will also bring more focused attention to this aspect of election administration. Language assistance will no longer be something that is addressed only once a decade and then shelved. And language assistance will also require more flexibility on the part of LEOs and their staffs. To date, some portion of local need has been met by LEOs doing more than what is just required by law in many places, a reflection of the public service orientation of election officials. Although nonresponsive or negatively responsive poll worker actions have been documented, we believe them to be the exception, not the rule.

CONCLUSIONS

Federal policy through Section 203 of the VRA remains the dominant force driving language assistance in voting across the states today, but other federal rules and some state laws and local choices supplement this. Major challenges related to language assistance provision today center on growing, fluctuating, and unmet needs; on resistance to the provision of services; on funding, especially for poll workers and interpreters; and, where paper ballots are used, on design. The factors that appear to aid language assistance at the local level primarily concern collaboration and network relationships with third-party groups and resources broadly understood, especially leadership. Although innovation in the form of language assistance was initially driven by national level politics, it no longer is. The driving force for language assistance largely began with federal involvement in reauthorizations of the VRA—Congress established what is required—and the Department of Justice enforced this. But these requirements were limited to particular groups; and states and localities, though not allowed to do less, can do more. Aside from federal requirements, then, the driving forces of what happens at and within the local jurisdictions above and beyond federal requirements are related to local resources, needs, and networks and collaboration.

Finally, we add another important consideration that may inform our understanding of innovation in language assistance specifically: the value of inclusiveness. The United States does not, de jure, have a national language, but its de facto language is English. As citizens of a nation of immigrants, many LEOs of both major political parties and a variety of political ideologies have chosen to embrace the value of inclusiveness when engaging in efforts that sometimes go beyond what is required of them by law. And there appears to be nothing that stops them from embracing both inclusiveness and integrity at the same time, seeing these as complementary values at the heart of their work rather than a source of conflict.

NOTES

1. The classification scheme used by the US Census involves responses to two questions. The first asks whether a language other than English is spoken. The second ask whether the respondent speaks English very well, well, not well, or not at all. The categories that are counted in favor of determining that language assistance is needed are well, not well, and not at all.
2. The VRA prohibits assistance from a voter's employer or a voter's labor union, or an agent of either.
3. The political subdivisions required to provide language assistance under either of the national language assistance provisions of the VRA are catalogued in table C.15 in appendix C.
4. The methodology is described in appendix C. Respondents were relatively evenly divided about whether language assistance posed a challenge in their jurisdiction. Open-ended responses indicate that the administrators who stated that language assistance coverage did not pose a challenge for their jurisdiction said so because they were not required to meet federal standards, and the administrators who stated that it was challenging are working in jurisdictions where language assistance is required.
5. The most recent reauthorization of the VRA included a procedural change in the method of collecting data used to determine whether language assistance is required. The new method uses the ACS data rather than data collected through the long-form decennial census, and language assistance coverage determinations will now be made every five years.
6. See county level data presented in table C.16.
7. Table C.17 displays the array of state and federal requirements across California's fifty-eight counties.
8. Accessed from www.sos.ca.gov/elections/laac/.
9. Accessed from www.kingcounty.gov/depts/elections/about-us/newsroom/news -releases/2016/april/29-voter-engagement.aspx.
10. See "Civil Rights Groups Sue Secretary of State for Depriving CA Voters Language Assistance," press release, Asian Americans Advancing Justice–Asian Law Caucus, April 23, 2018, www.advancingjustice-la.org/media-and-publications/press -releases/civil-rights-groups-sue-secretary-state-depriving-ca-voters#.WxRSly -ZPOQ.
11. New languages include Bengali, Burmese, Gujarati, Hindi, Indonesian, Japanese, Lao, Mien, Mongolian, Nepali, Tamil, Thai, Telugu, and Urdu; expanded coverage will begin for Hmong and Punjabi.

6

Administrative Innovations in Counting Ballots: How Election Results Are Verified

In the 2018 midterm elections, new scrutiny was paid to the administrative processes that determine how ballots are counted and how long this process takes. Polls close at different times across the states; and these closing times, combined with time zone changes, always produce a wave of media reporting about election results that moves from east to west throughout the evening across the country. Some jurisdictions indicate that results will become available at the time that polls close or within an hour after closing. Early results jibe with media preferences; the media's role historically has been to try to predict and announce winners as quickly as possible (Frankovic 2003). The public eagerly anticipates the results of each election and have become accustomed to instantaneous reporting of winner and losers. Yet the process is complex and detailed. Public trust in these results, and in the electoral system more broadly, is a reflection of the accuracy of these results, the framing of the media, and aspects of individuals who make up the public (Alvarez, Hall, and Llewellyn 2008; Edelson et al. 2017; Hamner and Hernnson 2014; Hernnson et al. 2008).

The reality is that the accurate counting necessary to determine the results of elections may take many hours and even days or weeks. In this chapter, we take up the reasons why ballots may or may not be counted, and the pressures that have pushed innovations that affect how we perceive the counting process. We consider how responsibility for counting ballots is a function of voter actions, election administrator actions, public policy, deliberate attempts at misinformation by parties and third-party groups, or a combination of these factors. We provide an overview of the complexity and constantly evolving nature of the balloting landscape, including the implications of centralized and decentralized intergovernmental arrangements, the administration of provisional ballot requirements, and the emerging use of audits for process improvements.

Almost two decades since the passage of the Help America Vote Act (HAVA) and its requirements for centralized voter registration lists, states and localities have arranged their counting processes in different ways. Provisional ballots provide a fail-safe opportunity to cast a ballot under particular circumstances and demonstrate a political compromise with expansive administrative implications. Auditing practices demonstrate new and increasingly popular efforts to ensure accurate outcomes as well as process fidelity, including election system security. We explicate the influence of politics, professionalism, resources, and needs in this aspect of election administration, both in terms of how these factors shape innovation and how these innovations have been used to define and measure successful election administration efforts.

HISTORY

How ballots are counted in US elections has changed significantly since the founding of the nation. At different points and in different places, people counted pebbles or beans or corn, listed voice votes, counted party-generated ballots, and eventually counted government-produced secret ballots (Bensel 2004; Keyssar 2000). In the modern era of election administration, the forms that ballots take continue to vary—paper ballots with preference indicated by a marker, punched cards, and electronic ballots predominate. Each of these has been associated with more or less accuracy (see, e.g., the work done by Ansolabehere and Stewart 2005).

But perhaps the most significant part of the election system is the actual counting of ballots. There are several stages involved in whether what we commonly call a "vote" is counted. And at the outset, it is important to establish precise terminology. What we commonly call a "vote" is actually an attempt to vote—the attempt is counted if it is cast in a timely manner and cast by an eligible voter. There are five sequential subsystems that determine whether a vote attempt results in a counted vote: (1) the counting and canvass process itself; (2) the use of provisional ballots; (3) whether vote attempts are contested; (4) whether recounts are required; and (5) the auditing processes.

Typically, counting begins when the polls close and after the last voter has voted. The specifics vary from state to state; however, the process is essentially as follows. Within polling places, the number of ballots cast is reconciled with the number of ballots issued. Ballots and the accompanying reconciliation documentation are transmitted to a central location, either physically or over secure telephone lines, or both.[1] Appropriately cast mail ballots, early ballots, absentee ballots, provisional ballots, and military and overseas ballots are counted as well; in some places, counting these can begin before Election Day or before the polls are closed, and may continue past Election Day, depending on state law and when ballots are received and/or postmarked. Next is the canvass, which is a review and verification of the vote count. Canvassing boards are often made up of political party representatives, though this also varies and may include other third-party groups. Decisions in these cases are usually made on the basis of available evidence for the intent of the voter; and if intent cannot be determined, then the ballots are not included in the final count. To ensure fairness, most places include bipartisan teams for making these determinations. This approach is important because experimental evidence suggests that in the absence of clear decision rules, people conducting hand counts and recounts are susceptible to subconsciously making decisions that would benefit their own party (Kopko et al. 2011).

The canvass is an integral part of electoral integrity. Although law and practice vary, the purpose of the canvass is to ensure that all ballots cast that should be counted are, in fact, counted. In most places, this integrity is augmented by attention paid to transparency by having election observers present to witness the canvassing process. Most people believe that the Election Night results released in the media represent the end of the electoral process; however, it is the canvass and certification that result in the selection of elected officials and decisions on ballot measures. These are critical, albeit little understood, parts of the electoral process and are fail-safes designed to ensure integrity and safeguard public trust and confidence in the electoral system, processes, and outcomes.

All the ballot counts together constitute the canvassing report. These reports give final results for the local offices, while local votes for other higher-level elections are sent as part of the canvassing report for totaling. On Election Day, the results that are released are unofficial. The final official results may take weeks to be determined, as the results proceed through certification, which is finalized by a state-level authority, usually a state board.

However, before certification occurs, election results may be contested. Although not typical, when contests arise, they are usually initiated by a losing candidate or some other group or party with "standing" (or a significant stake in the outcome). State laws vary in terms of who may do this and when, like so many other parts of the electoral process in the United States. In a contest, a judicial determination is made about whether there was a flaw in the election procedures sufficient to change the results of the race. In the case of recounts, each side will have representation presenting evidence; and the determining body, usually but not necessarily a court, will rule in favor of the original winner, a different candidate, or may rule that the election must be reheld. This last option was the outcome of the contest in the Ninth Congressional District in North Carolina after the 2018 midterm election.

Recounts may also occur before certification. The recount is an administrative, not a political or judicial, procedure. These occur to ensure that the initial counting was done properly—or, if triggered by a close margin of victory, as statutorily defined. Audits may include a full or partial recount, or may look at some other aspect of election administration altogether.

Perhaps the most notable recount and contest in modern American history was the Florida case of *Bush v. Gore* (2000), which presents the perfect illustration of the complex nature of American elections. Problems with the 2000 election involved equipment (and by extension, vendors and public–private dynamics); differences in intrastate and interstate rules and procedures; state certification procedures; the requirements of the Electoral College; the role of politics in what many feel should be value-free public administration; and checks and balances across and within the different levels of government. Simplifying all these issues to the extreme, questions over voter intent because of ballot design and "hanging chads" led to recounts across Florida counties using plans and procedures that varied. Experts argued that the differences in local processes would have resulted in different interpretations of ballots cast, would have affected voters differently, and would have led to different statewide outcomes. Because of the results from other states, this would have produced a different outcome in the presidential election. The certifying official, who was the Florida secretary of state (SOS), was institutionally and politically aligned with one of the candidates, and the Supreme Court's ruling was based at least in part on statutory timing requirements interpreted first by that SOS.

PROTECTING ACCESS

The provisional ballots of the modern era of election administration are an innovation initiated in the states and subsequently mandated by federal action through HAVA. Before HAVA, about one-third of states used provisional ballots through provisions similar to HAVA.[2] Ballots were segregated and counted after voter eligibility was demonstrated. At the other end of the spectrum, another third, including Florida, provided no recourse for voters who believed that they were registered but whose names did not appear on the voter rolls. In the middle, most states permitted counting provisional ballots if cast in the wrong precinct but in the correct jurisdiction.

The concept of a provisional ballot illustrates the political forces at play in resolving the debates raised in the aftermath of *Bush v. Gore* about how to guarantee access to all eligible voters and how to protect against voter fraud. The concept that no one would be turned away from voting in their state was particularly important in light of the removal of many eligible voters from the rolls (sometimes referred to as purging) as electronic databases were compiled. Political response to intense public scrutiny of the decision in *Bush v. Gore* led to the passage of HAVA in 2002. HAVA, in part, provides that potential voters have the right to fill out and submit what is now referred to as a provisional ballot.[3] The effect of this legislation is that voting citizens will have the right to a provisional ballot, so no voter will be turned away from a polling place and no voter will be disenfranchised just because their name does not appear on a registration list presuming they are actually eligible to cast a ballot in that election.

The provisional ballot is essentially a fail-safe or last-chance tool with which people can cast ballots when circumstances create doubt about their eligibility; the most common issue in the states before HAVA was that a voter properly appeared in the wrong precinct or that a person was not actually registered to vote. The concept of the provisional ballot was a political compromise that struck around whether HAVA would specify methods of voter identification at the polls and, if so, which methods of voter identification would be required. Summarizing the debate in very broad strokes, the Democrats wanted to preserve the status quo and allow states the freedom to determine identification requirements; the Republicans wanted a national voter identification requirement that included a photograph, such as a driver's license.

The HAVA compromise was the provisional ballot, which would be issued if a potential voter's name did not appear on the rolls and/or the voter's identity was in question. This could occur in the obvious situation where the person did not have the required identification, but also encompassed other common situations. Among these are that errors existed with a voter's name or address (quite common for movers and for recent marriages), or that the person's name did not appear on the voting rolls at all. Prospective voters would also be issued a provisional ballot if they requested an absentee ballot but did not return it and appeared at the polls to vote in person, or if their eligibility was challenged. Once a provisional ballot has been cast, the potential voter has time to come back to the appropriate local election office to demonstrate eligibility to have the ballot counted. Under HAVA, potential voters also have the right to know whether their votes have been counted.

The HAVA provisional ballot requirement does not apply to some states; exceptions are made for states that had same-day registration at the passage of HAVA,[4] and states that did not require registration to vote.[5] According to data collected by the US Election Assistance Commission (EAC) through the Election Administration and Voting Survey, of the states that did provide provisional ballots in the 2016 presidential election, half the ballots were cast in the state of California, and another quarter between Arizona, New York, and Ohio.

The EAC has tracked the rate at which these ballots are counted or rejected since the onset of their use in the 2006 presidential election. Over time, the number and proportion of those that were counted has increased steadily. Nationally, in almost half the cases, ballots were rejected because no evidence could be found that the expectant voter was actually registered in that state. Other reasons for rejection include ballots that were cast in the wrong jurisdiction or precinct, voter identification that was not produced in states that require it, and other technical requirements that some states place on voting (e.g., matching signatures and the use of the proper ballot envelope). Note, however, that different states utilize different criteria for determining whether a provisional ballot that is cast will be counted, as prescribed by state election codes. These reasons are laid out with the corresponding states in table 6.1. For all states that issue provisional ballots, ballots are not counted if the voter has already voted or if the voter submits clarifying eligibility information past the deadline. In some states, voting in the wrong jurisdiction is a disqualifier, and states of course have different approaches to jurisdiction-based voting. A lack of proper identification and a lack of signature match are reasons that provisional ballots are not counted in some states. In a few states, provisional ballots can be rejected if the information on the application for that form of ballot (typically an affidavit) is incorrect.

Jurisdictions have to evaluate documentation in order to accept provisional ballots, and this evaluation interacts with the time limits that states impose on the review process. The time period available for election officials to review the necessary proof that the ballot can be cast and counted varies across the states. These are depicted in table 6.2. Most states begin holding review panels, often convened by the board of elections, starting on the day after the election. There are some exceptions, and the process may not begin for as few as two days or as long as thirteen days after Election Day. The shortest period for accepting and reviewing documentation for counting

TABLE 6.1. The Most Common Reasons States Do Not Count Provisional Ballots

Reason	Number of States[a]
Already voted	All states that issue provisional ballots
Information provided after deadline	All states that issue provisional ballots
Not registered to vote	36
Ballot cast in wrong jurisdiction	26
No proper identification if required	13
No signature / no match if required	9
Affidavit information incorrect	7

Source: Review of provisional ballot statutes reports by the National Conference of State Legislatures (2015).

a. States identify multiple reasons in state election codes; some use general ballot provisions to address situations that generate provisional ballots in other states.

TABLE 6.2 Provisional Ballot Verification Timelines

Day on Which Cure Period Ends	Day on Which Cure Period Can Start	
Election Day	**Election Day +1[a]**	**Election Day + 2**
+1	1 state	
+2	3 states	
+3	8 states	
+4	2 states	
+5	2 states	
+6	4 states	
+7	6 states	
+8	1 state	
+9	1 state	
+10	3 states	
+11	2 states	
+12	1 state	
+13		
+14	6 states	
+15	1 state	1 state
+16		
+17		
+18		
+19		
+20	1 state	
+21	1 state	
Indefinite period identified in law	3 states	

a. This count may include Election Day.

Note: To create this table, the assumption is made that Election Day is a Tuesday for a presidential general using all calendar days unless specified otherwise. The table does not include four states that do not implement provisional ballots according to this type of schedule.

provisional ballots is one week, and the longest period is about three weeks, but typically this period lasts one week.

It is also important to note that states have different rules for assessing the validity of provisional ballots, sometimes referred to as "curing" the provisional ballot. In some states, voters bear the responsibility for the cure and must produce the documentation needed to resolve their identification or other discrepancies. The period for resolving discrepancies can be as short as 24 hours, and may require voters to return to the polling location or appropriate election office. In others, election administrators resolve discrepancies.

What is important about this variation is its impact on the strength of HAVA and the provisional ballot requirement itself. Provisional ballots were intended as a backstop to protect voters who did not have the identification that was increasingly a requirement post-2000. The concept itself was an innovation designed to provide voters and election officials with a method of resolving questionable cases of voter identification and protecting the voter's ability to cast a ballot and have their vote counted. The variation of administrative processes across states may actually dilute the protective effect of the provisional ballot for voters.

Early national efforts to encourage and train local election officials on how to educate voters about and administer provisional ballot processes now seem fairly basic; but when these first occurred, the EAC (2008d) provided useful information to localities through "quick start" guides. As simplistic as some of the advice may seem, these guides touch on issues that most jurisdictions still struggle with today.

One is the perceptions that outside observers have when watching voting in a polling place on Election Day, and the perspectives that they bring to their interpretations of what they observe. Election workers are trained to err on the side of the voter and to provide an opportunity for a provisional ballot if there is any question about the voter being able to vote in that particular location. An observer could conclude, incorrectly, that poll workers are trying to entice voters to vote in locations where their votes cannot be counted. More broadly, election jurisdictions struggle to establish systematic data collection vis-à-vis provisional ballots for troubleshooting and continuous process improvements.

States must also provide a way for people who cast a provisional ballot to determine whether the ballot was counted, and if not, why not. Early research on provisional ballots showed that, at the state level, their use was higher in states that had some kind of provisional allowance pre-HAVA, and that the acceptance rates in those states was also higher. Further, much like mail balloting, there was significant variation within states in these same figures (Shaw and Hutchings 2013).

Since the passage of HAVA, there have been a handful of state court cases related to provisional ballot implementation, including who has access to records about them, how and by when they need to be resolved, and what is to be done if ballots are cast in the wrong precinct. The right/wrong precinct cases are the most common. This is not surprising, given the combination of precinct-based voting, American mobility, and periodic redrawing of precinct and redistrict boundaries. Courts across the country have generally agreed that provisional ballots are to be counted if cast in the correct location (i.e., poll site or precinct) and not otherwise.[6] At least one court has determined that provisional ballots are protected by privacy laws.[7]

Not least, at a system level, reporting about provisional ballot results may also affect the ways in which we understand proper or effective election administration. In some early reports and studies of election administration, a variety of inappropriate or undesirable election administration activities were attributed to high rates of provisional ballots cast, accepted, and rejected (Weiser 2006). High rates of provisional ballots cast have been used to imply that election administrators were inept at voter check in or in training poll workers, and that election processes were not followed. In particular, high rates of provisional ballots cast have been used to imply that election administrators used their discretion to issue ballots to those not entitled to vote. High rates of provisional ballot rejection have been used to imply that provisional ballots were issued inappropriately. High rates of provisional ballot acceptance have been used to imply a deficiency in some other part of the election administration process, such as a faulty voter registration list. As these contradictory illustrations indicate, the interpretation of provisional ballot figures is not necessarily straightforward and is subject to mischaracterization. The vast majority of states offer provisional ballots, and the data should be considered carefully. At least, we should acknowledge that these ballots are always part of the total count.

ACHIEVING ACCURACY

Election officials are also critically concerned about accuracy. One way states work to ensure accuracy is through election audits, and discussions about methods of election auditing have become more frequent. In over half of all states, audits are legislatively mandated as a part of the counting process that must occur before certification. In these cases, some small percentage of ballots cast are essentially recounted for accuracy of tabulation; if a problem is detected, this triggers an administrative recount. Most often, these are done using a hand count.

Although audits are typically thought of as reviews of financial reports and accounting procedures, in the case of election administration, the term should be understood more broadly as an accuracy check. It is also clear that an election administration audit does not encompass a financial audit, which in public service is an entirely different animal altogether. Election administration audits include a review of counting accuracy after an election, and also of procedures used, processes, and justifications for rejections of ballots.[8] In a form of audit that occurs before the start of election days, voting systems are tested.

Auditing beyond the typical review during canvass and certification is an innovation that the field has not yet fully embraced. Aside from election administrators themselves, audits are often conducted by outside groups with no stake in the results. In the case of election audits, the groups involved in the auditing process have usually included a combination of sampling procedures and/or software (developed by outside groups), and representatives of the state's chief election official, and have been carried out either with or without observers present. Auditing is a growth area for innovation in election administration, but it will be constrained to the extent that the necessary resources are not available, particularly at the local level.

CONTEMPORARY CASES

Today, counting ballots has increased in complexity, and this trend will only continue. As different methods of convenience voting proliferate and states adopt multiple methods of voting, the counting process will need to take all these into account. There are differences in provisional ballot allowances and practices across the states, including use and allowance rates and identification requirements; recent challenges to certification of results and recounts; and new and emerging practices for auditing. From this array of counting innovations come a series of unintended consequences, some good and some bad.

Divergent practices across the states confound the ability to establish reasonable cross-state comparative measures and to analyze data in terms of their relationships to political factors, professionalism, resources, and needs. We created proxy measures for each of these areas related to counting ballots for a cross-state examination of the major components of innovation and their effects on these factors. We looked at counts of court cases related to provisional ballots and recounts, as well as types of state audits. There were no significant relationships among the bivariate analyses for these proxies and our measures of innovation. We believe, however, that the real story to be told lies in the details of the particular cases. In the next subsection, we discuss a few cases that illustrate counting innovations and the complications and solutions that arise from them.

Provisional Ballots

Not all voters are open to casting a provisional ballot when offered one. In one county we observed on Election Day in November 2016, we watched their board of elections grapple with a situation in which a hopeful voter was registered in another county but claimed that her registration had been changed on time and that she should be allowed to vote in the new county. The poll worker in charge could find no record of the voter in the ePollbook system and offered the hopeful voter a provisional ballot instead. The voter refused the provisional ballot repeatedly, which resulted in the coordinator of the precinct making contact with the local election official (LEO), whom we were shadowing. The LEO said that the voter needed to cast a provisional ballot, and the information was repeated to the voter. She refused again, and then contacted the American Civil Liberties Union, which in turn contacted the LEO and the county's election board. This all occurred within the space of an hour. After investigation, the LEO's office determined that the voter had changed residency status in the county after the deadline for the presidential election. The voter continued to claim she still had the right to vote there, and she never agreed to complete the provisional ballot, insisting for the remainder of the day that she be given an "actual" ballot (which she did not receive). The undercurrent in much of her refusal to fill out the provisional ballot was distrust—she did not believe it would be counted. In this case, her fear was both correct and founded; she was not eligible to vote in the county in that particular election. However, the fault was her own and not part of some deep state conspiracy to keep her from voting on Election Day.

One of the problems with provisional ballots is that most voters, when offered one, are still not sure what they have been given or what they should do with them. This disconnect is particularly significant for LEOs, because most provisional ballots are offered to voters by poll workers who are essentially volunteers. In many instances, poll workers are required by state election law to work an entire Election Day, including poll site setup, serving voters, and closing the polls, and in some cases counting and transmitting results. If the polls are open, for example, from 6:00 am to 9:00 pm, the practical significance is that poll workers arrive at 5:00 am and depart at the earliest at 10:00 pm and often later. Even in a very large jurisdiction, compensation is minimal (e.g., $200 for the day, or about $13 an hour for a typical 15-hour day). Poll worker training is conducted in every jurisdiction that uses poll workers, and poll workers are trained on the circumstances under which provisional ballots should be issued, and when they cannot be. State law typically requires that voters complete an affidavit or similar form involving an oath that attests to their identity and address. State laws differ, however, on what happens after a provisional ballot is completed. In some cases, voters must return to the polls with the specified identification; in others, election administrators resolve discrepancies by reconciling competing information using voter registration lists.

On the same day in another county across the country, the county experienced essentially a catastrophic infrastructure failure. Eight years earlier, the state had gone to a statewide consolidated registration system and ePollbooks, and it had a software update immediately before the election, which the LEO decided not to use because the poll workers had not yet been trained on it. On the day of the 2016 presidential election, the old system went down, and the LEO was faced with the prospect of using the new program. The LEO did not feel that the poll workers were adequately trained on the system (or in some cases at all), and instead went to provisional ballots, which the poll workers were trained to handle. In this case, the provisional ballots served as a critical backup for a catastrophic technology failure.

In another jurisdiction we visited, provisional ballots were also used to address technology failures on a primary Election Day. As an example, a particular jurisdiction had just moved to the use of poll pads (a form of electronic pollbook or electronic tablet). The new poll pads did not seamlessly align with their previous voter registration system. For several voters, party affiliation did not transfer from the former system to the poll pads. In that jurisdiction's primary election, party affiliation is critical because they have a closed primary system. In the cases where the poll worker could not determine party affiliation using the poll pad, the poll worker had the voter fill out a provisional ballot instead. The devices were then sent to the central office for investigation. However, the LEO noted to us that, regardless of how helpful the provisional ballot turned out to be in the end, the situation "led to more work for us and frustrated the affected voters."

We also observe that the effects of negative voting experiences extend beyond the individual voters who interact with poll workers or other election staff about provisional ballots. Although the vote itself is a private act, conversations in polling places can be overheard. One upset voter (whether their view is correct or not) can, and does, affect other voters in the immediate vicinity and perhaps more broadly. Increasingly, voters complain through social media; sometimes these experiences are picked up and circulated more broadly through the news media, both inside and outside the poll site. A loss of public confidence in the provisional voting option is both ironic and unfortunate.

Certification

The last few years have been witness to several interesting recount and certification cases, though none, of course, eclipses the 2000 presidential election. People in the State of Alabama inadvertently received an important lesson on certification after the 2017 special election for the US Senate between Roy Moore (R) and Doug Jones (D). After the election, Moore, a twice-disgraced Alabama Supreme Court chief justice famous for installing a 2.5-ton marble monument to the Ten Commandments inside the state capitol, claimed that there was systematic voter fraud during the election and filed a lawsuit, hoping to delay certification. But the court, as well as the Republican secretary of state, disagreed. The attention paid to the case was significant for several reasons. Political interest was piqued by Moore's notoriety and also by the possibility of a Democrat winning a Senate seat in a solidly red state (which was the ultimate result). Simultaneously, public attention shed light on a part of the voting process that most people do not know about or pay attention to. Discussion about, and confusion over, the meaning of certification was rampant across the state, and conspiracy theories abounded on all sides. For some, this only reinforced distrust in the election system.

The State of Virginia held an election at the same time as the Alabama race, and two seats in the Virginia House of Delegates would have made the difference in the control of legislature. The seats both went to the Republican candidates, giving them control of that legislative body. As in the Alabama case, lawsuits were filed to hold up the certification process. The Virginia State Board of Registrars acknowledged that there was an ongoing investigation related to an election administration problem (voters assigned to incorrect districts), but nonetheless decided that they were obligated to certify the results according to state law.

In another instance from the 2018 midterm elections, the Democratic Party in North Carolina filed complaints about the election for the Ninth Congressional District after the Republican candidate won by a narrow margin. The claims of election fraud were substantiated and tied to the Republican winner, and the state board refused to certify the results. The new Democratic leader of the US House of Representatives also refused to seat the winner. The state board of elections then called for a special election, which was held in May 2019. The Democratic candidate decided to participate in the new primary, and the Republican candidate did not; the general election was then scheduled for September 2019.

Recounts

Recounts may happen for a variety of reasons, which vary across the states. In the 2016 presidential election, the Green Party, which supported Jill Stein, sought recounts in several key states, including Michigan, Pennsylvania, and Wisconsin. Michigan started a recount but never completed it. Pennsylvania rejected the request. Wisconsin conducted a recount that yielded over 100 additional votes for candidate Trump. Despite the public rhetoric that the purpose of the recount was to address potential election administration problems, a federal election official noted to us that it was really politics that drove the decision to do this: "If you look at what happened in Wisconsin with the recount, they had paper ballots and conducted audits at a high level and they still got sued. It was all for publicity and money and politics. Jill Stein came out the big winner of all of that."

In 2018, the potential for recounts in Florida and Georgia were prominent in the news. In Florida, the most closely contested race was for a US Senate seat held by a Democrat and won eventually by the Republican governor. A recount was held, but not all the counties were able to have their recounted votes included in the final recount. Two counties did not finish at all, and one county finished but submitted the results 2 minutes after the deadline, so those votes were not accepted. The consequence was that the incumbent was unseated and the former Republican governor won the seat. The Georgia governor's race featured a Republican candidate who was the sitting SOS and the state's chief election official against a Democratic candidate popular in the state's urban areas. The results of the race were close, but not close enough to force a runoff election. The issue then became whether absentee and provisional ballots would tip the scale. They did not.

Audits

Perhaps the most talked-about audit model today is Colorado's risk-limiting audit (RLA) procedure, which was rolled out in 2017 as an initiative of the Colorado SOS alongside significant local cooperation. The RLA is an extension of Colorado's existing auditing practices. Even before its implementation of the RLA, Colorado was engaged in a variety of types of audits, including equipment security audits in 2014 and 2015 and annual chain-of-custody audits for ballots and tabulations and other elements of the election system. One state official with whom we spoke noted that "we do random audits every year. We have to do 3, but usually we do 4—we look at seals, seal logs, chain of custody, and TrustedBuild [their chain-of-custody voting system process]. Part of the logic and accuracy process is to make sure there is no breach in the chain-of-custody process. We have processes in place for the voter equipment and the ballots. We have strict rules about this."

What makes audits interesting today is the introduction of RLAs.[9] In this situation, a statistical confidence level is set (e.g., Colorado chose a 91 percent confidence level) to ensure that the audit result will verify whether the correct candidate won the election (meaning that the unit of observation for the audit is a particular race). Based on this, a number of ballots for auditing is selected, and then ballots are randomly chosen for the audit. The election administrators then take the ballot-tracking number and find the original ballot (note that this number is not tied in any way to any voter). The ballot is then checked to determine if the intended vote cast was counted in the exact same way. This is different than the traditional election ballot auditing procedure, which uses a fixed number or percentage of ballots for accuracy checks.

The State of Colorado took years to roll this process out. It started with a pilot process in one county. It then applied for and received grant funds from the EAC to expand its pilot to six counties, but its first attempt to do this was limited to one additional county. It worked with vendors to determine how best to design an election management system to handle an RLA, and it worked with local election officials to more seamlessly implement it. It also formed partnerships with universities to make this work happen. Finally, several years after their initial pilot, it went statewide with the new auditing system.

In spite of the current attention paid to the use of RLAs in elections and the value of the results, federal election officials believe that this is not enough. In one such conversation, federal officials advocated for some form of process audit in addition to auditing practices that focus on results. We were told that the election administration community "should analyze the whole process from beginning to end—this is how you discover where there are issues." In response to this, another noted that "if you just audit the results at the end, all you know about is tabulation, not who got the ballots, whether they got the correct ones, and so on."

The problem, of course, is that these things take time and financial and personnel resources, all of which are in high demand and low availability in election administration. Election officials note that RLAs are only as good as their risk limits and their attention to detail, and they have critiqued low-cost quick fixes that have been attempted in this arena as insufficient. Media and advocacy attention directly on election administration has increased significantly of late, and this increased attention has generated additional visibility about the systems that are involved. However, this visibility has not translated into monetary support. The essential functions of LEO offices are still funded locally in most places, with limited infusion of money from the states or federal government. In a world of competing priorities, though almost everyone will agree that elections are an essential component of American democracy, neither localities nor the states nor the federal government have committed the necessary resources to realize the level of service and system confidence they desire.

ANALYSIS

Understanding the current landscape and innovations vis-à-vis counting ballots is a story of politics and resources, compounded by increasing complexity. Transparency and an assurance of the integrity of our election system, and of counting in particular, are paramount in the current political climate. Aside from the Electoral College, which is significant because of increasing disparities between popular and electoral votes in recent presidential elections, the architecture of what is possible related to counting is constructed almost exclusively by state institutions. The administration of counting, however, is almost exclusively a local function. The exception to this was *Bush v Gore*, an important exemplar of the potential for the national government to move in and make decisions.

Aside from the architecture of the federal system, politics in this process is important in two ways. First, politicians have used fears about the fundamental accuracy of the counting process as a way to attempt to leverage outcomes. Fear about accuracy cuts both ways; some argue that particular practices disenfranchise, and others argue that other practices are necessary to prevent fraud. Second, political bodies mandate whether any particular practice is established. All states have established certification periods for counting ballots, and all states with provisional ballots have established cure processes. Specific approaches to auditing, such as RLAs, also require state legislative approval in most cases.

Although the need for judicial interpretation of these administrative processes is rare, cases such as *Bush v. Gore* illustrate the collision between state legislative intent, local administrative practice (and resources), and judicial principles of equity and equal protection. Local election offices are at the epicenter of this debate about the federal system. Election administrators abide by the rules, but they are under intense pressure to meet tight deadlines, particularly in very populous states. The balance of competing interests to ensure public trust in the integrity of the system needs to be struck in the political arena. This balance occurs alongside all the other ideological debates, including historic controversies about the reach of the federal government and national regulation, as well as the roles of states and localities. Although provisional ballots are an example of a state practice that has become institutionalized at the national level, and certification periods exist in every state, local variation in administrative practice remains.

Professionalism is quietly essential to this process. Colorado is a leader in the auditing process because it has the interest, capacity, leadership, resources, and skills to design and implement complex administrative procedures. We believe that most, if not all, election officials are interested in accuracy; however, it takes the strongest professionals to engage in innovation in this particular area. It is worth mentioning that the leading election administration professionals engaged in RLAs have been visible on the national, regional, and state conference circuit, where they are invited to professional associations with local, state, and national election officials to talk about the RLA process. National third-party funding organizations such as the Democracy Fund have made a recent investment in promoting RLAs as well as other forms of election certification and office performance; the timing of their entrance into this aspect of election administration strongly suggests a network effect and the related effect of professionalism.

The role of resources is more straightforward than in some of the other topic areas that we cover. Money buys and support systems. Human error in counting is real, and measuring systems increases accuracy, despite the fears that some may have. Certification and curing provisional ballots cost money. Audits cost money. New systems also require time to develop, pilot, implement, and test for reliability and accuracy. Notably, here, as in the other illustrations set forth in this book, innovations such as RLA require a sustained level of commitment and support from top leadership. Although perhaps less glamorous, poll worker training about how to correctly administer provisional ballot rules requires the same level of commitment and support. Both need to occur consistently and over multiple election cycles to take hold and begin producing desirable results.

Finally, this is also a story about need. Provisional ballots were needed in the US election system, which many states recognized. Rules are different from place to place, and are sometimes implemented differently even in the same place. We live and vote in a country that is now more mobile and more integrated with personal technological assistance than ever. Humans are a part of the system, and no matter how well meaning, human error in a system like this one is inevitable. Provisional ballots serve as a check on systemic, human, and technological errors, and they make the process fairer for everyone. State policy decisions about timing have imposed constraints, including decisions about the timing of and time allotted to counting, certification, and curing provisional ballots. In an era of potentially declining trust in electoral integrity, strong audits are needed to shore up trust in election administration specifically and trust in government more generally, as well as to guide internal system improvements.

CONCLUSIONS

Counting ballots is no longer about tallying pebbles, corn, or slips of paper. In today's landscape, it includes making sure that all ballots that are turned in and should be counted are—and are counted correctly. It involves administrative certification of results. It may involve recounts and contests. And in most states, in some form or another, it involves auditing the count as well as the procedures that it took to get to the count to ensure that the system is accurate. Counting well ensures the integrity of the election system.

In the modern era of election administration, political controversies have highlighted the details of the counting and auditing processes, and have focused attention on the need for change. Indeed, the modern era of election administration began in 2000 with such a political controversy, which led directly to the adoption of HAVA and the provisional ballot requirement. Innovation vis-à-vis counting and auditing procedures and the diffusion of best practices that come from innovation require a number of things. Most critical among them are resources and professionalism. Governments must invest more in election administration to ensure continued accuracy in counting and to shore up trust in the system. Professionalism must also be undergirded and enhanced across the country to enable these practices to spread.

NOTES

1. Portable storage devices for electronic data, such as memory cards, are commonly used, and are transferred from voting machines to counting locations through an exacting chain of custody process.
2. These states and jurisdictions were Alaska, Arizona, Arkansas, California, Delaware, the District of Columbia, Iowa, Kansas, Maryland, New Mexico, New York, North Carolina, Oregon, South Carolina, Virginia, West Virginia, and Washington.
3. HAVA Section 302.

4. Idaho, Minnesota, New Hampshire, Wisconsin, and Wyoming.
5. North Dakota.
6. See *Hunter v. Hamilton County Board of Elections* (OH); *Kindley V. Bartlett* (MO); *Florida Democratic Party v. Hood* (FL); *Bay County Democratic Party v. Land* (FL); and *Hawkins v. Blunt* (MO).
7. *Mah v. Board of County Commissioners* (KS).
8. Although not an audit per se, LEOs also conduct logic-and-accuracy testing on voting systems well in advance of Election Day. If logic-and-accuracy results do not fall within parameters prescribed by the vendor and approved by the state and/or national voting systems certification guidelines, equipment must be adjusted before it can be used in an election.
9. For additional detail on RLAs, see Morrell (2019).

7

Technology, Integrity, and Security: How Equipment and Preparation Matter

The election technology arena is fertile ground for innovation. Election jurisdictions are searching for new equipment to replace the electronic voting systems purchased by states since the implementation of the Help America Vote Act (HAVA) in 2002, which remain essentially unchanged from the initial systems used to replace punch card and lever machines. Innovation in election technology is also occurring in response to the voting public's pressure to have greater confidence in election results and election security, and at the same time these citizens expect to participate in a voting experience that reflects the typical use of technology in their daily lives (e.g., online banking, scanned entry to events, and more). For new equipment and for existing election systems, election officials continue to face public challenges that call into question the integrity of the voting process under conditions of stress, including natural disasters and cybersecurity threats. A new technological context has emerged to address the election "transactions" that occur in this very visible environment, with collaborative arrangements across institutions and sectors leading the way. The new methods of operation and new models of governance that have emerged around these issues provide a unique lens for viewing the story of innovation in election administration. Embedded within the concept of innovation are underlying questions about preparedness—whether election administrators and the broader community are prepared to both prevent and respond to emergent threats, and what that means.

This chapter begins with a discussion of the development of the election equipment environment in the modern era—including the development of new federal organizations, funding, certification, and the election system market—and presents three illustrations of approaches that election administrators are using to address pending issues. The chapter then turns to election preparedness generally and to cybersecurity concerns in particular and the collaborative institutional architecture that is emerging to engage with this new environment. We then apply our innovation analytic framework to these changes to further develop our understanding of how innovation happens across the election administration system.

The environment in which this all takes place is rapidly evolving. As with so many things in the administration of elections, it is impossible to capture a static picture that will remain true even within a six-month window. Thus, our discussion in this chapter uses conditions present as of the time of writing to illustrate larger points about innovation, with no expectation that the examples we draw upon will be au courant even by the time this book is printed.

THE ELECTION EQUIPMENT ENVIRONMENT

Election administrators face several challenges with respect to the equipment used to operate elections: these include financial barriers, integrity concerns that pertain to both existing and new equipment, and the nature of the election technology industry itself. These challenges are relatively intractable and not particularly new. They are also certainly predictable, given the degree to which the equipment environment has shaped our understanding of innovation. The most significant modernization of American voting systems occurred in years after the 2000 presidential election, which pointed out the limitations of punch card voting systems and later underscored the importance of ballot design. Under HAVA, more than $3 billion was granted by the federal government to the states for the purchase of electronic voting systems, among other purposes. Most states replaced or updated their voting systems relatively quickly; by the end of 2008, states had spent 70 percent of appropriated funds (Burris and Fischer 2016). The two most common equipment approaches included either machines that can scan a paper ballot (optical scan machines) or touch screen machines (direct-read electronic machines).[1] The majority of these also incorporate some form of paper record that can be used as a paper audit trail.

Election officials and others in the election community have expressed concerns about aging election systems for at least the past decade, and their intensity has grown. Operating systems are at or near the end of their useful lives according to any estimation of how long that ought to be; many of the devices in use today have exceeded them (Hitt et al. 2016; Norden and Codrington 2015, 2018; Presidential Commission on Election Administration 2014). As one election official noted, "We update our office computers more frequently now," especially in comparison with voting equipment. In using aging equipment, election administrators face issues with both hardware and software. Older systems are more likely to fail, and they may also be more vulnerable to hacking or other forms of electronic tampering.

How to pay for new equipment is a significant issue, and local jurisdictions experience this pressure most acutely (Hale and Brown 2013; Montjoy 2010). Most of the funds allocated under HAVA have been depleted in all but a handful of jurisdictions. By 2014, two-thirds of states had less than 10 percent of their HAVA funds remaining, and an additional 25 percent of states had less than half of these funds (EAC 2014).

By any measure, the acquisition of new voting equipment will be an expensive proposition. In addition to the costs of purchasing new equipment, jurisdictions must also consider costs associated with proprietary software updates and other types of maintenance. Replacement costs are difficult to determine, and estimates vary widely. The Brennan Center for Justice forecasts costs at above $1 billion, in range of $580 million to $3.5 billion; other estimates place the replacement cost toward the high end of this range or more (Hitt et al. 2016). In early 2018, Congress released $380 million remaining in HAVA funds to the states, with the requirement that the funds be spent within five years. These funds were targeted at security improvements. Yet it seems unlikely that these funds will make a significant dent in modernizing or safeguarding the election system infrastructure. The 2018 release of HAVA funds has helped this in some cases across the states, but these funds are inadequate and are just a one-shot infusion of resources that cannot, by definition, solve a long-term problem.

Election system integrity is another concern, and is closely related to public confidence in elections. The Election Assistance Commission (EAC) addressed system integrity from its first days as a federal agency through the establishment of a national testing and certification program founded on the federal Voluntary Voting System Guidelines (VVSG). Election system certification is a collaborative process, in which federal agencies, states, local jurisdictions, and technology experts have worked together to develop the VVSG. Voting system certification laboratories are certified by the EAC under guidelines that it develops along with its partners, which include the EAC Standards Board, the EAC Board of Advisors, and the Technical Guidelines Development Committee (TGDC). The TGDC works with the National Institute of Science and Technology (NIST) to advise the EAC on VVSG. The TGDC consists of representatives from across the election administration network, including the National Association of State Election Directors, technical experts, and members of the EAC Standards Board and Board of Advisors. Together, the Standards Board and Board of Advisors are broadly representative of both the local election official (LEO) and chief election official (CEO) communities.[2]

Election administrators and vendors alike have expressed concerns about VVSG, and the majority of states do not require wholesale compliance with these federal guidelines. In 2014, twelve states mandated compliance, and twenty-two had adopted some form of the federal guidelines (Hale and Brown 2013). One concern that election administrators and vendors have expressed about VVSG is that certification is expensive. The certification cost can range from $50,000 for a simple change into the millions for an entire system. Certification is also time consuming; it can take two years or more to complete all the various steps, including preparation and reporting results.

In some ways, real innovation may only be happening now, given the decisions made post-HAVA about how to design and implement the requirement for the federal VVSG. One former national election official told us, "when . . . HAVA passed in 2002, it had things backward. Instead of first doing the first set of standards and requirements and getting those out so the manufacturers could build equipment, they told everyone they had to have new equipment by a certain day. States in turn bought old, legacy equipment that some states are still using today." The practical effect of the lag in developing the VVSG was that vendors would retrofit existing equipment rather than design wholly new election systems (Davidson and Wilkey 2019).

Another concern, and perhaps a more technical one, is that the VVSG themselves do not pair well with the extensive array of readily available commercial off-the-shelf (COTS) equipment used in elections, such as printers, scanners, standard personal computers, and tablet computers. Further complicating the issue, the COTS technology used in many election operations may be implicated in the election security chain. Decisions made by the EAC, and informed by the TGDC and NIST, about what constituted a voting system and what did not were made before the widespread use of COTS equipment in election operations.[3] The path-dependent nature of subsequent processes has had the effect of creating multiple classes of "certified" equipment used in elections. An election system may be able to present its EAC certification as a badge of operational integrity.

In addition, the political environment has not been entirely friendly to the development of voting systems standards as a result of partisan congressional wrangling over the existence of the EAC itself, which manifested in withholding appointments for years and in introducing bills to end the agency. The partisan implications of the election environment are acknowledged in the structure of the EAC; its four commissioners are presidential appointees made on recommendations from the US House and US Senate, one of each party from each chamber, for a total of two Democrats and two Republicans. In 2009, the number of commissioners fell to two, so the EAC was operated without the three-member quorum necessary to take action. Moreover, from 2012 until the end of 2014, the EAC operated without any commissioners, as arguments were mounted on both sides of the political aisle to either keep or disband the agency (Martinez 2013). Thus, from 2005 through 2015, the VVSG remained stagnant.

TABLE 7.1 Major Points of Vulnerability across Election Subsystems and Actors

Election Administration Element	Type of Disaster		
	Natural Disaster	Physical Attack	Cyberattack
Voter registration	CEO		LEO CEO Vendor
Get out the vote	Candidate Party	LEO	Candidate Media Party
Ballot creation	LEO CEO Vendor	LEO Vendor	LEO
Ballot delivery	LEO	LEO USPS Vendor	LEO Vendor
Ballot marking	LEO Voter	Voter	Vendor[a]
Ballot return	USPS	LEO USPS Vendor	
Ballot counting		LEO Vendor	LEO Vendor
Reporting			LEO CEO Media
Certification/audit		LEO CEO	

a. This is only relevant in a few places, depending upon the equipment used.

At the end of 2014, three EAC commissioners were appointed. With a quorum, in 2017, the TGDC and EAC made progress by releasing basic principles for VVSG 2.0. These guidelines represent countless hours of interaction with election administration stakeholders. Table 7.1 illustrates general categories of factors to consider when developing new voting systems. Among these are high-quality design and implementation; transparency; access and privacy; accuracy and auditability; security; and integrity. The guidelines are presented in table C.18 in appendix C. The guidelines are general in comparison with the volumes of documentation that will constitute the final standards, and they could be considered a list of rather obvious characteristics that should be included in a "good" election system.

Despite their apparent simplicity, however, the VVSG 2.0 guidelines demonstrate a significant step toward the next generation of voting system standards, even though the full guidelines have not been issued. The Presidential Commission on Election Administration (2014) recommended streamlining the certification process in its recommendations for election administration across the country. Streamlined processes for development of standards and for certification would benefit the election community. These guidelines represent a public and published first step in this process, and they should provide some stability and assurance to election stakeholders about the principles that are guiding voting system development.

Technical development aside, the ability of the EAC to act on VVSG has also been a political challenge. Separate bills were introduced in late 2017 to terminate the EAC (HR 634; introduced by Gregg Harper, R-MS) and to reauthorize the agency at least through 2022 (HR 794; introduced by Robert Brady, D-PA). Interestingly, the reauthorization proposal would establish new funding for voter registration system improvements, mandate state reporting, and mandate reports to Congress on cybersecurity. And yet, in early 2018 the EAC found itself once again without a quorum due to the nonrenewal of the appointment of Commissioner Matt Masterson, who was the appointee of the speaker of the US House of Representatives (Paul Ryan, R-WI). In late 2018 the full complement of commissioners was named, and in 2019, Commissioner Masterson ultimately landed at the Department of Homeland Security with responsibilities for election cybersecurity; until those decisions were made public, speculation ran rampant that the EAC would be eliminated.

The long-term effect of these political choices has been to solidify the initial VVSG, even though technology has changed significantly; as a consequence, the election administration community has been stymied as vendors and jurisdictions wait for guidance. Other aspects of VVSG also remain stagnant. Vendors are also able to pay testing laboratories directly, and the EAC's role has always been nonregulatory. Thus, the EAC has no statutory authority to collect fees or to serve as the intermediary between vendors and the testing and certification labs.

The voting system standards environment has become infinitely more complex since 2016. In the months leading up to the 2016 presidential election, concerns about the security of individual voting machines that had lingered from the 2000 election cycle mushroomed into broader concerns about cybersecurity. Public attention focused on election cybersecurity, in part because of the high-profile media attention during the 2016 presidential election (and since then), and media attention to claims of involvement by foreign actors (Russia) seeking access to online voter registration systems. Media attention has also been focused on intergovernmental disagreements about transparency related to cybersecurity data and other intelligence gathered about the attempts of foreign governments or other bad actors to influence American elections. Media attention has also begun to focus on the use of paper ballots, in the form of a return to paper ballots or a requirement that all electronic election equipment be supported by a paper backup record. This backup record, typically known as a voter-verified paper audit trail (VVPAT), currently exists in one form or another in most states, but not in all. In 2018, five states (Delaware, Georgia, Louisiana, New Jersey, and South Carolina) conducted elections using direct recording electronic machines (touch-screen, or DRE machines), which are accompanied by no such paper trail. Nine other states (Arkansas, Florida, Indiana, Kansas, Kentucky, Mississippi, Pennsylvania, Tennessee, and Texas) used a combination of paper ballots and electronic machines without VVPAT (Verified Voting Foundation 2019). In 2016, about 20 percent of voters cast ballots on paperless equipment, in counties and towns across fourteen states; that is expected to drop to 12 percent in 2020 and include perhaps as few as eight states (likely—Indiana, Kansas, Kentucky, Louisiana, New Jersey, Mississippi, Texas, and Tennessee) (Norden and Codrington 2018; Norden and Cordova 2019).

Election officials face real constraints in obtaining new equipment from the private sector, which for all intents and purposes has been the exclusive source. The election equipment market offers limited equipment options. Three major vendors dominate the supply side of the voting system market, providing equipment to an estimated 92 percent of eligible voters. These are Election Systems and Software, at 44 percent; Dominion Voting Systems, at 38 percent; and Hart Intercivic, at 11 percent (Hitt et al. 2016). Incentives for new election system vendors to enter the market are limited, given the relatively small and essentially static nature of the market of fifty states and US territories, variations in state and local requirements embedded in state election laws, and the episodic nature of elections. Because of this fragmentation and uncertainty, the election equipment market has been observed to be generally resistant to innovation overall (Hitt et al. 2016). Election officials also face complexities in attempting to match their election systems with the ancillary technology used in election operations, such as electronic pollbooks (which hold voter registration data), Election Night reporting packages, and election management systems developed in house. As we discuss later in this chapter, it is also unclear how to obtain new equipment that includes appropriate and timely security assurances.

The public procurement process itself is also problematic. Procurement of election systems is done locally in some states, but typically requires extensive state-level authorization or at least coordination. Even in states where LEOs have considerable influence, CEOs and state procurement offices substantially direct the acquisition process or control it outright. All public procurements are time consuming. The subject matter expertise and technical capacity needed for effective technology acquisitions is particularly lacking in government, and this deficit is distinctly acute where public offices seek innovative solutions (Bennett 2019). Many election jurisdictions may lack the capacity to participate effectively in acquiring sophisticated information technology systems. This is true at the state level, but particularly true for smaller jurisdictions, which make up the vast majority of the nation's more than 8,000 election jurisdictions.[4] Election administrators sit at the intersection of these factors, where it is difficult (if not virtually impossible) to determine (independently) how to obtain and afford new equipment and how to assure operational integrity and timely, appropriate security. Election officials must rely extensively on private-sector expertise, and equipment vendors are integral actors in acquisition and maintenance. They have also evolved into problem solvers for local and state election offices (Lichtenheld 2019).

Regardless of the type of equipment used, election officials will need to defend their practices to a skeptical public, and this will translate into pressure on vendors for solutions. The news at the national level for the capacity of the EAC to support a positive environment for election administration was positive by the start of 2019. The future of the agency was unclear with the removal of Commissioner Masterson, but by the start of 2019 two new commissioners were appointed. This has allowed the EAC to expand its reach and continue its mission, which provides a more stable environment for innovation to enable it to grow—or not.

In 2019 legislative pressure continues to mount for voting processes that rely more clearly on paper ballots as a response to cybersecurity and hacking concerns. The For the People Act (HR 1, 2019) and the Securing America's Federal Elections Act (the SAFE Act, HR 2722, 2019) propose congressional authorization to establish EAC regulatory oversight as well as to extend that oversight to a broader array of election-related vendors, products, and services.

These proposals appear stymied in a divided Congress. However, a week after the 2019 November general election, a policy advocacy group released a report calling for a sweeping new framework for federal oversight of election vendors, including the establishment of best practices, certification, and federal enforcement (Norden, Deluzio, and Ramachandran 2019). The Brennan Center for Justice policy report builds on HR 1 and HR 2722, and calls for expanding the oversight authority of the EAC beyond the voluntary certification of voting systems to include regulatory authority, a new definition of the types of vendor products and services that are covered, and new categories of oversight for all types of vendors. New types of vendors that would be subject to federal scrutiny include companies that provide or maintain voter registration databases, software for ballot programming, electronic pollbooks, Election Night reporting services, and postelection audits. Among the policies and practices that all vendors would be required to disclose and submit to federal scrutiny include cybersecurity practices that vendors use to protect their own technology infrastructure and data, foreign ownership interests, personnel policies and procedures that safeguard against inside attacks, cybersecurity incident responses, and their supply chains. The report argues that the willing participation (voluntary compliance) of states and localities in new practices could make a considerable impact, and that significant steps could be taken by the EAC without the need for new congressional approval that would authorize regulatory oversight; among these would be to extend the VVSG to include best practices for cybersecurity, ownership transparency, personnel security measures, and supply chain management. Although HR 1 and HR 2722 would accomplish many of the Brennan Center's recommendations—including EAC regulatory oversight and oversight of a broader array of election-related vendors, products, and services—the Brennan Center report adds a call for ongoing certification of vendors and ongoing monitoring, best practices for personnel actions, and supply chain management.

In spite of the public attention and system constraints, or perhaps because of them, election officials are adapting their operations by leveraging structural flexibility and functional capacity through new organizational relationships and arrangements. In the sections below, we feature innovations in data standardization, online voting, and new customized voting systems that make use of open source software and novel procurement strategies. We focus here on these particular innovations because of their scale and likely long-term influence in setting the stage for future iterations of voting systems.[5]

DATA STANDARDIZATION AND
FEDERAL PROGRAM SUPPORT

The concept of data standardization is relatively invisible, but it supports the spine of systems that process election transactions across the maze of organizations necessary to accomplish voter registration, casting ballots, and counting and reporting returns. In this area of election operations, the federal government has played a key role in facilitating data standardization efforts. Election transactions accomplished through electronic transfer have been greatly facilitated by efforts of the Federal Voting Assistance Program (FVAP). FVAP is a program of the US Department of Defense, and it administers the Uniformed and Overseas Citizens Absentee Voting Act (UOCAVA) around the world. UOCAVA and FVAP grew out of absentee voting options in the 1940s and 1950s that were intended to facilitate voting by uniformed military personnel and US citizens living outside the United States. Today, the FVAP effort reaches voters in all fifty states and US territories, and it involves partnerships with election officials as well as the Department of State, the Department of Justice, and the US military. This complex environment provides an interesting laboratory for innovation that reaches across the nation and around the world.

Technological solutions lead FVAP efforts to communicate with voters and facilitate their registration and voting across this complex array of organizations. In 2009, the Military and Overseas Voter Empowerment Act (known as MOVE) established FVAP's ability to explore and test possible technological solutions to voting system issues. The FVAP experiences are instructive about the complexities of the election data environment and the barriers that exist to effective data transfer and communication.

One such initiative, the Electronic Voting Support Wizard, explored the use of technology to support the ability of local election jurisdictions to offer UOCAVA voters an electronic ballot. The experience with the Electronic Voting Support Wizard sharply focused attention on significant underlying issues with data exchange in election administration systems. These issues include incompatible languages and data formats across existing commercial and public information technology systems. Incompatibility within states encumbers local efforts to collect data from diverse sources such as departments of motor vehicles, public service agencies, tax offices, and the courts; the intricacies of these relationships from the perspective of LEOs challenge resources and capacity. At the local level, data sharing is also essential across and within the voter registration and election administration functions, which are sometimes conducted by entirely separate offices. Data sharing is impeded by incompatibility across states and between states and the federal government, including the various agencies that administer UOCAVA (Council of State Governments 2017).

To address these issues with data incompatibility and facilitate data exchange, FVAP formed a partnership with NIST to create the Data Migration Tool (DMT). Through the DMT, data can now be imported in a specific format, and they can then be exported into the NIST Common Data Format (CDF; Council of State Governments 2017). The goals of the CDF, which is formally known as the Election Results Common Data Format, are to provide a single format that equipment manufacturers can use in voting equipment, that election administrators can use in their offices, and that other stakeholders such as media and government offices can use (NIST 2016).

The DMT initiative evolved over multiple iterations and is the outgrowth of a cooperative agreement between FVAP and the Council of State Governments (CSG) that formed the CSG Overseas Voting Initiative. The results of the DMT project will be linked to another NIST system, the Materials Data Curation System, which has a purpose broader than elections and exists to encourage collaboration across sciences and academic research. The FVAP/CSG data management tool is focused on ballot data; however, the extension of the concept across other and even all election data is an obvious opportunity.

The CDF specification 1.0 facilitates interoperability across the election system. In election systems, interoperability also has implications for equipment innovation, because election results can be "reported directly from election offices, regardless of manufacturer" (NIST 2016, 7). This CDF encompasses major data elements and permits flexible reporting, ranging from very granular levels to highly aggregated levels. It also encompasses device types, types of ballots and contests, and geopolitical units of geography, including the ability to reconfigure these.

It is difficult to overstate the importance that the CDF will have for innovation in election administration when it is finally completed. The institutional geography of elections illustrates why the CDF is such an important development. The internal architecture of any election requires mapping where people live against the political and physical world. These interact with election laws in fifty different states, which specify different ballot styles, including various types of elections (general and special elections, open and closed party primaries, runoffs and retention elections), rules for ballot measures, and the relationship between the jurisdiction boundaries and the boundaries of representation (whether an election represents all or part of one or more jurisdictions). Common data can enable information sharing across election systems at a level and in a manner that are simply unprecedented.

Successful implementation of the CDF suggests that the need for customized or proprietary software will decline, as will the need for customized reporting formats. In addition, it will be easier for jurisdictions to combine and transfer information between equipment provided by different vendors and between multiple versions of equipment and software. More broadly, development of the CDF has been picked up by third-party nonprofits that advocate the value of the tool within the election community, illustrated through the detailed discussion by Owens Hubler and Patrick (2019) about the work in this area supported by the Democracy Fund. Of course, the development of the CDF requires a deep understanding of a common language and agreement about terminology in the field. Political considerations do not appear to present roadblocks to the CDF; however, finding a common language that derives from state election law and policy and that serves a national audience may prove to be intractable.

PILOTING APPROACHES TO ONLINE VOTING

It is a measure of innovation itself that the term "online voting" actually encompasses a number of methods of remote voting. Early research in the field acknowledged the dominance of in-person, place-based Election Day voting practices around the country (Carter and Baker 2005). The term "convenience voting" was coined to refer to a number of election administration practices that did not fit that traditional model. These included voting that did not take place on Election Day, or did not occur at traditional polling places—for example, vote centers (Gronke et al. 2008; Gronke and Stewart 2013; Stein and Vonnahme 2011, 2012). Early labels have given way to increasing specificity as election practices have evolved rather rapidly.

Today, online voting refers to voting that does not occur at a polling place, and that is facilitated by the Internet. As with other approaches to voting, electronic or online voting takes many forms. The Congressional Research Service (Burris and Fischer 2016) reports that options range from the electronic provision of blank ballots via email, facsimile, or website to end-to-end Internet voting, in which a voter accesses, completes, and casts the ballot online.

The concept of online voting has been described in various ways by scholars and in academic and policy studies (see, e.g., Alvarez and Hall 2003, 2008; Flack, Gold, and Helbick 2004; and Pew Center on the States 2012). These studies and others argue the benefits of convenience and yet raise security concerns. Throughout, the concept of end-to-end Internet voting and the use of any technology connected to the Internet are linked to available technology, or what may seem to be reasonably feasible in the future. It is worth noting that the groundbreaking work in this area by Alvarez and Hall (including the study of successful implementation in Estonia) began shortly after HAVA and the American transition to electronic voting machines. However, the first generation of electronic voting systems were not equipped to facilitate secure Internet voting; this consequence is an artifact of the state of technology at the time, including the use of legacy systems, a reflection of policy preferences of state and local election officials, and a reflection of public opinion.

Use of the Internet to facilitate voting is most common for military and overseas voters and has been fostered by federal requirements. UOCAVA requires that military and overseas citizen voters receive a ballot by some electronic method, and states are required to comply. However, UOCAVA does not mandate the return of voted ballots via Internet connection, so that approach continues to be rare for any voter. In 2018, three states offered the option to return voted ballots via a Web-based portal. About 40 percent of states (twenty states and the District of Columbia) allowed some voters to use email or facsimile to return voted ballots, and another 13 percent permitted transmission of those by facsimile. In nineteen states, an option to return a voted ballot by electronic means is not available. In 2016, as many as thirty states reported offering some form of online voting; however, the meaning of this term is not always clear. What is clear is that the tools developed for the use of the Internet to return voted ballots were developed for military and overseas citizens, and that end-to-end electronic transfer of election information is limited almost exclusively to UOCAVA voters. So far, no state system offers end-to-end electronic voting using the Internet outside that context (Burris and Fischer 2016; National Conference of State Legislatures 2018b).

Federal activity has spurred some innovation targeted at making online voting secure. Defense authorities were required by HAVA and under several defense authorization bills to pursue studies of end-to-end Internet voting, including demonstration projects; this spurred the development and testing of the Secure Electronic Registration and Voting Experiment (known as SERVE). These projects were controversial and were terminated in 2015 (Burris and Fischer 2016; Federal Voting Assistance Program 2001, 2015; Jefferson et al. 2004).

Some states have experimented with electronic ballot transmission. For example, Alabama implemented a pilot program for the Internet return of voted ballots, which was limited to the March 1, 2016, primary; however, the project has not been repeated. Florida took a more comprehensive approach and created the Military and Overseas Voting Assistance Task Force to study, among other issues, the feasibility of developing an online voting system. The task force's report, which was issued in 2017, did not recommend pursuit of the initiative "due to the formidable challenges" posed by system requirements, including "ballot integrity, security, technology, and privacy," along with cost (Florida Department of State 2017; National Conference of State Legislatures 2018b).

Online voting is not yet a reality, although the concept has great intuitive appeal as people continue to use the Internet for all manner of personal transactions, including financial matters. In practice, public opinion about election security exists with any form of Internet-facilitated voting (Horwitz 2016). Among these are the ability to authenticate voters, public records access requirements, ballot secrecy requirements, and the ability to change ballots, along with cyberattacks. This risk is currently mitigated by the extent to which systems do not an provide end-to-end service, in comparison with methods that provide the ability to obtain blank ballots online. However, current cybersecurity concerns may stymie this aspect of innovation for at least the near term.

CUSTOMIZED VOTING SYSTEMS
AND OPEN SOURCE SOFTWARE

Local election officials have been leading the way in innovation in the election systems environment. The limitations of the private market for election equipment have spurred local initiatives in Los Angeles County, California, and in Travis County (Austin), Texas, that have received considerable public attention. In both states, and independently of one another, LEOs have engaged in multiyear processes to develop proposals for local voting systems.

In both cases, a fundamental reason for seeking to develop what would be, essentially, a brand new type of system is the belief that no current vendor would be able to meet the needs of voters and administrators in these jurisdictions (Wogan 2014).

The size and diversity of these jurisdictions illustrate the magnitude of these needs. Los Angeles County has slightly less than 5 million registered voters; it is the largest election district in the nation, and its registered voter population is larger than the population of forty-two of the fifty states. Los Angeles County is home to 88 cities and 500 political districts and deploys 25,000 volunteers and 5,000 voting precincts on Election Day; the election system serves 16 languages in addition to English under the Voting Rights Act of 1965 and California law.[6]

Travis County, Texas, is not as large, with about 775,000 registered voters; however, it is still quite large relative to other election jurisdictions. Travis County is in the top 1 percent of election jurisdictions by number of registered voters; jurisdictions in the top 1 percent provide services to more than 25 percent of the nation's voters. The number of foreign-born residents in the county increased by 17.5 percent from 2012 to 2016, and in 2016 more than 30 percent spoke a language other than English at home (US Bureau of the Census 2016). Notably, Travis County has registered nearly 90 percent of its eligible voters.

Both Los Angeles County and Travis County based their voting system concepts on open source software platforms and the intention to combine open source software with COTS hardware. In the words of one election official familiar with both projects, these approaches will "break the mold of the traditional voting system acquisition model" by providing independence from traditional voting system vendors and flexibility in procurement.

Open source platforms may be less costly in the long run, and that is certainly one of the points noted in favor of spending time and money to develop these for use in elections. It seems reasonable to assume that costs incurred now will generate valuable information for future development efforts in these jurisdictions and have the potential to benefit the election environment more broadly. However, cost savings in the short run are by no means certain.

A more reliable value of an open source platform lies in its public transparency. This transparency allows for, and indeed encourages, public involvement in design and troubleshooting and in system revisions. And this transparency holds great appeal for the broader election community beyond election administrators. Voter advocacy groups on multiple sides of any of the contentious issues of the day should find increased value in citizen input and oversight generally, and in public scrutiny of various stages of election operations, including the processes of voter registration, voter identification, and ballot tabulation. Government officials in offices related to elections—such as county commissioners, who approve a significant proportion of the funding for elections across the country—should find value in transparency as well.

Although these projects have not been the subjects of a systematic analysis of procurement aspects, to the extent that they generate comprehensive understanding and agreement on goals and terminology across stakeholders, they will address significant concerns about procurement capacity and enhance capacity for election administration and for public service offices generally.

The innovative approaches taken by Los Angeles County and Travis County are different, although there are similarities. The outcomes have been different in each case. The major points of each are summarized in the next subsections.

Los Angeles County's Voting System Assessment Project

In 2009 the Office of the Registrar-Recorder / County Clerk in Los Angeles County, California, embarked on a multiyear project to build an entirely new sort of voting system. The concept of the Voting System Assessment Project (VSAP) uses human-centered design principles. The intention was to create a new relationship between the election process and the voter, and between election office and vendors in terms of design, ownership, and long-term control.

The Los Angeles County VSAP project is intended to be integrated with other county reforms, most notably the change from neighborhood polling sites to regional polling centers. The system uses touch screen machines and records votes on paper ballots that are fully auditable. This modernization is actually quite significant given that, in 2017, the county still used a modified punch card system dating from the 1960s. The VSAP will meet federal requirements, including making voting materials available in multiple languages and simplifying the process for voters with disabilities.

The project's design focused on several concepts, including public ownership and operation, and transparency and security to support voter confidence that ballots are cast and counted as intended. The county designed the specifications for the system using a competitive bid process. Throughout, the focus was on how voters experience and interact with the equipment and the steps in the voting process. The Los Angeles County Registrar-Recorder / County Clerk notes that "in LA County, we started by designing around the voter experience rather than starting with designing a technological solution. We wanted to get the voter experience right and then to have the technology respond to what ends up being defined as the ideal voting experience."

The Los Angeles County design approach focused on components that could be purchased separately. The approach also integrated the new system with other system improvements, and multiple appearances before the county supervisors to establish a "vote center" model—which would determine the number of machines needed (and their cost). The system is also required to meet California state system-testing requirements.

The Los Angeles County VSAP timeline began in 2009 with the concept and progressed to a $15 million contract with a human-centered technology design firm. The process went through multiple iterations, dozens of prototypes, and feedback from more than 3,500 voters. Election officials across the nation have watched this project with great interest; it has been labeled "transformative" across the board.

The first rollout of the VSAP occurred during the California primary in June 2018. The election itself was marred somewhat by reports of 118,000 names missing from voter rolls. The negative publicity that followed could have spelled the end of the project after nearly a decade of effort. A week after the election, however, the Los Angeles County Supervisors approved funding for the county registrar-recorder's proposal, which may reach upward of $280 million, noting in their decision that the voter roll mishap indicated the need for new equipment. A contractor was selected that meets the system requirements, and the county developed a contract approach that is performance based and contains protections for the county (Hernandez 2018; Logan 2019).

VSAP continues to be developed. Today, VSAP stands for Voting Solutions for All People. The assessment phase has been completed, and the acronym has been reconfigured to reflect the philosophy of the project as implementation continues. The equipment was used in nearly fifty polling locations throughout Los Angeles County during the 2019 general election and will be used exclusively at all polling locations beginning with the 2020 March primary election.

The Travis County, Texas, STAR-Vote System

Travis County, Texas, also began its quest to develop a new voting system in 2009. The project seed grew from a conference presentation made by the Travis County clerk's request to the technology community for help. At that time, Travis County used a direct-read electronic voting system and had previously used an optical scan system. As the time to transition to new equipment approached, the clerk wanted to establish a next-generation system that would be secure, cost-effective, and robust.

At the request of the clerk, in 2012 faculty from Rice University convened a team of cryptographers, statisticians, and developers; and in 2013, this team presented the initial project criteria to a national election voting and technology workshop. Criteria included cost-effectiveness and use of COTS tablets. The system had to incorporate online voter registration that supported a vote center concept across the county. The system had to be reliable across an election, even in the event of a power failure. A critical element was that the system created a clear, verifiable ballot and a receipt for the voter. The team publicized its work through conferences that combined practitioners and academics (e.g., Bell et al. 2014). The initial cost to design and build the system that was referred to as STAR-Vote compared favorably with a standard system ($10–12 million, compared with $14–16 million) but did not include support and maintenance. Exemplifying the values of the local jurisdiction (and many others in the election administration community), "STAR-Vote" stands for secure, transparent, auditable, and transparent vote.

Travis County issued a request for proposals in late 2016, but responses were insufficient to proceed. Today, Travis County is still in need of new voting equipment that will ensure a voter-verified paper audit trail and that has contemporary security and audit features. Ultimately, work on STAR-Vote was suspended because it lacked a vendor to build the system.

It might seem that the suspension of the Travis County STAR-Vote project could be considered an innovation failure. However, in the rich information environment that supports innovation, the STAR-Vote experience is simply one more step along the path. Travis County clerk Dana DeBeauvior noted that the STAR-Vote experiment influenced the national conversation about voting systems through its focus on the potential cost savings associated with the open source approach, and by calling attention to security measures beyond vote recounts (*Election Administration Reports* 2018a). The project has also contributed to national conversations about election technology, as several features of the STAR-Vote system are also incorporated into the VVSG 2.0 Guiding Principles, which were issued in 2017.

ELECTION SECURITY IN NATURAL
AND INTELLIGENT DISASTERS

Innovation is also evident in the area of election security. All election technology and equipment exist in a larger context of actions and events that, on one hand, have absolutely nothing to do with elections and, on the other hand, could be specifically intended to disrupt them. Crises and attacks on elections come from a combination of natural disasters and intelligent attacks. Since 2000, several natural disasters have disrupted elections. Public concern about intelligent (human-made) disruptions of elections came into focus with the transition to election voting systems after HAVA, and most recently as a result of claims of foreign interference with the 2016 presidential election. We examine both here, and note that both have primarily had an enduring public effect beyond that on elections.

There are similarities and differences between natural and intelligent disasters. Election systems have been disrupted by both—by natural disasters, from hurricanes to floods, and by intelligent disasters, from terrorist attacks to cyberattacks. Both natural and intelligent disasters present an array of vulnerabilities across the election landscape. These vulnerabilities are displayed in table 7.1 as points in the US election system across various election subsystems, primary actors in the subsystem, and types of vulnerability. Vulnerability is assessed as a function of the probability of an event and its importance for system integrity. High-probability events are those that we know have happened and that will continue; low-probability events are those that seem unlikely. High impact reflects the severity of damage and also the duration of the resulting incapacity. There is a high probability of a cyberattack on a voter registration system, which would be of great importance for system integrity, for example. At the other end of the continuum, a physical attack on a local election office during the certification period or during an audit is relatively unlikely and would be of comparatively limited duration.[7]

As the environment evolves vis-à-vis election cybersecurity, the characteristics of natural disasters and policy approaches may be relevant for future consideration. We can learn about innovation from the methods that organizations use to mitigate, plan for, and operate in degraded environments as a consequence of natural disaster or intelligent action. Disasters significantly affect the operations of governments and elections, whether natural or human-made. The potential for these types of events requires that election administrators develop operational contingency plans and focus on security to prevent degraded election environments if possible and to ensure seamless responses when they occur. It is now also clear, since the 2016 presidential election, that bad actors—including other governments and criminal actors sometimes tied to these governments—can have an impact on US elections, either directly or indirectly. We next briefly discuss the types of disasters, and focus on the ways that election operations are implicated.

Natural Disasters

Natural disasters disrupted national, state, and local elections in 2005, in 2012, and again in 2018. In September 2005, Hurricane Katrina created challenging conditions for election preparation and election operations in the November 2005 election (see, e.g., Vanderleeuw, Liu, and Williams 2008). Some of these are relatively simple to understand, even though they were not simple to fix— for example, damaged or missing polling locations in New Orleans. Others are less obvious; thousands of Louisianans were left homeless and evacuated to Houston and other locations, and parish (what counties are called in Louisiana) offices faced significant challenges in executing voter registration and election activities. In 2012 Hurricane (and Superstorm) Sandy affected nine states and the District of Columbia in late October, and President Barack Obama declared a state of emergency in most of these areas. However, on November 5, these jurisdictions nevertheless held the presidential general election and races for other offices. Residents of some states were permitted to vote at any polling location. In some affected areas, eligible voters were permitted to vote in the presidential election by email or facsimile, although these methods were not acceptable as a matter of general practice. In the 2018 midterm elections, Florida and parts of Georgia were drenched by Hurricane Michael, which arrived during the early voting period. In counties throughout the Florida Panhandle and in the adjoining Gulf Coast region, and also in southwest Georgia, election offices and residents were without power, food, or water for extended periods.

In all these circumstances, election officials relied on prior planning and worked together to create methods of restoring office functions and serving voters, using unorthodox methods in extreme circumstances, including electronic voting. In short, even in the midst of natural disasters, elections have been held, and held successfully; at the heart of these success stories are strong plans and the strong leadership that are the hallmarks of highly skilled professionals.

How this success is possible may depend upon the specific circumstances of a natural disaster. Natural disasters typically fall into one of three categories—those that are forecasted, those that are not, and epidemics. Forecasted natural disasters, as the name implies, include events that meteorologists can typically anticipate, and they usually include such things as hurricanes and major snow or ice emergencies. These can allow organizations to prepare or even pre-position material or personnel in anticipation of the need.

Nonforecasted natural disasters are more nuanced. Although forecasters can usually predict a coming storm, it is harder to determine whether, when, and where collateral consequences may occur. Hurricane Katrina in 2005 was an example of such a combination event; the hurricane was forecasted, but the failure of the levy system in New Orleans was not. Similarly, although scientists are better able to determine when an earthquake may occur, that technology is still far from perfect; it remains challenging to predict whether and where tsunamis may result when seismic disruption occurs under bodies of water. Our understanding of long-range weather trends has improved; however, understanding when a drought will happen is not yet a perfect science, nor is being able to determine whether a drought will produce fires significant enough to qualify as a disaster. The fires in La Plata County, Colorado, in the summer of 2018 are an example.

Understanding the onset and nature of epidemics still remains a mystery. Epidemiologists have improved their understanding of the spread of disease, but predicting an initial outbreak is not possible. Epidemics may also exist in a gray area between natural disasters and intelligent disasters. Governments store diseases for study, and individuals and governments have been accused of releasing them to strategically annihilate or cripple certain people or groups of people.

Intelligent Disasters

Intelligent disasters present similar but perhaps less familiar circumstances, and may involve actors not typically engaged in natural disaster responses. Intelligent disasters can be classified in three categories: nonviolent, violent, and those caused by government interference. Nonviolent intelligent disasters usually involve some form of cyber disruption that accesses computers and other electronic media for information. Nonviolent intelligence disasters may also encompass drone use. Violent intelligent disasters may also include drone use, but may also include some form of boots-on-the-ground military or quasi-military operations (gendarme, paramilitary, etc.), or terrorism. Government interference that produces disaster conditions is predicated on the use of government power to disrupt normal services or operations for residents in such an extreme way that it produces a crisis.

Intelligent disasters in elections in the American context can be the result of actions by those both in and outside of the United States. One illustration is the New York City primary election of 2001, which took place on September 11. The primary included highly contested races for the New York City mayor, public advocate, and other offices. Poll sites opened at 6:00 am in more than 6,200 locations all across the city, throughout Manhattan and the other four boroughs. That same day, the terrorist attack on the World Trade Center towers in lower Manhattan was unprecedented as an occurrence and in its magnitude. The effects were devastating in and of themselves.

In the midst of this disaster, the intergovernmental interplay illustrates a number of points about complexity and authority vis-à-vis elections. Governor George Pataki declared a state of emergency for the entire state. Upstate New York counties do not open the polls for primary elections until noon, so voting had not yet begun; voting there was halted by virtue of the governor's state of emergency. A judge in New York City ordered the polls closed in the city, where voting was under way. The state legislature rescheduled the primary for September 25, two weeks after the attack. A runoff election was required for the Democratic candidates, and that was scheduled for October 26. The regularly scheduled election occurred on November 6.

The events of September 11, 2001, continue to influence election operations in New York City and around the state. Three times in the intervening years, (2007, 2012, and 2018), New York's election dates have been moved from September 11. In 2007, the deferral to September 18 was determined by the New York state legislature, and cost an estimated $1.2 million in notices to voters. In 2012 and 2018, the deferral was again determined by the legislature, and state and local primaries were moved to September 13. Attention to the effect of possible terrorism on elections has not been limited to New York, or to elections on or near September 11. In 2004, the

Department of Homeland Security (DHS) considered ways to delay the November presidential election, as the first presidential election since the terrorist attacks. Some scholars identified points of disaster vulnerability in the federal election calendar (Fortier and Ornstein 2004), and called for intervention by Congress to establish national protocols for these types of events (e.g., Goldfeder 2005).

Across all components of the election subsystem, including actors and points of vulnerability, no part of the election administration system is fully secure on its own. Yet the security constructs vary somewhat in different areas; some parts are uniquely vulnerable to physical attacks, and others to cyberattacks. The threshold distinction for cyber vulnerability is whether the systemic element or election transaction touches the Internet (whether electronically or through human action). For many jurisdictions, registration and results reporting are potential areas of vulnerability. These systems likely use electronic data transmission that may be accessible online either in whole or in part, and in some cases and some places information is stored only electronically. Alternatively, some parts of the overall election process are most likely primarily vulnerable to physical threats, whether they are intelligent or occur naturally. These are aspects of the election process that most people never think about but are nonetheless critical for election operations and therefore for security considerations. Examples of these aspects could include warehouse operations for equipment storage and the delivery of poll site supplies, including voting machines. A perfect example of this occurred in 2010, when the election equipment warehouse in Harris County, Texas (in which Houston is located), caught fire, destroying more than 10,000 pieces of election equipment less than two months before an election.

It is worth noting that the ubiquitous nature of technology, which has been the subject of innovation in other aspects of the election administration environment, increases electronic vulnerability. Broad generalizations are almost certainly incorrect when referring to the nation's election system. In most cases, none or few components of the process of casting a ballot are online, although online portals for registration are an obvious exception. And yet it is also the case that likely every LEO and CEO office uses email, which alone provides another point of entry for electronic contact. Because the nature of threats is so broad, and interactions between humans and equipment are ubiquitous, contingency planning is particularly important. In the next subsection, we discuss current efforts to address these concerns.

Contingency Planning

Contingency planning for both natural and intelligent disasters is not new, and is not new for the election community. Election officials can access a wealth of threat assessment and disaster planning activities that have been designed by federal agencies—such as the US Department of the Army, Department of Commerce, and Department of Defense—and by humanitarian organizations such as the Red Cross to address the range of disaster types (e.g., US Department of the Army 2003; US Department of Defense 2009; Glaser 2005; Humanitarian Practice Network 2010; Kent 2011; Quarantelli 1991; Stoneburner, Goguen, and Feringa 2002). As a part of its clearinghouse function, the EAC has assembled an extensive collection of continuation-of-operations plans (COOPs), which have been developed by state election offices and local election jurisdictions; one example is the plan developed by the Office of the Supervisor of Elections for Pasco County, Florida (Corley 2016). The Election Center (2016) also has developed a practical checklist on this topic, the *Elections Security Check List*. The major elements of the COOPs are representative of traditional disaster management concepts, which emphasize cross-functional planning, communication, and implementation. Established scholarship on disaster response policy and intergovernmental and cross-sectoral response is expected to inform the emerging scholarship on election security as well (Birkland 1997, 2006; Comfort 1999, 2002; Comfort and Kapucu 2006; Comfort and Resolihardjo 2013).

The EAC has also made available a general process outline that election officials can use in creating a natural disaster preparedness plan for their jurisdiction. The planning process begins with the identification of potential disasters and an exercise to create a minimum of five worst case scenarios. The next step involves creating a COOP for each of these scenarios. The process also recommends that specific plans be developed to address communication failures, polling place relocation, staff shortages, ballot shortages, and technology failures.

Organizations like the Election Center, International Association for Government Officials, and National Conference of State Legislatures offer sessions at conferences to educate election officials about the need for contingency planning, and to introduce the tools needed to both plan for and positively respond to degraded environments. Broadly, the techniques of the first responders and emergency management units that act to provide relief from a wide range of natural disasters (fire, flood, blizzards, hurricanes, and more) are readily available for adaptation to election operations.

CYBERSECURITY AND ELECTION ADMINISTRATION

The issue of election cybersecurity first rose on the national scene during the 2016 presidential election cycle. Reports of "Russian hacking" dominated the national news in the wake of publicized cyberattacks on databases at Democratic National Committee headquarters and at public offices and private firms that support electronic voter registration databases. DHS and the Federal Bureau of Investigation began working with targeted states and localities on possible security threats specifically from cyberattacks.

In late 2016, DHS reported consideration of election systems as critical infrastructure in accordance with Presidential Policy Directive 21 (2013), and made this designation in early January 2017 (DHS 2013, 2017). The designation provides DHS with access to information that states and localities use to manage elections, including state agency databases. The scope of this designation under the 2013 directive is broad, and it includes "at least the information, capabilities, physical assets, and technologies that enable the registration of voters; the casting, transmission, tabulation, and reporting of votes; and the certification, auditing, and verification of elections."

The array of facilities, equipment, and locations covered by the critical infrastructure designation is similarly broad. Critical infrastructure includes technology and systems used during early voting and on Election Day to maintain voter registration databases and voting systems and to manage elections, including systems that audit and display election results, and that conduct post-election certification and validation. The scope includes voting systems and equipment and the storage facilities for these, polling places, and centralized vote tabulation locations. Also in scope are the information technology infrastructure and systems that support these, without regard to whether they are in storage on public or private property and whether they are used on Election Day proper, during early voting periods, or after the election has concluded.

The critical infrastructure designation was controversial, and the election community was not unified about its views (e.g., the different analyses of McCormick 2019 and Schneider 2019). Concerns included relatively technical matters of scope, and also political concerns about governance and authority. Nominally, state participation with DHS is voluntary. However, an important caveat (or incentive) is that DHS will not provide cybersecurity information or other related resources to states that do not volunteer their participation. The volume of information and activities covered by the critical infrastructure designation may be unduly burdensome for states and localities. In addition, whether the designation requires reporting and what that might look like is also an open question.

Another open question (at the time of writing) is whether the critical infrastructure designation also provides the federal government with new access to state information that it may not already be able to obtain, including databases of public assistance agencies, vital statistics bureaus, and motor vehicle licensing agencies. It is also unclear whether states that volunteer can determine their own scope of information sharing, and whether volunteer involvement with DHS carries with it the requirement that states conform to a federal cybersecurity standard.

The potential loss of subnational autonomy was cited by detractors as a central concern, as is the potential for partisan interference. Direct federal regulation of the conduct of elections is extremely limited, given the constitutional imperatives that establish significant responsibility in the states. The EAC has no regulatory authority, although it is an independent bipartisan agency. Partisan political interference is a concern because DHS is an executive branch agency under the direct control of the political party in the White House. DHS secretary Jeh Johnson attempted to dispel these concerns in his press release announcing the critical infrastructure designation, disclaiming that the designation represented a federal takeover or that it changed the roles of state and local governments in election administration (DHS 2017).

The influence of the critical infrastructure designation was felt quickly in the election administration community (Choate and Smith 2019). The EAC devoted a portion of its first summit of 2018 (in January) to election cybersecurity, and the Election Center (the short name for the National Association of Election Officials) made cybersecurity the topical focus of its opening 2018 conference (in February). At these meetings, and subsequently, DHS representatives explained their function and approach; LEOs and CEOs expressed fundamental concerns. Initially, however, the quality of federal support that was available was unclear, as were whether strings were attached and what those would look like.

Some state and local election officials were excited by the opportunities provided by the designation, while others struggled to become engaged in the conversation and expressed frustration (and sometimes outright dissatisfaction) with federal officials who came to national and regional conferences to discuss "how they could help." At one conference, in January 2018, a DHS official noted that DHS was supporting security clearances for election officials to permit enhanced information sharing. Adding a bit of fuel to any potential discord, the next month, DHS reported very publicly that election systems in more than twenty states had been touched electronically in some way, but it declined to identify these states or to offer specifics about the contacts and the results. Media accounts were widespread and damning to election administrators. Election offices had only a limited ability to respond to prove a negative.

EMERGING INFRASTRUCTURE AND GOVERNANCE

Since that time, cooperation has evolved, and collaboration has begun. The installation of former EAC commissioner Masterson at DHS with election cybersecurity responsibilities was a positive step toward bringing these diverse communities together. Anecdotally, many of the election administrators involved in these efforts are positive about the joint work, but simultaneously some who are not a part of the conversations remain skeptical and frustrated. There is no clear threat analysis that can be applied nationally, however, because of the diversity of laws, procedures, and practices both across and within the states.

DHS has worked closely with state election directors and representatives from some of the larger election localities across the country to better understand the diverse nature of election administration and identify ways in which their efforts can assist local election administrators (Masterson 2019). The risk mitigation framework for election security revolves around the concepts of defense, detection, and recovery, all within the overarching principle of resilience. The resilience risk mitigation framework acknowledges that defense is essential and yet not sufficient; it is impossible to achieve a perfect defense against electronic attempts to penetrate anything.

An institutional architecture for election security has evolved and will focus on the efforts of the Election Infrastructure Subsector Government Coordinating Council (EIS-GCC) and the Election Infrastructure Information Sharing and Analysis Center (EI-ISAC). The charter of the EIS-GCC is to enable "local and state governments to share information and collaborate on best practices to mitigate and counter threats." A list of the member representatives and ex-officio members is shown in table 7.2, and illustrates the potential for extensive collaboration across public organizations in different branches and at different levels of government. The intergovernmental representation is weighted in favor of state election offices (fifteen positions) and the federal government (eight positions). Local election offices are represented (nine positions), and this representation was hard won.

The EI-ISAC is modeled after existing ISACs, and its evolution illustrates the influence of path dependence in relation to earlier risk mitigation strategies. The ISACs are developed by the Center for Internet Security (CIS), which is a partnership of public agencies and private firms. Broadly, the role of an ISAC is to monitor threats to systems, detect common issues across states including attacks, and support risk mitigation efforts. ISACs exist for major sectors of the economy; the financial services industry, for example, has the Financial Services ISAC. The EI-ISAC grew out of the existing Multi-State ISAC, which works with the state-and-local sector generally, and represents the unique character of the election environment relative to other public functions that are administered at the state and local levels. Organizations

TABLE 7.2 The Intergovernmental Configuration of EIS-GCC Membership

Types of Members	Federal Agency	State Election Officials	Local Election Officials
Voting members	3	15	9
Nonvoting members	8		
Total	11	15	9

include federal government agencies, nonprofit professional associations for state officials, and other third-party groups.[8] The organizational partnerships within the Multi-State ISAC combine an expansive scope of information technology and administrative expertise.

To some extent, these organizational arrangements reflect the fusion center concept established by DHS and the Office of Justice Programs (OJP) in the Department of Justice (DOJ). These centers were established as early as 2003 in the aftermath of the terrorist attacks on America on September 11, 2001. Fusion centers are physical locations for interagency information exchange and collaboration vis-à-vis disparate intelligence gathered across the network of participating agencies. The centers fill a gap identified by the 9/11 Commission by providing a formal mechanism to link state and local leaders with frontline security personal and DHS. The partnership between DHS and the OJP is intended to provide a consistent, unified message (National Commission on Terrorist Attacks Upon the United States 2004; OJP 2006).

The fusion center concept was hailed as an innovation when states first began to establish these centers in 2004 and 2005. Today, there are seventy-two centers across the country, including those in states, tribal jurisdictions, territories, and large urban areas. The National Network of Fusion Centers coordinates information from the various centers. This center concept appears to have widespread support. The OJP chronicled laudatory comments from lawmakers and senior officials, who noted the accomplishments of fusion centers at various events commemorating the tenth anniversary of 9/11 (OJP 2011).

The proliferation of working groups, task forces, councils, and centers that have evolved in relation to election cybersecurity suggests new coalitions among existing actors. And a growing list of groups are involved in the field; organizations currently involved are listed in table C.19 in appendix C. The intersection of these groups has created the potential for novel arrangements, given the singular focus of most on security, technology, or elections. State chief information officers, for example, are now beginning to meet regularly with state election officials. Common understanding and communication can produce new capacity in and of itself. These interactions may establish new opportunities for states and localities to improve their investment in technological capacity, which is far outstripped by that of the private sector.

Formal and informal protocols are beginning to take shape, although this aspect of the field is very new and is rapidly evolving. The CIS (2018) published its *Handbook for Infrastructure Security* (version 1.0). The material presents information about how cybersecurity and elections intersect, and why this matters; a description of major election components and their risks depending on connection to networks or other systems; and crucial activities and best practices in election infrastructure security to use in mitigating system risk. Additional protocols are likely to follow as the field develops.

Three observations seem important to make about this emerging work. First, the material emphasizes that one-size-fits-all approaches are not appropriate; there is no single approach to election security, and each jurisdiction must make unique assessments. Second, the materials clearly define the elements of the election system that are not in scope. Defined as out of scope are the topics of registration eligibility; identification verification, unless specially about the accuracy and availability of voter registration rolls; campaign system and information security; and accuracy about candidate and issue information, including social media (CIS 2018, 6). Third, the materials reflect the beginning of a common language about election security that focuses on connectivity to networks and other systems, rather than on a particular method of election (e.g., early voting, vote centers, and mail ballots). This is an important bridge to build within the election administration community on this particular topic, and in the field more broadly.

The classification of election systems (or components) by types of connectivity allows election administrators to group their processes according to risk type, catalog appropriate activities, and simplify the steps needed to manage risk. The classifications are (1) network-connected systems and components, whether the connection is intermittent and regardless of network ownership; (2) indirectly connected systems, which typically involve the introduction of threats through removable media; and (3) nondigital election components, such as purely paper-based steps in a process, which were defined as out of scope (CIS 2018, 8).

In conjunction with these efforts, several national tools have been identified to assist election administrators. Among these are engaging in activities like network penetration checking and receiving training (e.g., a certified information systems security professional). At the state level, some associations have begun training in election security. The Florida state association began with a focus on training for small and midsize counties that have fewer resources to engage in risk assessment and mitigation efforts. In addition, the association has suggested that smaller counties enter into memorandums of understanding with other county offices that use similar technology for loans of equipment and staff during emergencies.

The current effort of the Council of State Governments (CSG) exemplifies how an organization in the collaborative space around election administration is poised for further engagement in this arena, given its role for state governments across the country, and also illustrates the limitations. In late 2017, the CSG established an advisory board of state and local election officials and technology officers and representatives of election professional associations, and this advisory board met periodically. Stakeholders conducted interviews with state-level partners that included representatives from the governor's office, both houses of the state legislature, state election officials and technology officers, and state associations of local election officials. The format generated the skeleton of a general framework for communications and planning

(Council of State Governments 2018a, 2018b). Their plan had been to engage in efforts in pilot states to enhance coordination and communication, but the politics involved in onboarding all the stakeholders proved significantly more difficult than anticipated, and this stalled the process.

Related but different in focus and scope, the Belfer Center at Harvard's Kennedy School of Government targeted cybersecurity as a technological specialization within the election administration field. *The State and Local Election Cybersecurity Playbook* (Belfer Center for Science and International Affairs 2018) is widely regarded in the election community as the seminal work in the election cybersecurity field. The Belfer Center has also initiated training with groups of election officials and other stakeholders in state and local government using tabletop exercises that simulate actual (and rapidly changing) conditions—a model borrowed from military planning exercises and underscoring new and evolving sector partnerships, sharing, and borrowing. As both the CSG and Belfer Center initiatives indicate, the success of cybersecurity planning and preparedness depends upon developing new relationships within state government that include state chief information officers and state technology directors, as well as emergency preparedness teams generally, and that bring these resources into local jurisdictions.

At the local level, election administrators have been encouraged to focus on assessing risks and vulnerability for their operations in a variety of ways. Some have suggested contracting with local sheriff's offices to also conduct security checks for physical security threats. Others believe that the most significant threat to security across the election administration system are the election office staff members themselves, who remain largely uninformed and unprepared to engage in protective behavior or effectively respond in an emergent crisis. The voter registration database in Cook County, Illinois (in which Chicago is located), was an early target of cybersecurity attacks. The county's election officials developed a detailed account of their observations and concerns and presented this, along with recommended protocols, at numerous conferences and meetings of election officials and other stakeholders around the country (Praetz 2019). In smaller jurisdictions in particular, election administration offices are not staffed internally to support all components of their operation, and thus another focus for identifying and mitigating risk is collaborating across all parts of local government working on an election. Finally, a concern that has been touched on is threats from insiders who have access and knowledge and some motivation to cause harm.

ANALYSIS

Two opposing forces are at play in studying election administration contingency planning and security. On one hand, actual problems and risks are not fully known. This is always a concern when trying to predict the future;

here, it is also a consequence of working with information such as security protocols for physical environments, hardware, and software. On the other hand, public analysis of past security risks (threats, attempts, and breaches) and current risks must, by definition, take place within an unclassified world. We may believe we have mapped the population of potential risks and have full knowledge of what is involved, but we cannot know this for certain (and if we actually believe this, we are probably wrong). As the field of election security continues to evolve, it will be important to consider the implications of research conducted about other nations, and the effects of possible interactions of trust, perceptions, participation, and corruption (e.g., Herron, Boyko, and Thunberg 2017; Massicote, Blais, and Yoshinaka 2004; Mitchell 2006; Norris 2004, 2014).[9]

These inquiries may offer important insights into the questions we ask about election security in America. Decisions about election security are always political ones, not simply technological ones made in a political vacuum. The political context for understanding election security therefore includes not only the typical understanding of partisan alignments but also a sophisticated consideration of the intergovernmental complexities of America's fifty-plus state election systems alongside the national role. The critical infrastructure designation of election systems, made in the waning days of the Obama administration, was highly charged along ideological lines but not necessarily a partisan issue. The continuation of this designation brought stability and new challenges.

Discussions about election security issues are likely very frustrating for the general public. Election officials are participating in regular briefings from DHS staff about intelligent threats and activity; many have obtained security clearances to be able to participate, and the federal government has facilitated this process. However, much (if not all) of the information that is shared within those briefings cannot be shared publicly. The most consistent information is that attempts to breach any type of electronic security occur constantly—it is not a case of whether, but when—and that a constant state of readiness and planning is required. Also, elections are not actually conducted on the Internet—many of the security risks are quite ordinary and can be mitigated by following standard information technology (IT) protocols.

Several aspects of the voting system projects undertaken in Los Angeles and Travis counties that were discussed earlier in the chapter stand out as case studies of innovation in the field of election administration. One is the focus on public ownership. Both counties were intent on moving away from the traditional vendor relationship. The public governing structures here were also remarkably supportive over an extended period. Another is the degree of cooperation, collaboration, and governance required. New governance structures are emerging in the form of the EIC-GCC, and others may be on the horizon. The EIC-GCC builds on fusion centers and the ISAC structures to create new collaborations and venues for information sharing. This extension of the fusion center innovation helps states and particularly local governments leverage resources and gain capacity.

Large-scale projects such as this require LEOs (and CEOs) to engage in what we term "parallel processing" of multiple streams of information. Technical specifications, the political process, voter confidence, legal requirements, and operational dimensions must all be navigated, and with different groups of stakeholders. This processing ability is a resource that we find associated with the innovations discussed in this chapter in particular.

Both projects also illustrate concerns with transparency, in two ways. One is through transparency in the voting experience. The other is through a very public process of design. Transparency is related to accountability as well. Here, both voting systems also relied on paper ballots as auditable election transactions to establish a very public method of accountability. The aspect of public investment here is also innovative. Both of these projects break new ground in their willingness to consider, and then approve, public investment.

These projects also clearly illustrate the factors of the networked innovation model. The networked nature of these initiatives is clear and extensive, and expands the election system infrastructure even further. The types of guiding principles illustrated by the cybersecurity structures discussed in this chapter bring real impetus to innovation. Research in other areas of public policy (see Hale 2011) demonstrate that these principles serve as a form of synthesized information. When widely acknowledged across a networked environment, guiding principles and model programs support and foster innovation that is consistent with network values. These kinds of interactions within a policy community have clear influence on policy innovation in two specific ways: dissemination of information by and to diverse organizations across a policy arena over time actually creates synthesized information, and the information is vetted for accuracy and fidelity to policy system concepts. As a result, synthesized information becomes denser as time continues. The discussions in the cybersecurity realm will likely reflect this change as the field matures.

Each of these innovations was widely discussed throughout the election administration community. Thus, the strengths and weaknesses of different methods of dealing with technology challenges have been the subject of numerous conference panels and workshops. Jurisdictions listen to and learn from each other. As more than one election official has noted over time, both the Voting System Assessment Project (now Voting Solutions for All People) and STAR-Vote were successful regardless of whether they were implemented (or how) because these projects changed the conversation about what was possible and paved the way for new ideas.

New governance structures are evident in each of these local initiatives and include significant and influential development, implementation, and outreach task forces; these governance structures continue to evolve. The cybersecurity framework builds on existing fusion center infrastructure, and establishes a unique adaptation of its multisector infrastructure for the election community through the EI-ISAC.

The political and resources dimensions are also expansive and intertwined. Both local election system initiatives relied on county funding. We resist the temptation to compare the projected price tags in terms of cost per voter, because such a blunt instrument obscures very real and important considerations. However, our conversations with election officials and others throughout the election community did not indicate that procurement cost per se would be a negative factor. In terms of the internal resources necessary to support such an initiative, both counties are at the top of the financial brackets, and both have staff resources to coordinate development and testing over time. Political permission appeared to have been favorable in both cases. The Los Angeles County project also mobilized additional political support through legislation to adopt vote centers and early voting, and these were integrally connected as one overall project.

Time was required for both projects to develop and to become sustainable through the political process and the development process, which were intertwined. Time supports the information sharing that is required for innovation to take hold. Governance structures reinforced the projects over time by providing the stability and structure that enabled information to flow between stakeholders.

Resources have played out in a number of ways. Almost without exception, LEOs note that the most challenging resource need in the field of cybersecurity is the need for IT support. For some offices, the need is for more IT staff members. However, for most, the need is for any staff. Even offices with relatively high numbers of IT staff, such as large CEO offices and the largest local jurisdictions, feel unqualified to act alone. The role of professionalism takes on a different dimension in this area of innovation. The role of professional associations seems to shift toward connecting with additional technical expertise, and then working to package it for their members.

When asked about how they might spend the HAVA funds that were released in mid-2018, the common responses were to hire project managers to design and implement security projects and to work with vendors to do the same. More than one election administrator noted, wryly, that even if there were consultants "who knew elections," the line for their services would be so long as to be useless. Thus, election officials in state offices seem to be considering hiring additional IT staff. At the state association level, leaders focused extensively on cybersecurity issues throughout 2018. It was difficult, in fact, to find a conference agenda that did not include this topic. State associations also have developed training programs in this area, focusing on the basic principles of identification and assessment.

Innovation in technology is driven by all the components of the theory of change. Need fuels change; resources are required—human, financial, and temporal; professionalism and the development of networks are particularly pertinent in today's environment vis-à-vis security; and politics either enhances or dampens innovation, depending on the will of the leadership. LEOs and CEOs around the country are in a tough position. They must engage in innovations for change, but they are dependent on a resource- and information-limited environment that constrains their ability to adequately respond to anticipated needs.

NOTES

1. See Saltman (2006) for a detailed chronology of the development of modern voting systems.
2. The EAC Standards Board is made up of 110 people, including 55 CEOs and 55 LEOs. The EAC Board of Advisors is made up of 35 people who represent stakeholder organizations at the national level, including members from both inside and outside the federal government. For more information, see www.eac.gov /about/board-of-advisors/.
3. The EAC definition of a voting system is: "The total combination of mechanical, electromechanical or electronic equipment (including the software, firmware, and documentation required to program, control, and support the equipment) that is used to define ballots; to cast and count votes; to report or display election results; and to maintain and produce any audit trail information; and the practices and associated documentation used to identify system components and versions of such components; to test the system during its development and maintenance; to maintain records of system errors and defects; to determine specific system changes to be made to a system after the initial qualification of the system; and to make available any materials to the voter (such as notices, instructions, forms or paper ballots)." This definition can be found at www.eac.gov/assets/1/1/Glossary percent20ofpercent20Keypercent20Election percent20Terminology percent20in percent20Englishpercent20topercent20Spanish.pdf.
4. The vast majority of America's election jurisdictions have fewer than 50,000 residents (93 percent, by count); the election jurisdictions with fewer than 50,000 residents make up about one-third of the registered voters, and the nation's sixty-five most populous election jurisdictions account for about 45 percent of all registered voters (Brace 2017).
5. It is worth mentioning that we expect that changes in technology will continue, and that there are any number of smaller-scale processes that are gaining traction in election offices—e.g., the use of quick response codes and intelligent barcodes on mail, and applications that voters can access in order to find their polling places and learn about wait times there.
6. These languages are, in alphabetical order, Armenian, Bengali, Chinese, Cambodian/Khmer, Farsi, Gujarti, Hindi, Japanese, Korean, Punjabi, Russian, Spanish, Tagalog/Filipino, Thai, Urdu, and Vietnamese.

7. A mark next to the name of an actor denotes the potential for vulnerability, not necessarily evidence that an existential threat has already occurred. Note that there is some element of threat in all parts of the election administration system, but it is not useful to simply state that the entire system is vulnerable in one way or another.

8. The MS-ISAC is made up of DHS; NIST; NGA; NASCIO; National Council of ISACs; US-CERT; ICS-CERT; Stop, Think, Connect; Global Cyber Alliance; and Public Technology Institute.

9. See Norris (2014) for an introduction to the extensive literature on international elections and the significant literature on electoral integrity and trust.

8

Measurement and Innovation: How We Know That We Are Doing What We Think We Are Doing

Innovation often flows from combinations of building blocks, of which some already exist and others are in their infancy. In this way, innovation leverages existing capacity and can contribute to the creation of new capacity. Measurement in the context of innovation in election administration is such a building block—a subtle driver of change, influencing and affected by all the other major influences discussed in this book. This relationship may seem unusual; yet many innovations in election administration can be traced to measurements of policy activity and policy change that have in turn shaped the field. These measures are driven by political forces and reflect the ways in which we conceptualize success. For example, for much of our history, our measurements of election operations targeted voter participation through measures of those who were turning out to vote, primarily reflecting the success of campaigns in mobilizing voters. In the not-so-distant past, in the years leading up to the Voting Rights Act of 1965 (VRA), measures of participation and particularly of voter registration were indicative of systematic discrimination against African Americans and other groups; these measures focused significant public attention on methods of implementing state laws and fueled political forces that led to the adoption of the VRA.

We define measurement in an expansive way to refer to systematic activities that generate understanding about system processes and outcomes related to a particular topic.[1] Measurement includes counting but does not stop there. In the field of election administration, even in the period since the passage of the VRA, measurement has continued to focus primarily on outcome measures, such as voter turnout and voter registration. More recently, measurement approaches have emerged that look beyond the proverbial black box of an election office to examine implementation—including, but not limited to, process design and methods of administration and various cost-efficiencies. As we have illustrated earlier in this book and elsewhere, this effort is "wickedly" complicated by the diversity inherent in local election systems and the diversity in local–state intergovernmental arrangements that exist within each state. General comparisons across states are rarely meaningful and often misleading, though almost everyone who studies elections and election administration in the US context engages in this, ourselves included.

This is not to suggest that the measurement of election administration is a futile exercise. On the contrary, measurement is important for an analysis of innovation and for our understanding of the possibilities and constraints of the American federal system. At the local level, measurement reflects the results of administrative choices in exercising discretion and implementing policy changes prescribed by state legislatures and, in some cases, state election offices. At the state level, measurement reflects states' efforts to navigate the intergovernmental maze that characterizes the American federal system in general and elections in particular. In general, good measurement can facilitate evaluations and decision-making based on data rather than anecdotes, and can facilitate valid and reliable comparisons. Measurement can also identify trends over time and facilitate determination of the impact of rules and process changes. Not least, measurement can encourage new research and better data collection by researcher or administrator reflection on the measurement process and results.

Systematic measurement of election operations is relatively recent and represents considerable innovation in its own right. We trace the evolution of publicized measures of election administration performance that address the modern era. These begin with data sets and have moved to include indices, process measures, and the development of common terminology for the field. It is significant, as the figures in the book bear out, that universal process maps that apply to election administration do not exist, and there is little agreement about common terminology; nascent efforts in these areas are discussed later in this chapter.[2]

In our chronology, we describe several measurement approaches that have guided development of research and practice. These include key formative tools such as the Election Administration and Voting Survey (EAVS) and the Common Data Format (Owens Hubler and Patrick 2019), and indices such as the Democracy Index (2009), the Election Performance Index (Pew Charitable Trusts 2016a; Stewart 2019), and the Election Administration Professionalism Index (Brown and Hale 2019). The evolution of measurement approaches also includes the development of surveys of voter perceptions and reports that synthesize information from the election community, such as the Presidential Commission on Election Administration. We also highlight the development of a collaborative research project about costs and resources in election administration (Hale and Brown 2019). Each of these projects illustrates the extent to which political influence, networked relationships, needs, and resources relate to the innovation theory-of-change model. These projects also illustrate different challenges that measurement poses in election administration, in breaking new ground without common terminology or common conceptual frameworks. These projects have engaged election officials in the coproduction of measures and approaches, and they have shaped the way that we measure the field.

THE EVOLUTION OF MEASURING
ELECTION ADMINISTRATION

The timeline of measurement in the modern era of election administration can be traced to the Help America Vote Act (HAVA), its charge to the new Election Assistance Commission (EAC) to report to Congress about the nation's election administration activities, and the embedded reporting requirements inherent in its new requirements for statewide electronic voter registration databases and voter registration list maintenance. The key measurement initiatives in the field begin with the EAC's signature national survey, the EAVS. Over the next nearly twenty years, the conceptualization of measuring election administration has expanded as election system stakeholders have considered additional lines of inquiry. The discussion that follows tracks these developments; additional information is noted in table C.20 in appendix C.

The EAC is authorized by Congress to collect information about election administration and to distribute that information nationally. Congress's mandate specifically concerned federal elections and voters covered by the Uniformed and Overseas Citizen Absentee Voting Act (UOCAVA). The EAC has chosen to go beyond this to collect information about elections from local election jurisdictions, state offices, the District of Columbia, and the US territories that can be used to better understand the context in which administration takes place, and to form a basis for improving election administration across the country. Through the EAVS, data collection capture information beyond voter registration and voter turnout. The EAVS was first administered in 2004, and has been administered every two years thereafter. EAVS data are publicly available on the EAC website. The categories of the 2018 EAVS broadly include voter registration (overall numbers, same-day registration, forms used, and removals); UOCAVA data (registrations, Federal Post Card Application data, ballot information, information about Federal Write-in Ballots; domestic civilian voting by mail data; votes cast (total, in-person, precinct, and polling place information; and poll worker information); provisional ballot data; voter participation and election technologies (total participation, pollbooks, voter technology use, and the location of the vote tally).

The concept of a national survey of election operations does not seem particularly political. Yet the process of developing an instrument and including stakeholders in this process took years. Stakeholder involvement was particularly critical because responses are voluntary. The EAC used a collaborative process to develop the EAVS and relied on the participation of state and local election officials across the election administration community (Greene 2019). The EAVS has been systematically revised through collaborative working groups of election officials in partnership with academics and private consultants (e.g., ForsMarsh Group) under the direction of the EAC. The EAVS is widely acknowledged as the only national data set on election administration for all election jurisdictions. Despite this comprehensive and important endeavor, it is not without particular limitations, most notably missing and inaccurate information. Many argue that these gaps are the consequences of the EAC's lack of ability to compel responses. And perhaps most important, the EAVS has served as a springboard for other measurement surveys and indices.

After the EAVS, the Survey of the Performance of American Elections (SPAE) was fielded to capture opinion data from the perspective of self-reported voters. The SPAE evolved from a collaborative effort of researchers led by Charles Stewart III at the Massachusetts Institute of Technology (MIT) to measure a variety of concepts related to the voter experience. Samples of 200 voters from each state are drawn for an Internet and/or telephone survey that is administered through a vendor. Information collected includes voter opinion and recollection information on topics related to voter intent, registration, check-in, how respondents cast their ballots, difficulties, lines, equipment, quality of experience in voting, and voting integrity. Publicly available data from the SPAE start in 2007 and continue through the 2016 election. Where the EAVS and the indices that follow from it focus on administration and policy, the SPAE focuses on voter opinions and perceptions about their election experiences.

In 2009, after several years of discussion at multiple academic and professional forums, the Democracy Index was published as a policy reform effort to develop a new measure of election performance and new ways of thinking about the components of a "good" election (Gerken 2009). The Democracy Index creates a ranking index to indicate how well jurisdictions performed against three broad goals: that every eligible voter who wants to register can do so, that every registered voter can cast a ballot, and that every ballot is counted properly (Gerken 2009, 27) as the voter intended. Elements of the Democracy Index were proposed as items of interest to all voters, and included concepts such as the length of time it takes to vote, how many ballots are discarded, how often machines break down, how long it takes to cast an absentee ballot, and so on. A goal of the Democracy Index was to encourage Congress to adopt legislation that would mandate that the EAC establish jurisdiction-level measures of election performance on these and similar items; its normative orientation was to shame local election jurisdictions into improvement in a "race to the top." US senators Barack Obama (D-IL) and Hillary Clinton (D-NY) each introduced legislation to establish such an index, as did New York City mayor Michael Bloomberg, but all these proposals were unsuccessful.

A successful avenue to promote a new approach to measurement was found, however, with support from a major private philanthropy. The Election Performance Index (EPI) built upon on the Democracy Index and the work of the new Caltech/MIT Voting Technology Project. The Voting Technology Project explored the experiences of the Florida 2000 presidential election and identified links in the chain of voting activities where the voting experience went awry (or could). The combination of these initiatives guided the development of the EPI as a tool to gauge the voter experience in registration, voting, and balloting, and the performance of the election administration system in the areas of security and convenience. The EPI was established by Pew Charitable Trusts and was first reported in 2013 (for a detailed accounting of the development of the index, see Stewart 2019). The EPI's seventeen indicators were constructed with input from state and local election officials and academic researchers. The concepts and categories captured by the indicators include jurisdiction participation in the EAVS; disability- or illness-related voting problems; registration and absentee ballot problems; use of online voter registration; use of postelection audits of voting equipment; turnout; voter registration rate; residual vote; use of voting information lookup tools; voting technology accuracy; and voting waiting times. The EPI also includes the proportion of absentee ballots, mail ballots, uniformed and overseas citizens ballots, and provisional ballots rejected or unreturned, and voter registrations rejected. EPI results have been reported for elections since 2008.

Several practical concerns have been noted about the EPI. A good portion of the measurement items rely on the EAVS. However, as noted above, participation in the EAVS is not compulsory. Election officials at local and state offices have expressed concern about the accuracy of the EAVS data (Brown, Hale, and King 2019), as have researchers. It is also evident that some indicators are beyond the control of the local election officials who conduct elections. Some of the indicators reflect administrative activities, but others reflect policy choices made by state legislators and state election offices, and still others reflect voter behavior.

The indicators of the EPI are not partisan, and the EAVS was not initiated as a partisan tool. However, the EPI's state-ranking approach has been used in some quarters to score political points vis-à-vis the concepts of "winning" or "losing" or "improving" or "lagging behind." Among practitioners and researchers, it is the consensus that the EAVS has improved since its inception, and by definition, the EPI has also improved over time.

Periodic reviews of the underlying measures are conducted by the EAC utilizing panels of election officials and ForsMarsh research staff as well as other stakeholders. A recent example is the working group convened to review the data collected about UOCAVA voters (also known as part B), which led to revisions in phrasing of some questions and the addition of others (Council of State Governments 2016).

At the time of writing, the administration of the EPI is directed by MIT professor Charles Stewart III. Through the MIT Election and Data Sciences Lab, which he directs, academics and election officials provide advisory feedback about the EPI generally and about some of the indicators. This type of stakeholder review lends credibility to the EPI as an iterative, transparent measurement approach that seeks input from the election community, even though it may not be universally endorsed.[3]

The next significant step in the evolution of election administration measurement came from the Presidential Commission on Election Administration (PCEA), which produced a conceptual classification of categories of election reform that showed promise as best practices for the future. The PCEA was developed through an executive order from President Obama to study election administration practices around the country. Commissioners traveled across the country, holding hearings and talking with voters, election officials, and other experts, and observing election offices and polling places. In 2014 they issued a report providing an overview of the differences in election administration across the country, discussing challenges related to resources and technology, discussing the impact of law and professionalism, and issuing recommendations and identifying best practices (Presidential Commission on Election Administration 2014). Policy activity or administrative implementation toward or away from the PCEA's recommendations could be noted as an indicator of progress, and representatives of the PCEA have appeared on multiple occasions before regional, state, and national associations of election stakeholders to discuss the recommendations.

In another development, the Bipartisan Policy Center joined with Charles Stewart III of MIT and other researchers to conduct a national survey of lines in elections. The long lines research is an offshoot of one of the PCEA's recommendations: that voters should not have to wait in lines any longer than 30 minutes (this was also a recommendation from the Democracy Index). The project gathers data from jurisdictions around the country from eleven states and over 4,000 polling locations, using counts of people waiting in line to check in each hour (for a summary to date, see Stein, Stewart, and Mann 2019).

A significant challenge in measuring and understanding election administration data is that there is no single format or system for reporting data from election offices; this is reflective of other aspects of election administration. The Common Data Format (CDF) is an effort by a collaboration of stakeholders called the NIST Interoperability Public Working Group and hosted by the National Institute for Standards and Technology (NIST) to develop a unified understanding and system for data reporting. The overarching goals of the group are to develop a common format that can be used for election equipment and software interfaces across states, jurisdictions, and vendors. The first version of this focuses on results, votes cast, and election events; versions related to voter records, business processes, and voting methods are under way. Other areas of consideration include a CDF for ballots and ePollbooks (NIST 2016; Owens Hubler and Patrick 2019).

Not least in these election administration measurement efforts is the federal Government Accountability Office (GAO). Over the years, the GAO has been perhaps the most prolific research body related to cataloging and describing government activity in election administration. At the direction of congressional requests, the GAO has been charged with studying a plethora of topics—from election administration policies, registration, and turnout to innovations like mail ballots and vote centers, to standard practices like absentee balloting, to equipment, to the effects of get-out-the-vote efforts, to costs and budgeting, and more. A simple Internet search on the GAO Web page for the term "election" yielded 5,212 reports, 620 testimonies, 8 comment letters, 11 memoranda, and 591 other products.[4] Narrowing the scope to the phrase "election administration" yielded 4,834 reports, 533 testimonies, 2 comment letters, 6 memoranda, and 502 other products. Although few of these are specifically about election administration and measurement, as we intend in this volume to be, it would be an understatement to note that the GAO is both prolific and underappreciated in this area.[5]

The chapter turns now to two recent illustrations of the contemporary status of measurement issues in election administration. The first is an index of election administration professionalism, necessitated by our belief that an integral component of innovation is professionalism and its causes and consequences. The second is an exploratory initiative to capture meaningful data about how America pays for elections, differences across jurisdictions, and the influence of those differences, if any, and another significant and integral component of innovations. These illustrations highlight the iterative, synthetic, and endogenous nature of innovation, and how current projects build on earlier efforts. In a networked environment, these iterations over time and the interplay among actors with competing viewpoints have been demonstrated to generate capacity to implement policy and develop structures that facilitate the creation of new capacity for future efforts.

MEASURING PROFESSIONALISM
IN ELECTION ADMINISTRATION

The EAVS and EPI created a platform for thinking about a different way to understand election performance measurement. The EAVS's national data set provided the basis for the further development of tools and indices, and it also provided the opportunity to combine election administration data with other data sets, such as those of the US Census. The Democracy Index offered a normative view of what might "matter." A third-party philanthropic organization, Pew Charitable Trusts, provided the shell of a method to compare state performance. A previous Pew project, known as the Government Performance Project, developed an index to compare the states on their performance in a variety of administrative categories (finances, human resources, infrastructure, technology, etc.). This project's approach, titled "Grading the States," included a fifty-state report card and policy briefs, along with events and meetings to facilitate information sharing across states and aimed to promote innovation through a collection of proven management practices.[6] The EPI built upon this approach to generate the first index in the field to compare state election operations.

The EPI focused on one aspect of election performance—states as a whole—and compared them with each other. The indicators combined state legislative policy choices (e.g., mail ballot options) with voter behavior choices (e.g., I did not vote because I was sick), along with aspirational elements about technology, such as whether a state had developed a state election website and its particular features. Local administrative activities that could directly affect the operation of an election were not as obvious in this state-level aggregation, and the results of this measurement strategy presented a picture over which local election officials had little control (and in some cases, none).

Another school of thought approached the idea of election performance as a matter of capacity, a major element of which is the concept of professionalism. Conceptually, capacity is the ability of government offices to perform what is asked (Honadle 1981), and is essential for innovation to occur. Professionalism has many different components and is complex and sometimes nuanced, requiring an index as opposed to a single measure to capture the various factors of influence and that define the concept (for an index of legislative professionalism see, e.g., Squire 1992, 2007). The impetus behind the Election Administration Professionalism Index (EAPI) was to identify components of administrative practice that reflect, broadly, administrative decisions that support the capacity to perform. The foundation of the EAPI rests on interoffice and interpersonal relationships that facilitate training and other forms of information exchange, and opportunities for interaction with the election community and the larger conversation about this field of public service.[7]

The EAPI is intended to identify capacity, regardless of policy direction, and its components are not attributable to political ideology or policy choices. One important component established in other studies of administrative professionalism and capacity was the activity of local election officials together and with the state and national community (for a discussion of this concept in the criminal justice policy arena, see Hale 2011). The goal of the EAPI is to establish a unified measure to better explain and array the elements of capacity, antecedent conditions, covariates, and consequences. These interactions are critical to the networked public service environment, collaborative administration, and agency interoperability (Agranoff 2007, 2012, 2017). Building on the path established by the EPI, the professionalism index presented here is a part of a work in progress. Our goal in creating it is to develop a measure that could be captured over time, across states, and ultimately across lower-level election jurisdictions within states.

The EAPI is related to two important measures of election performance. Criticisms of various attempts to gauge administrative performance at the state level aside, the best-known state-level indicator of election performance today is the EPI. Figure 8.1 provides a scatterplot of the professionalism index and EPI across the states. The correlation between professionalism and EPI is fairly strong, and the pattern between the variables is clear.[8] What is less clear is the causal direction between them. Professionalizing an elections staff ought to lead to enhanced performance, and enhanced performance may then provide more interest in enhancing the professionalism of others within the system, leading to more and better training and national attention, and so on. We should expect that a collection of factors would be mutually reinforcing (see, e.g., Rainey and Steinbauer 1998, and their study of the relative

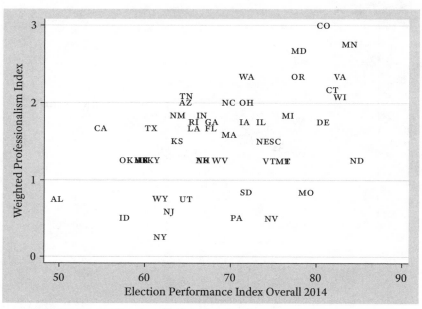

FIGURE 8.1 Professionalism Index by Election Performance Index

importance of key leadership attributes in relation to public organizational performance). For election administrators, a variety of characteristics are important—office leadership, resources, networking opportunities, advanced education, and experience with technology—each of which is an element of professionalization, and some are reflected in the institutional infrastructure snapshots that were captured by the EPI. Although the causal relationship is probably impossible to determine given the endogenous nature of these concepts, and our inability to measure these with precision, the correlation is not surprising, and it suggests that the EAPI reflects some attributes of "good" election performance that others in the field find valuable.

Professionalism is similarly related to turnout, which is the historic measure of election success, although it may have little to do with election administration activities per se (see figure 8.2).[9] It is possible that professionalism of election administration may have an impact on election outcomes. The logic may be that more professionalized administrators will, through neutral competence and greater efficiencies, enhance local trust in the election system and thereby increase turnout. But the opposite could also be true. To the extent that turnout is a proxy for need, turnout may indicate the need for more or enhanced election administration professionalism. These relationships may also be wholly endogenous. These are questions to be considered further in a different volume.

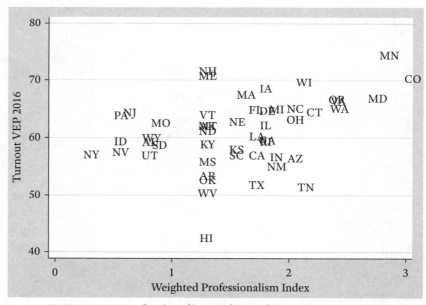

FIGURE 8.2 Professionalism Index and Voter Turnout, 2016

We also examined possible relationships between election administration professionalism and two other variables that are critical for our innovation theory of change: party politics and resources.[10] It could easily be argued that states that are controlled by one party or another may be more or less interested in investing in the professionalism of election administration in the state. Perhaps one party might be interested in investing in the professionalization of election administration to safeguard the integrity of the election system. Or another party might be interested in highly professionalized election administration to ensure neutral competency and by extension safeguard the voting rights of all eligible citizens.

Similarly, it could be argued that state resources should be related to professionalism levels. The more money a state has in its coffers, the more able it will be to hire highly qualified professionals and/or support further training of that workforce. In addition, wealthier states ought to be able to spend more money on travel and, in particular, on participation in communication forums and events, networking, and information sharing. Further, states with greater income inequality may be more or less interested in enhancing election administration professionalism, either to lift up or suppress the engagement of lower-income voters.

What these comparisons indicate is that the EAPI is capturing some of the sense of state approaches to election operations, and some sense of whether voters participate in the process, but that there is more to learn about the capacity of election administrators. As we continue to refine the EAPI, it is important to examine similar issues over time and at the local level, given that election operations are inherently local. Although such indices are imperfect, they do serve an important role in measuring government capacity and functioning generally, as well as election administration specifically. No measure is perfect, and in measuring election administration specifically, it is critical to select indicators that are as politically neutral as possible in order to develop the clearest, least biased, and potentially most useful tool.

EXPLORING HOW TO MEASURE
THE COST OF ELECTIONS

Attention has focused recently on measuring the "cost" of elections and, in some quarters, the "cost per vote." How America pays for elections is confounding. As if American election administration systems were not already complex enough, the intersection of these systems with intergovernmental budgets is particularly challenging. Measuring election administration costs is important for election officials both in local jurisdictions and in state election offices. Across the country, election officials are seeking information to use internally in their offices to improve their operations. They are also interested in developing information for presentations to funding sources and policymakers, and they want to be able to compare the relative efficiency or effectiveness of various methods of conducting elections, such as voting by mail, vote centers, and early voting in traditional precincts. In terms of public administration principles, this information is essential for public decision-makers as they consider whether to adopt or amend their processes. And yet this information is quite difficult to obtain, and even more difficult to compare within states, let alone across the country. Not least, the terms "cost," "election," and "vote" remain undefined.

As has been noted with respect to measurement generally, election officials are reluctant to engage in comparative conversations about election performance for fear of being portrayed in the media as wasteful or worse. As one local election official noted, "We provided detailed cost information to our state office, only to have the data used to grade us and rank us in the newspaper." Another local official commented that "cost per vote" was used by state election officials to identify jurisdictions that were relatively higher in cost and therefore supposedly poorer stewards of public funds, but without consideration of varying demographic and geographic constraints across jurisdictions.

This type of publicity is not uncommon in public service, and, indeed, transparency is a core value of public management. Transparency is also a hallmark of professionalism. And yet election officials around the country are hesitant to share cost information for fear that the media or others will misunderstand or misinterpret the information.

At a more fundamental level, it is difficult to develop cost information that can be used accurately for comparison and very easy to develop cost information that does not produce true "apples to apples" comparisons, given the wide variation among both state and local election administration and state and local budgeting practices. States differ in the institutional structures that administer elections and the responsibilities allocated to various local offices. States also differ widely in policy that establishes methods of election, such as early voting, OVR, vote centers, voting by mail, same-day voter registration, and options for equipment. It is fundamentally difficult to define what an election is, or to identify specific cost areas. Election officials at all levels and across the country concur that the "cost" of an election and the "cost of elections" are two different concepts, and that both concepts depend on how "cost" and "election" are defined. For some, an election is a time-specific event, for others it includes the year-round costs of voter registration and other office administration, and for still others it includes the cost of purchasing election equipment and/or election system maintenance. The cost of serving voters is dependent upon many factors, including population density, the degree of additional language support, the election equipment, and the method(s) of election used, to mention only a few.

As a result, there is a deficit of cost information in the election administration community at the most basic levels, both within and across states. Measuring costs in elections is extraordinarily challenging, and a key aspect of this exploration has been to identify those challenges and present them in a way that will further advance the field. The GAO, like several other interested research and third-party groups, has also attempted to quantify the field, and it has expressed how challenging, and ultimately unfruitful, its efforts have been. Despite these challenges, the topic remains at the top of the election administration agenda as local and state election offices think about purchasing new equipment, and as policymakers weigh trade-offs between new methods of voting, election security, and established processes.

Measurement Illustration: Investing in Elections

Investing in Elections (IIE) began in 2017 as an applied research project to generate information about election costs and resources that could be useful for local election officials (LEOs) and chief election officials (CEOs) in analyzing internal election operations, gathering funding support, advocating for (or against) policy change, and addressing policy implementation issues.[11] The IIE process and findings illustrate the importance of network-level collaboration and the iterative nature of the process of developing tools and methods that support change.

The importance of the topic has been percolating through the election administration community for several years on agendas at national, regional, and state conferences and at working group meetings of election community stakeholders, including members of the Election Center and other professional associations. One impetus for these discussions was the publication by a national professional association of a summary of state laws regarding reimbursement practices for special elections (National Conference of State Legislatures 2018a).[12] After the publication of this summary, election stakeholders discussed the costs of and investments in election operations and infrastructure at Inclusion and Integrity, a national symposium of local, state, and national election officials, academics, research funders, vendors, and other stakeholders. The data collection process was structured to model collaborative efforts that have been proven to advance capacity and to acknowledge the interconnectedness of public organizations and the public service environment. Scaffolded presentations incorporated new information at each step along the way, and they included structured opportunities for conversations and an iterative process of dialogue throughout a network of organizations in the election policy space.

Over the next two years, a steering committee of academics and election community stakeholders made twenty-five presentations at meetings of election officials and stakeholders. These included plenary presentations at state

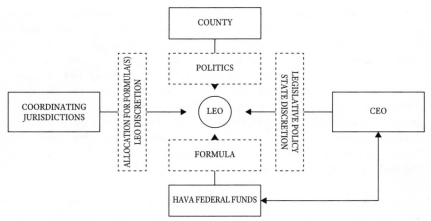

FIGURE 8.3 Model of Local Election Jurisdiction Funding Streams

association meetings in four states, at national and regional conferences, and at a national symposium on election administration data and reform. The steering committee also met with hundreds of election officials through focus groups.

Findings bring the resource challenges facing LEOs into sharper focus. A model of LEOs funding streams presented in figure 8.3 illustrates possible sources of revenue for local offices as well as the gatekeepers for each. For all LEOs, revenues and expenditures are guaranteed to fluctuate from year to year and sometimes widely, depending on the number and type of elections. Unanticipated expenses for special elections or other emergent conditions are also typical.

County budgets are the primary source of revenue for local election offices. County funds are typically controlled by boards of county commissioners or supervisors who are, by and large, partisan elected officials. Local offices may also receive state funds, subject to state legislative policy decisions; it is also theoretically possible for local jurisdictions to levy fees or taxes on the general public in support of elections, although this does not appear to be common and the ability to do so would also be a matter of state legislative policy (i.e., the degree of authority granted for local home rule). State reimbursement practices vary widely and are largely insufficient to reimburse local offices in full for the expenses incurred in conducting elections. Reimbursement practices are geared toward considering elections as special events rather than toward election administration as an ongoing public service. State reimbursement may be authorized only for particular types of elections (e.g., special, run-off, presidential) or for specific supplies and equipment (e.g., postage, ballot materials, poll workers). Across the board, states do not reimburse general operating expenses or voter registration activities, including list maintenance. States served as the pass-through for federal HAVA funds to purchase new voting equipment; largely, these funds have been spent. Local offices also charge coordinating jurisdictions—such as school boards, cities, and special districts—for running elections. The ability to recover expenses from coordinating jurisdictions is a matter of policy, and LEOs have some discretion in deciding the amounts of recovery. For most offices, the costs of elections are not absorbed by other entities. And regardless of the source of funding, political obstacles need to be navigated. Some of these are relatively within the immediate operating sphere of the LEO (e.g., billing coordinating jurisdictions for election expenses), and some are not (e.g., a local share of HAVA funds).

Despite wide-ranging differences across states in the structures and methods of election administration and resource acquisitions and expenditures, analysis of the general level of local funding allocated for election administration is revealing. Funding is low by any measure, given the results of a study of the share of county general administrative funds allocated to election administration in 2016 (Hale and Brown 2019).[13] In our comparison of county election expenses with county budgets for general administration across six states, election budgets represent less than 1 percent of total county administrative expenses—the median proportion of election administration budgets as a share of county expenditures was 0.54 percent (0.0054). Median election expenses for the bottom quartile counties are 0.78 percent (0.0078); for the top quartile, they are 0.59 percent (0.0059). For counties in the bottom quartile, election expenses ranged from 0.13 percent (0.0013) to 12.4 percent (0.124). For counties in the top quartile, election expenses ranged from 0.02 percent (0.0002) to 2.5 percent (0.025).

Study of local election budgets and resources is now proceeding in several directions. Studies in Wisconsin have been influential in policy decisions (Government Accountability Board 2013). Within-state mapping and analyses have been conducted for California (Hill 2011) and North Carolina, with an emphasis in the latter on the compensation of local election officials (Kropf and Pope 2019; Mohr et al. 2019). The importance of procurement practices is the focus of another line of emerging research (Bennett 2019). Systematic research has also begun to examine the costs of special elections in California and the financial ramifications of adopting different methods of voting in these types of elections (Logan 2019). The findings from the IIE project will support these efforts and will potentially help further specify the work that is to come.

ANALYSIS

Measurement touches election administration in both internal and external ways. Elections in and of themselves are inherently a measurement exercise.

Beyond that, measurement can (and should) be used for planning, reflection, process improvements, enhanced efficiency, and most obviously, reporting. Like so many parts of the election administration system, the ability to accurately measure and reflect reality is evolving, and innovation in measurement exists and is expanding. What is measured, who does it and when, and why it is undertaken may (and some would suggest must, by definition) have an impact on the conclusions that are drawn. And measurement is itself an area of and for innovation.

Measurement is implicated in each aspect of our innovation theory of change. Politics may be involved, and certainly does play a role in motivating questions asked of the GAO and in decision-making about the advent and evolution of the Election Administration and Voting Survey. In less obvious ways, politics is involved in who funds what research undertaken by third-party groups and university researchers. Certainly, whether and how results are used to shape policy is inherently political.

Networks and professionalism are also intricately tied to measurement. Self-measurement that involves any degree of sophistication and accuracy requires training and is enhanced through information networks. Scholars use their own information networks to modify research ideas and questions, think about designs, share findings, and critique their own work. New studies have derived from points raised in the various measures of election administration and election performance; for example, the opportunities for error in a typical chain of election activities involving mailed ballots (Stewart 2010), and the length of time that voters wait in line to vote (Stewart 2013), as well as countless other studies cited throughout this book. Professional networks and organizations are sometimes used to foment ideas, collect data, and disseminate results about this work, and to refine its focus.

Much of this work is driven by need and supported by resources. When problems arise, particularly those that may potentially influence the quality of American democracy, the need to understand—almost anything related— is critical and immediate. The array of intergovernmental and networked institutions, power, and people involved in questions pertaining to election administration require innovative approaches to measurement and modifications of research-as-usual approaches, particularly when comparison is involved. And measurement in and of itself is necessarily resource dependent—on time, on money, and on people.

Exploratory endeavors such as Investing in Elections are also important to our study of innovation because they attempt to map new ground and to meet specific needs in the field. The findings illustrate why such media-attractive numbers (e.g., cost per vote) or other oversimplifications cannot be compared across states or across jurisdictions within states because of differences in approaches to balloting, how offices related to elections are structured, jurisdiction size, and attendant concerns about costs and efficiency—and most important, because even at the jurisdiction level, costs are allocated and captured differently. Without further research to specify points of comparison, research in this area will remain inherently unreliable and potentially harmful.

More broadly, in thinking about the influence of the federal system as an aspect of the political environment, the efforts of the national government and local election officials have provided essential platforms. At the national level, the EAVS provided the initial articulation of the most critical dimensions of election administration and was the initial effort directed at creating a national picture of the work of thousands of election jurisdictions. The EAVS also reflects the political calculus of HAVA, which was to place implementation details of its prescriptions for provisional ballots and new voting systems firmly in the hands of the states. Reflecting that political calculus, state and local compliance is voluntary; the EAVS is an easy target at times for that reason. State CEOs may be able to incentivize LEO compliance, but many have not exercised their limited resources in that way.

The balance between national and local efforts remains imperfect, and yet the EAVS serves as the backdrop for the development of a host of other measurement approaches over time. The Common Data Format is an illustration of a second-generation effort to build on what the EAVS can reveal, by addressing the very real and intractable problems with language and terms that vary across states. The resolution of these differences will go a long way toward increasing the utility of the EAVS. And as the EAVS more accurately captures the local election administration landscape, the accuracy of other measurement tools such as the EPI and EAPI can be expected to increase as well.

Beginning at the local level, the IIE project has begun to map LEO resources. As with the EAVS, the results will be refined over time, and should also foster additional research as new areas of inquiry are identified. The IIE project is a voluntary effort supported by the professional association of election officials, which has increased interest in participation.

Mapping new territory is important—although the idea of an election is quintessentially American and part of our common lexicon—we have documented relatively little about the institutional, financial, and human resource arrangements that are involved. Increased understanding of the election administration environment can make an important contribution to the political discussions that shape the field and that frame what is possible for innovation.

Not least, in the complex landscape of election administration systems and subsystems, measurement is integral and intractable. It challenges the idea of "science as usual" approaches to problem formulation, research design, data collection, analysis, and feedback, and instead is itself a process that is evolving and inherently innovative. Simple tools may be employed, but sophisticated and agile analyses are required to identify the nuance needed to properly understand and interpret results. It must be the case that innovation drives measurement, and measurement drives innovation.

NOTES

1. Measurement here is not counting per se, although that is one aspect.
2. Efforts in this area were first made through contracts made by the Government Accountability Office and are being continued by the Democracy Fund.
3. One of the authors, Kathleen Hale, is a member of the MIT Election and Data Sciences Lab's Advisory Board. The information presented here does not constitute an endorsement by the MIT Election and Data Sciences Lab to review the EPI or to use any particular process, approach, or timeline.
4. Accessed at www.gao.gov/search?q=election&Submit=Search.
5. See, e.g., among many others, GAO 2012, 2016, 2017, 2018.
6. The GPP was conducted over a fourteen-year period ending in 2010; additional information is available in the project archives at www.pew.org.
7. A description of the construction of the current professionalism index is included in appendix C.
8. $R^2 = .469; p < .001$.
9. $r = .368; p < .001$
10. Statistical models did not demonstrate significant relationships using typical state-level measures of party influence or control, and general resources levels such as the Gini coefficient and median income.
11. The authors are the lead researchers on IIE, which is affiliated with the Election Center's Professional Measurement Project initiative. Auburn University faculty members have a decades-long relationship with the Election Center, in the design and delivery of professional certification for election administrators and voter registrars, election equipment vendors, and election monitors.
12. The specific meaning of "special election" varies somewhat across the states according to state election law; here we use the term generically to refer to elections that are scheduled outside the "regular" schedule prescribed by a state's election code.
13. County election budgets were obtained from public websites; county administrative budgets were as reported by the 2016 US Census. Median county administrative expenses are $51 million, and median county election expenses are $274,528. The six states are not named because anonymity is a condition of the IIE project; election officials express concern that financial information will be used to rank jurisdictions or develop a comparative "cost per vote" metric that does not reflect actual operating conditions. These concerns appear to be well founded, given the variations identified in this chapter.

Conclusion:
The Future of Innovation
in Election Administration

Innovation in election administration in America is a story about context. What is possible in one place and at one time and under a particular political configuration may not be possible in another. And what is possible at one level of government, or in a particular county or state, may not be possible in another.

Throughout this book, we have delved deeply into particular cases across the dimensions of the election administration process where innovation has taken place or is ripe to do so. These include registration, convenience voting, language access, ballot counting and audits, equipment and security, and measurement. The nuances in these cases pinpoint critical catalysts and inhibitors of change and innovation. Collectively, they contribute to answering the "how" questions about registration and voting that are so difficult to address, and they focus on methods and approaches to design and implementation in complex systems.

In the first section of this conclusion, we revisit the cases presented in the introduction and follow them through from the point of view of prospective voters and election administrators. Next, we discuss the recent political context and events that will shape election administration during the 2020 election and beyond. We then review the innovation theory of change and conclude with a discussion about the broader implications of our research for understanding election administration as a series of intergovernmental networks in the American federal system, and what this suggests for innovation.

ELECTION ADMINISTRATORS AND VOTERS

At the start of this book, we introduced twenty people whose interactions with election administration systems and subsystems typify some of the problems faced today. We bring them back here in order to discuss how various innovations help or do not help these people address the situations they face.

Overall, the innovations we discuss in this book help voters and the people who work on elections. But unfortunately, sometimes these innovations occur at the margins. Problems are not completely resolved. Political decisions create new dilemmas. Innovation diffusion is limited, such that some people can take advantage of innovations but others cannot, all depending upon where they live. Although these inequities may seem unfair, they are a natural and legal consequence of the constitutional arrangements that structure US elections today. As the legal framework for elections in the United States evolves, so do the administrative challenges faced by election administrators and voters alike. Developing new approaches to solving administrator and voter problems is a function of many factors.

VOTER REGISTRATION AND VOTERS: MAYA MARTINEZ AND JOHN SMITH

For Maya and John, the innovations discussed in this book could have a direct impact on their experiences at the polls. The accuracy of voter rolls improves with the implementation of online voter registration (OVR) and electronic pollbooks (EPBs), as well as with third-party data management support, such as the National Change of Address system and the Electronic Registration Information Center. Automatic voter registration is expected to have the same effects. EPBs can access a sophisticated statewide data set that can determine where exactly Maya is supposed to vote. If the state permits, the EPB can be used to update her voter registration on-site in real time. If the state uses a precinct-based voting model, the EPB can generate documentation that shows Maya where to vote. If the state makes use of National Change of Address data, and participates in third-party programs for data-matching support that address this type of inconsistency, John is much more likely to have questions about his voter registration record resolved before he gets to the polls. If Maya and John need to change their registrations, in states with laws that permit same-day registration, Maya and John can vote as they had planned. John can see that times have changed in some ways. His grandmother would find it easier to navigate the logistics of registration and casting a ballot through changes like automatic voter registration and voting by mail (VBM). However, though the poll taxes and violent intimidation of her youth are gone, she still may face basic hurdles in registration and in voting, including her ability to access the Internet and to provide the new documentation now required. It may require time and money to obtain the documentation that she needs in order to register to vote, depending on the laws in her state.

All across the country, these and similar situations occur when voters go to the polls to vote. Whether Maya, John, or his grandmother are able to vote, the administrative processes that local election officials must follow are a function of state election law and of administrative decisions about how to maintain voter rolls. These matters affect different people in different ways, and policies and practices ought to be written in such a way that the least among us are not penalized or restricted because of their personal characteristics or circumstances.

VOTER REGISTRATION AND ELECTION ADMINISTRATORS: GEORGE MARKUS AND MARTHA PENDLETON

George and Martha are responsible for maintaining an intricate system of data and processes that ensure that Maya and John and John's grandmother can register to vote if they are eligible, that they can cast ballots, and that their ballots will be counted as cast.

With EPB links to a statewide voter registration database, George and Martha can use the experiences of these and similar voters in their state and in other states, as well as research conducted on these programs and their effectiveness, to make their case for OVR and EPBs, and for participation in third-party support systems. If adopted, these innovations would then change the training program that Martha runs. Although the implementation of new systems is never perfect, it is likely that in the long run these changes would make tremendous improvements in Martha's state. One issue that other jurisdictions have observed is that Internet connectivity is still a common problem, so they will need to consider this in their proposals, given that Internet connections are the backbone of EPBs and OVR.

CONVENIENCE VOTING AND VOTERS: CLAIRE MICHAELS AND PAUL RANDOLPH

Having access to mail balloting would allow Claire to vote without the hassle of having to apply for an absentee ballot. Claire may still need to be responsible for re-registering every time she moves. Vote centers or VBM would also help Paul, and early voting periods would help him in particular. In both cases, however, the current and immediate solution to their different problems is the same: given the rules in their state, the easiest thing for them both to do is to apply for absentee ballots and vote these ballots in the allowable period before the election so they are sure the ballots will be counted. Because Claire in particular is part of the activist community, the longer-term answer for her is to work with community and advocacy groups to push the state legislature to change voting rules so that she, and countless other voters, will have different ways to cast ballots that are more convenient for their individual circumstances.

CONVENIENCE VOTING AND ELECTION ADMINISTRATORS: JESSICA SADIE AND ANTHONY SMITH

Jessica's desire to move to VBM is unlikely to be met in the near future, unless her state association is able to coordinate with the chief election official and other state-level interest groups to advocate for legislative changes. These types of changes take a variety of resources that one election official alone does not have; change can come about through work with other election officials and other groups concerned about similar issues.

Moreover, Anthony is right to be concerned about the future of VBM. It does have some drawbacks, which may become more problematic for future generations; solving them through Web-based voting in the current environment is highly unlikely. Getting there will take the collective vision and commitment of multiple stakeholders and leaders, as well as resources. And given the designation of elections as critical infrastructure, doing so will probably involve Anthony working with other new groups through the Department of Homeland Security and the related information sharing and analysis centers. These changes will likely require him to develop new partnerships and networks and additional technical skills, and will also likely require new and different types of staffing. And these things will not only have an impact on Anthony's office at the state level; they will also have an impact on all the county offices with which he works, as well as their vendor partners. Future innovations in these areas will likely be long-term endeavors that require political goodwill, ongoing strengthening of networks and professional skills, demands of the citizenry, and financial resources and leadership.

LANGUAGE NEEDS AND VOTERS: SYLVIA MORENO AND JIM SMITH

Sylvia and Jim's grandfathers are fortunate that their native languages are covered by the Voting Rights Act of 1965, unlike many naturalized citizens whose native languages are not included in the four language groups mandated for assistance. They are also fortunate that they live in areas of the country where language assistance is required for their language(s). This is not the case everywhere or for all elections; in many places, the number of non-English-speaking voters is so low that, when coupled with the available technology for balloting, it is cost-prohibitive to provide translation services for election information and balloting. And language assistance is about more than the mechanics of services; Sylvia wants to encounter a voting experience that is welcoming, where she can be given the support she needs to ask questions, where she can have assistance to know the proper questions to ask, and where she can be understood.

LANGUAGE NEEDS AND ELECTION ADMINISTRATORS: DAVID CHEN AND MARY BLEDSOE

Unlike Mary and Jim's grandfathers, the voters in Mary's district do not get information and ballots in their non-English native languages. There is a real need for language assistance in areas without the population density that triggers mandatory support. In these instances, election administrators are faced with the competing challenges of limited budgets versus responding to the real needs of citizens who want to vote. They are also faced with policy limitations in providing assistance to Korean and Polish voters. Even where mandated by law, the story of non-English language coverage in American elections is one of needs versus resources, where innovation is driven and supported by local networks and third-party groups. David tried to solve these problems himself in what he thought was a direct, cost-efficient approach; but the political pushback that he experienced and that shut his program down highlights the importance of politics and outreach in any kind of innovation that is not motivated by response to a legal mandate. Election administrators need the capacity to anticipate when innovations will face political opposition and to navigate the thicket of involved organizations and competing interests; without this support, many good ideas fail to survive.

BALLOT COUNTING AND AUDITS, AND VOTERS: JANE WALKER AND LAMONT JACKSON

Innovation in counting is driven by the desire to overcome human error and the fear of a democratic failure. Jane has trust issues, and a well-done and publicized auditing system might help her and people like her overcome such fears. Lamont, like most people, needs education to understand the counting and certification processes. As a candidate, Lamont should be as informed as possible, both for his benefit and, most important, to be able to communicate accurately about the process. Jane and Lamont might be interested in watching the counting process at an election office at the end of the voting period on Election Day. Provisional ballots are widely and wildly misunderstood. Public education is important to inform voters and candidates that provisional ballots are a fail-safe for them, and that all provisional ballots are reviewed and counted if valid.

BALLOT COUNTING AND AUDITS, AND ELECTION ADMINISTRATORS: JOE STEVENS AND SONIA RIOS

Joe is a public administrator who is trying to practice the principle of neutral competence in the American intergovernmental framework, which is itself inherently contentious and political. Being an election administrator is hard, not just in terms of the nuances of the job but also in terms of the political savvy and credibility required to assure people with much at stake that the process was fair, whether they won or lost. He needs to enlist all candidates as system stakeholders in order to demonstrate the integrity of the process through publicity and transparency about office processes. And Sonia needs to network with other election administrators working in states that have implemented auditing processes to learn from their challenges and successes with their state policymakers. She can borrow from their strategies and use their evidence to convince her own legislature to move to a system that will reinforce integrity and shore up public trust. She can also gather information from other jurisdictions about best practices for poll worker training for the provisional ballot process.

ELECTION SECURITY, EQUIPMENT, AND VOTERS: MICAH BENSEN

Micah continues to watch the "news" through his social media feeds. On the most recent Election Day, his county's election director was on his Facebook Live feed several times explaining how the election office had prepared for Election Day, what was going on, and how long the lines were, and reassuring watchers that everything was fine. The local election officials' website had a diagram that illustrated the voting system's components, and it seemed from the diagram that the voting machines that accept and count ballots are not actually connected to the Internet. Instead, results would be transferred to USB drives, which would be physically carried by police officers to a central counting facility. At the same time, other people reported their concerns about malfunctioning machines. But Micah decided to go vote anyway, and his experience was typical of his past ones. He still does not know if he can trust the system, and what he sees in the media has not helped him make this decision. He is like many Americans today. Civics classes at all levels of school teach about what kinds of elections we have, but not how elections actually work. Encouraging young people like Micah to serve as poll workers may go a long way toward educating the future electorate about the process, and also about ensuring them how much more secure our elections are than the impressions they currently get from the media.

ELECTION SECURITY, EQUIPMENT, AND ELECTION ADMINISTRATORS: ALAN PARKER

After Alan's office received its funds under the Help America Vote Act (HAVA) from the Election Assistance Commission, he conducted a similar grant process with counties, allocating funds based upon proposals that included projected budgets. According to state law, the counties that did not spend all their funds by the end of the first fiscal year had to turn them back in. Because of this state rule, Alan is now facing the prospect of collecting unspent monies from the counties only months after distributing them. Although this rule was clearly identified in the proposal process, the county election directors are furious with Alan, particularly those in smaller counties that did not have enough capacity to engage the appropriate information technology specialists quickly enough to spend their allocations. They have asked to keep the monies for the next election cycle because of these limitations; however, Alan must have counties return their unspent grant funds, and then must initiate another proposal process with the counties for the next fiscal year.

After looking at the consulting assistance available, and at state office support, Alan will need to hire new help or expand the capacity of his office in some way. Expertise is hard to find, given the relatively low level of government compensation. The ways in which the second round of HAVA funds are being spent across the country are sometimes stymied by administrative rules such as this one, and these rules exemplify some of the structural problems inherent in the US system that make innovation challenging. Counties with limited professional election staff capacity are sometimes unable to respond quickly enough when presented with opportunities such as this one. Time, as a resource, is critical for successful implementation, diffusion, and adoption; administrative rules often get in the way.

Purchasing new equipment may be an appealing option for some counties; and if resources are available, this might be worth further investigation. In order to pursue the best value for his time, Alan should contact the procurement officers in his state and ask to meet with them. He may also want to include state information technology professionals. And he will also want to contact the current vendor(s) that provide hardware and software to the counties and get their input, along with the input of county election officials.

WHAT TO MEASURE:
STEVE EVANS AND MANDY ROGERS

Steve and Mandy have identified common and important questions, but they may be too early in their careers as researchers to fully understand the nuances of the questions that they have raised. The literature will help them focus this question more specifically and will allow them to proceed beyond the "wow—things are different in every state" stage. Surveys such as the Election Administration and Voting Survey may provide data that is a useful starting point for comparisons. In this way, they can appreciate, and add to, the body of knowledge related to election administration in the United States. Mandy's desire to systematically study whether inequality and questions of fairness continue to plague American elections in the modern era points to a much-needed area of research that has not recently received adequate attention. Particular instances of state implementation seem to indicate that inequality matters. In some states, for example, driver's license offices that issued voter identification cards to citizens without driver's licenses were authorized to operate only on some days of the week, or at reduced hours, in poorer, rural areas or areas with high proportions of minority residents.

WHAT TO MEASURE:
ELECTION ADMINISTRATORS—DONNA DIANGELO

As an election administrator, Donna understands the complexity of what is involved, at least at the jurisdiction level within her own state. She may not be able to adequately collect and analyze the necessary financial and operational data, and she may not be able to make clear comparisons. But even if she can do those things, she may still not be able to convince the public that she is not wasting public dollars in her election office. This topic of cost in the election administration system is fertile ground for improvement and innovation, but it is too often hampered by partisan politics, haranguing, and manipulation. Donna will benefit from dialogue with election administrators in other states and within her state association.

SUMMING UP THE CASES

As the cases and analyses in this book demonstrate, the policy decisions of Congress and state legislatures significantly influence the political opportunity structure within which election innovation is possible, but they do not wholly define it. National administration of elections is quite thin in comparison with other policy areas. The courts currently seem increasingly deferential to the states. And the states are increasingly dominated by one party. Partisan-led redistricting has effectively foreclosed the voices of many citizens. Citizens' initiatives have begun to appear on the ballot in some states; leading examples include rights restoration for felons (Florida) and the establishment of independent redistricting bodies (Ohio and Wisconsin, among others). This direct citizen action responds to ideological legislatures that have taken extremely partisan approaches to structuring the election sphere.

ELECTION ADMINISTRATION AND
THE POLITICAL LANDSCAPE

Throughout our research, we observed the influence of politics, professionalism, needs, and resources on innovation. At the time of writing, in mid-2019, the political landscape reflects conflicts about the US federal system and also about particular policies. The intergovernmental relationships structured by the American federal system open up space for local and state action. And yet change is not guaranteed. Under the federal umbrella, change proceeds differently in various policy areas. In the election administration arena, change has come about in swings of the pendulum toward and away from states' rights. Normative debates about access to, and participation in, the franchise have appeared to be settled more than once—by federal constitutional amendment, by federal law, and judicial interpretation—only to be later undone or mitigated by state or local decisions that exclude particular groups or make it more difficult to register or vote. Recent examples of this tension include the unsuccessful legal challenges that equate the most stringent state voter identification methods with a modern poll tax, and the success that states have had in proceeding with requirements for additional documentary proof of citizenship and partisan gerrymandering. State authority in election administration continues to prevail in many federal constitutional challenges. Judicial interpretations have reinforced the theme that some areas of state election policy are essentially political questions beyond the scope of judicial interference.

The norms and values that are embedded in the current federal system that shapes election administration are not unique to elections; nor is conflict between the states and the reach of national authority. New Deal programs extended broad and new benefits for income support and health care to older Americans and very young Americans; yet the authority of the federal government to institute these programs was very controversial, even in the face of national economic catastrophe. For example, the Social Security program, as one area of what we know today as social welfare policy, established definitions of work and defined eligibility requirements in ways that initially excluded some groups of people; particularly, occupations excluded categories of labor performed extensively (if not exclusively) by African Americans and women. Even today, some groups of people are still excluded, including those who perform labor inside the home (so-called women's work) and prisoner populations. Changes occurred over time to include new populations (those with disabilities and those on Medicare) and to expand funding. Social Security policy includes an independent administrative legal process for the denial of benefits, and a host of nonprofit organizations and independent companies designed to help people access benefits or appeal benefit denials. The policy is national in scope, and is administered on a national basis, with states grouped into geographic regions. Change to address initial policy and programmatic inequities took place incrementally over decades.

Oversight in the election administration policy area looks very different. The franchise applies nationally for federal offices and questions, and within states for state and local offices and issues. Yet federal administration plays a significantly smaller role. The Election Assistance Commission is a very young agency (2002) without regulatory authority; the Federal Election Commission, though older, has a significantly limited scope; states are able to make policy decisions as long as national constitutional protections are guaranteed. And the specifics of these constitutional protections continue to shift, slowly, over time. There is no national administrative oversight authority for election functions outside the enforcement authority of the Department of Justice. Since 2013 and the decision of the US Supreme Court in *Shelby County v. Holder*, state-level policy changes that potentially limit the ability of citizens to vote are possible because federal enforcement authority under the Department of Justice has been significantly weakened. It is still possible to challenge state practices under the Voting Rights Act, but the onus is on individual voters to bring challenges.

In this environment, election officials in both local and state offices face real pressures as they work to improve the ways in which they operate elections. Highly contentious political environments that produce much change increase pressures on election administrators. Election officials can mediate some of this; but if the volume of change is significant, they become, by the nature of the institutions where they work, unable to engage in activities to mitigate effects on policy and practice that may have an impact on potential voters.

Allegations of manipulation of the election system are commonplace, and contemporary cases range from concerns about voter fraud to the security of the election system itself. In the 2018 election cycle, for example, chief election officials in Georgia and Kansas were challenged publicly for their roles in overseeing local election processes and making controversial administrative rulings while also running for state office. In Georgia, during the 2018 general election, more than 50,000 voter registrations were removed from the voter rolls under the state's "use it or lose it" approach to purging voter rolls in the administrative process. This approach—which removes voters who have not voted for a period of time, after notifications—is now in force in a handful of states, and the Ohio variation has been upheld by the Supreme Court. In Kansas, Secretary of State Kris Kobach oversaw the 2018 elections while running for governor amid investigations into allegations of mishandling of the state's online voter registration process in 2016, after his involvement in the short-lived presidential commission to investigate claims of voter fraud, the Presidential Advisory Commission on Election Integrity. Even absentee ballots have come under attack. Though touted as a matter of voter convenience, the absentee process is receiving new scrutiny since fraudulent charges were brought in North Carolina's Ninth Congressional District for illegal ballot harvesting.

The cybersecurity concerns raised in 2016 also continue to percolate. The national government has taken a voluntary leadership posture in order to provide assistance to state and local election offices with strategies and tools for threat decision and mitigation, and states and localities have become engaged, in some cases despite earlier reservations about the intrusion of federal authority into state election operations. The 2018 and 2019 election cycles were remarkably free from cybersecurity breaches; however, threats persist, and it does not appear to be possible to eliminate them. Leading cybersecurity experts believe that Russia continues to post a significant threat; misinformation and disinformation distributed through social media are perhaps a greater threat than penetration attempts to gather voter registration files or similar data, but election officials cannot rest easy (Center for Internet Security 2019). Perhaps one of the most significant concerns to date is the impact that these intrusions have had on citizen trust in election systems specifically and government more generally.

INNOVATION AS A THEORY OF CHANGE

Despite these constraints, innovations in the election administration system are occurring at perhaps the greatest rate in the history of the country. This innovation is a function of four main drivers—politics, professionalism, resources, and demands—but no one of these is either necessary or sufficient. Drilling down more deeply, a variety of components of each of these four drivers serve as catalysts to and fuel innovation (see the summary table). These include some combination of political will, information exchanges through networks, staff capacity and expertise, financial resources, visionary leadership, time, and need. Innovations are also driven by different layers of government, and the attendant components necessary for positive innovations to emerge differ accordingly. Looking across the different drivers of innovation by category or components, they are all almost equally and differently

Table Summarizing Innovation Areas and Drivers

	Areas of Innovation in Election Administration					
	Registration eligibility and access	Convenience methods of voting	Language access and outreach	Provisional ballots, counting, certification, and auditing	Equipment security and integrity	Measurement and reflection on quality of practice
Dominant Intergovernmental Actors						
National		X	X	X	X	
State	X	X	X	X	X	
Local	X	X		X		
Nongovernmental	X				X	X
Dimensions of Factors that Influence Innovation						
Politics	Leveraging fear about access and integrity	Partisan views about access	Partisanship Immigration	Bipartisanship Allowable practices Leveraging fear about access and integrity	Partisanship State and local authority and expertise	Bipartisanship

Professionalism	Networks	Networks Internal capacity	Advocacy groups Public service orientation	Capacity Highly skilled workforce	Networks Capacity Highly skilled workforce	Capacity Partner organizations Networks
Resources	Financial	Financial Visionary leadership	Financial Visionary leadership	Vendors Financial Visionary leadership	Financial Visionary leadership Time	Financial
Demands		Geography	New and expanding groups American Community Survey estimates	Checks on errors Enhancing integrity	Outdated systems Outside attacks	Public attention Crises

important. Though different combinations of actors have emerged as dominant in these various areas of the election system, one common thread is that communication across these networks remains paramount.

Politics matters. At the national level, bipartisan agreement about system fail-safes, the importance of system information, and resources have driven diffusion of some of the biggest changes we have seen across the country. HAVA's requirements for provisional ballots, statewide electronic voter registration databases, and federal funding for training have fostered positive change and have created opportunities for collaborations that are platforms for further change, the latter around technology in particular. But partisan haranguing over issues like immigration, access, integrity, fairness, and accuracy has had the opposite effect, particularly when discussions play on fear and consequently stymie what is possible. Political control is critical to the point that it brings stability, but beyond that it stifles creativity. What is allowable by rule also matters a great deal—institutions can be constructed to build in the flexibility and time needed to support innovation, or the same institutions can be constructed to limit the possibility to experiment and grow. The nimble aspects of the election administration system should be fostered. The innovations discussed here are the product of strong local design and local implementation strategies, which are a benefit of a federal approach that is relatively hands-off in terms of operational details.

Moreover, politics is about ideology. By mid-2019, judicial decisions evidenced a tightening in the political arena that seemed compressed into a relatively short period. Various decisions supported state autonomy at the same time that the nation's demographics are becoming more diverse than ever; simultaneously, some state practices that limit political participation through methods of identification or gerrymandering appear intractable and beyond federal scrutiny. Techniques that administrators choose to explore, and that will ultimately be implemented, will have to pass political muster—and this may prove very difficult. We are perhaps in a period of political backlash about electoral rules.

Professionalism matters. Information sharing through networks drives election administrators to think about their offices and issues, and to think differently about potential solutions to these problems. Structured opportunities for election administrators to share and discuss practices have proven to be particularly important for all the innovations we have examined. Training and education have also provided important opportunities for administrators to reflect about public service values and the goals of neutral competence. Leadership and ethics training helps election officials to thoughtfully build the resilience required to stand up to political pressures so they can ensure that all people who are eligible to vote can do so.

Through conferences, meetings, and training, election administrators can share essential details of innovation processes, and answer the "how?"

questions. Developing the internal capacity of election offices and their staff and honing the skills of the workforce also make it more likely that successful and positive innovation can take place. When information sharing and improved capacity are added to a focus on community outreach, partnerships, and a public service orientation, the possibilities for positive innovation are substantial. Election officials are best situated to engage in innovation when they are well educated, trained, and connected.

Resources matter. In every single case we examined, having more money dedicated to the work that election administrators do made a significant difference in the development of innovative solutions to the problems that both election administrators and voters face. In chapter 8, we draw from preliminary research that finds that, on average, election offices receive 0.5 percent of their county budgets to do the thing that is the sine qua non of democratic states: run elections. And in many jurisdictions, this figure is even lower. If resources make a difference, and if we constantly underfund election offices, it is no wonder that the professionalization of the field of election administration has lagged behind so many other aspects of public service. And it is no wonder that election administrators face the challenges that we catalog here. But resources that drive innovation are not just limited to office budgets. Human resources are also critical, most notably the effect of having visionary leaders in positions of authority (or influence) in state and local offices who can see what is possible, and who have the ability and authority to arrange incentives, rewards, and timelines to achieve these things.

The information connections that are fostered by professionalism become even more important in the face of such limited resources. Local election offices, for example, are not likely to be able to hire their way into in-house capacity regarding voting systems technology procurement, cybersecurity management, or data matching for voter registration list maintenance. State offices have a greater ability to address these issues, but they are remarkably behind the curve. Not least, the federal government will not be able to fill this capacity gap, whether through the Department of Homeland Security (DHS) or the Election Assistance Commission (EAC), and it relies on third-party resources for much of the election effort. What local election officials and chief election officials have to be able to do is network, collaborate, and learn new vocabularies to leverage the existing capacity of their technology counterparts in other areas of local and state government, and with vendors. From our research presented here, we believe that the greatest return on investment will be found in fostering systematic relationships and protocols between local election offices and other local government units and with vendors.

Demands matter. The needs that voters, candidates, and election officials have and the demands on their systems are often the original catalysts for innovation in a particular area. These demands include factors such as increased numbers of voters, a small number of voters who live across a large geographic area, the access needs of voters (e.g., language and disability), and the mandate to respond to changing legal contexts, crises, failing equipment, or even attacks on the system. Innovation is less likely when things are running perfectly—why change what works?—and thus, hardships, though challenging, set the stage for changes to make voting more accessible, accurate, and fair.

Innovation also needs room to breathe. National drivers either force states and localities to act in new or different ways when congressional or court mandates are issued, or they incentivize behavior through the offer of money for particular activities. But national-level requests without mandates or incentives are doomed to stagnate or, at best, produce insufficient results. The increase in state power compared with that of localities in the election arena as a consequence of the mandates in both the National Voter Registration Act and HAVA has a two-edged effect on election administration innovation. On one hand, there is a potential for resources to be dedicated to greater consistency, training, and capacity building to help improve administration, and this can drive innovation. On the other hand, if states do not allow latitude for local offices to try new things, local innovations that respond to local needs may be stifled. And finally, despite what happens at the national or state level, in most places in the United States the primary drivers of high-quality election processes and innovation are the local officials who work under fixed time constraints, with small (minuscule) budgets and few personnel, and who nonetheless clearly are able to develop creative solutions for problems in their election systems and subsystems.

ELECTION ADMINISTRATION, THE FEDERAL SYSTEM, AND FUTURE INNOVATION

As a nation, America made the decision to create political and related election systems characterized by divided powers across all levels of government, with safeguards to combat authoritarianism. For the most part, this means we have single-member districts with plurality voting rules. These structures create a political system with two major parties in which leadership is fragmented, gridlock is common, and change is characterized by incrementalism. Achieving political compromise to improve election administration is made even more difficult in the current environment because Republicans and Democrats alike are also sure that their opponents are both wrong and corrupt (Lewis 2019). Further, the choice was made early on that the responsibility for elections should be held primarily by states and practiced by localities, with national influence exerted when states and localities chose to systematically violate any of the basic rights of citizens. Combined with the Electoral College system, these institutional and structural choices make the US election system truly and literally unique in a global sense.

The cases of innovation illustrated in this book have occurred against this backdrop. Innovation has occurred in spite of federal constraints, but also in response to them. Some of the innovations identified in this volume have occurred as part of the administrative responses necessary to implement federal legislative requirements—for example, establishing statewide electronic voter registration databases. States have been able to develop solutions that reflect their administrative capacity and voter demographics. And many of these innovations begin, spread, and flourish because of the absence of federal legislative requirements.

One of the arguments of this book is that innovation in election administration is supported by increased professionalism of the field. This professionalism is necessary in order for election officials to navigate the complexity of the intergovernmental terrain, the increasing complexity of information technology, and stakeholder relationships both inside and outside government. Professionalization in election administration has occurred in a context of conflicting norms and values, institutional relationships that are both embedded and emerging, and increasing complexity. And it has occurred in a political environment where different branches and levels of government have played (and continue to play) very different roles.

In some forums, it has been observed that election administration may not yet be a full-throated profession, although election officials behave professionally and execute their responsibilities in a professional manner. As a common language emerges for election operations, the nature of the election administration field will be shaped by election officials' actions and responses, which will influence both the possibility and probability of innovation.

The normative argument in favor of professionalism is that it builds capacity. The dark side is that it can create adherence to professional norms that conflict with the principles of public administration in a representative democracy. The role of technological expertise should be a concern regardless. The lack of technological expertise in government as a whole, and in election administration specifically, leaves this process at the mercy of private-sector actors, and also at the mercy of technical specialists. The motives of each sector may be pure; however, wholesale outsourcing strains democratic accountability in any policy area, and only a few in the election community are equipped and authorized to digest the actual details of electronic security protocols.

In favor of professionalism, more professional development—not less— can raise the capacity of election administrators to engage more productively with other stakeholders. Cross-jurisdictional exchange is essential, both within a state and across states. So is exchange within jurisdictions between other areas of government that can exchange information on routine operating matters as well as provide resources in cases of emergency. Debates have ranged across the election administration community since 2000 about what kinds of expertise are most valuable in designing election equipment (e.g., security, transparency, access); these debates have intensified with the introduction of cybersecurity concerns and expertise of the intelligence community. The capacity of election administrators must continue to expand to accommodate these new interactions. More broadly, the very nature of election administration is embodied in democratic principles. Transparency, trust, accountability, effectiveness, and efficiency are the hallmarks of an election office. These are actually the services that an election office provides to current and future voters, through the process of counting voter preferences on candidates and issues.

Governance remains a central question. And for the future, it is worth considering—who governs the field of election administration? The array of government offices with a claim on some level of authority over election operations has expanded considerably since 2000. At the state level, the authority of state offices has grown since the advent of HAVA, particularly with respect to the technology for voter registration databases and equipment requirements and selection processes. Federal authority also has expanded since the 2016 election and the concerns raised about election cybersecurity. DHS is a relatively new and highly visible player in the election arena. Relatedly, the profile of state information officers and technology professionals has increased through their national associations, the National Association of Chief Information Officers and the National Association of State Technology Directors. And yet the role of DHS is purely advisory. State associations of local election jurisdictions have become more visible. Collaborative groups of these associations have formed to engage in the policy conversations that will shape the field.

Not least, vendors and other nongovernmental actors play a significant role across all the election administration subsystems, and also help to promote innovation. The case of the new voting system designed by Los Angeles County illustrates this point perfectly. Los Angeles County has a highly professionalized election staff of hundreds, to serve nearly 5 million registered voters. Yet even with this internal capacity, its new system would not have been possible without consultants, researchers, and vendors to develop and refine it, without the voices of voters to identify their needs, and without political actors to support the project concept with staff, time, and money. Because the system is funded by Los Angeles County (the most recent appropriation after the 2018 election was roughly $300 million), the design was a public process. Other vendors were able to watch and borrow to improve their own systems, and other jurisdictions have begun to consider how to engage in their own design process or to adopt the one developed by Los Angeles County. Whether the existing federal involvement in election administration continues as is, or whether more power is subsumed by states or the national government, the role of vendors in this work will only expand. It is true that even though voting system vendors and other election equipment vendors are private actors, in the case of government contracts, they must operate publicly within the same constraints as other bidders. However, in a few cases, vendors are starting to play the role of election official—and this should give us pause.

The role of the judiciary also continues to evolve in the election administration arena as courts decide about the essential political character of state legislative actions that affect election administration. Cases that touch on the constitutionality of processes used to draw district lines, the structure and operations of state election boards, and state election laws and administrative procedures are just the most recent. These decisions and others to come will define the space in which election administrators can operate and innovate.

Against the backdrop of all these cross pressures, local election offices continue to assume new responsibilities in the form of unfunded mandates and continue their work despite, in many cases, stagnating resources. Future innovation will depend on local capacity, and therefore on professionalism. Innovation in election administration education has been evident over the past decade, as professional associations have established linkages with other institutions of higher education to bolster credentials and legitimacy.[1]

Most recently, groups that accredit public service education have observed the significance of professionalism in the field of election administration. The Network of Schools of Public Policy, Affairs, which is the national accrediting organization for graduate programs in these fields of public service, has established an organized section on Election Administration and Leadership to develop benchmarks for the field's graduate curriculum. This provides an opportunity to build additional credentials for students entering the field and will build capacity in the field over time.

As innovation in election administration continues, some questions will be privileged over others and some voices will be accorded greater credibility than others. The debate about technology and security is a clear example; this first engaged with advocates for voters with disabilities who gained rights under HAVA for all voters to vote privately and independently. More recently, technology officers, DHS, and EAC personnel are engaged in understanding the challenges of electronic voting systems. Security expertise seems poised to overshadow many other aspects of election operations, at least in the short term.

We view election administration in the United States almost organically. It is constantly evolving, responding to external and internal stimuli, and it is healthy. The people who support it are highly skilled, well intentioned, and growing with the system. In terms of practical concerns, local offices especially seek to grow capacity generally and the technological skills associated with security and general office operations specifically. There is a contemporary narrative about election administration suggesting that it is broken beyond repair or that it needs a vast intervention from the national government. These suggestions come from both liberals and conservatives. Some focus on a need for a nationalized system to protect voting rights, while others call for more stringent protections to safeguard its integrity from fraud.

We reject all these. Heterogeneity in US elections systems both reflects our diverse history and culture and serves as a critical safeguard against systematic intrusion by so-called bad actors that nationalized systems do not have. The key problems with developing a national system today are at least threefold: (1) it is easier for bad actors to understand the nuances of centralized systems and use that to their advantage; (2) it is possible for one party to exert too much authority over processes that might advantage that party; and (3) administrative resources directed to building a national election administration infrastructure would likely come at the expense of the local function and further formalize the hollow state of elections through increased reliance on vendors. System diversity poses challenges, to be sure; but the balance of diversity is positive and allows for the potential for more innovation, not less. A single, federalized system would allow for less creativity and innovation, not more. From a comparative perspective, the importance of states in decision-making about elections cannot be overstated. Aside from times when states or localities deny citizens' rights, clear instances in which national intervention is needed, state variance serves as an enduring check on national power. Surely what happens in some states with one-party entrenched power is an exemplar of what is possible in the absence of competition.

This is not to suggest that a national presence is not needed. Indeed, the innovations discussed in this book evolved within an architecture of national laws designed to guarantee access and promote participation, no matter the local configurations. There is a need for resources that only the federal government can bring. The EAC is the best contemporary mechanism to provide national support, but it is breathtakingly underfinanced in comparison with other federal organizations that are tied to other universal and critical aspects of American public life.

Failure to fund election administration at the local level in particular highlights a dark consequence for election innovation. Funding is needed in local offices to build general capacity and for new voting systems. Federal funding may be the most viable source of funding for equipment, given the magnitude of those costs; county budgets appear able to allocate additional resources to local election offices for general operating purposes, given the paucity of current levels. We should actively consider whether we really want to underresource government to the point that elections cannot actually be effectively conducted. The quality, quantity, and capacity of American democratic functioning are at stake, and they are worth far more than we currently give them.

NOTE

1. As one example, the Election Center's national Certification in Election and Registration Administration program is linked to a graduate certificate in election administration at Auburn University, and to graduate credit in Auburn's master's in public administration program. Courses offered by the International Association of Government Officials are linked to credit toward status as a certified public manager through George Washington University.

APPENDIX A

List of US Supreme Court and Federal Court Cases

Arcia v. Detzner, 908 F. Supp. 2d. 1276 (SD Florida), 2012
Arizona v. Inter Tribal Council of Arizona, 570 US 1, 2013
Baker v. Carr, 369 US 186, 1961
Benisek v. Lamone, 138 S. Ct. 1942, 2018
Bush v. Gore, 531 US 98, 2000
Crawford v. Marion County Board of Elections, 553 US 181, 2008
Citizens United v. Federal Election Commission, 558 US 310, 2010
Gill v. Whitford, 138 S. Ct. 1916, 2018
Husted v. A. Philip Randolph Institute, 138 S. Ct. 1833, 2018
Locke v. Farrakhan, No. 03-1597, 2004
Northwest Austin Municipal Utility District No. 1 v. Holder, 557 US 193, 2009
Reynolds v. Sims, 337 US 533, 1964
Shelby County v. Holder, 570 US 529, 2013
Scott v. Schedler, Civil Action No. 2-11-00926, 2014

APPENDIX B

Major Federal Laws

Americans with Disabilities Act. Prohibits discrimination against people with disabilities in all areas of public life, including public programs and services, and all public and private places that are open to the general public.

Help America Vote Act. Passed after the 2000 presidential election to reform the voting process; established the Election Assistance Commission as an information clearinghouse, statewide electronic voter registration databases, and distributed funds to states to facilitate the transition of the nation's voting systems to electronic voting equipment.

National Voter Registration Act. Also known as "Motor Voter," requires states to offer voter registration applications through state agencies that issue drivers' licenses or provide public services, and to register applicants that use a federal voter registration form. Prohibits states from removing registered voters from the voter rolls unless certain criteria are met.

Uniformed Overseas Citizens Absentee Voting Act. Provides for and regulates absentee voting by US citizens who are active members of the uniformed military services, the Merchant Marine, and the commissioned corps of the Public Health Service and the National Oceanic and Atmospheric Administration, their eligible family members, and US citizens residing outside the United States.

Voting Rights Act of 1965, and reauthorizations. Signature civil rights legislation to address legal barriers imposed by state and local authorities that prevented African Americans from exercising their rights to register and vote as guaranteed by the US Constitution.

APPENDIX C

Methodology

We began collecting data for this book shortly after the 2012 election and continued to do so through the 2018 election season. We utilize a mixed methods design, as we do with most of our work. We believe that the best approach to understanding policy and practice is to systematically analyze data to pick up patterns, and simultaneously to use rich, descriptive information from watching and speaking with experts to augment and interpret our other findings. We are also committed to applied research that engages practical settings common to stakeholders in public service activities (e.g., Brown and Hale 2015).

Mixed methods are widely used to study networks and governance questions, and they serve as a basis for developing grounded theory. We utilize these methods here to develop our model of network innovation and to delve deeply into organizational arrangements and processes (e.g., Fredrickson and Fredrickson 2004; Miles and Huberman 1994; Provan and Milward 2000; Weimer 2012). In practical terms, this means that our qualitative data collection is purposive, and it is designed to provide context rather than statistical significance. The extensive variation in practices across the states, which are embedded in state election laws and in some cases state constitutions, works against any large-scale quantitative analysis over time; our study of changing conditions works against that as well.

Where relevant, we provide a comparative state analysis (fifty states and the District of Columbia); at other points, we describe case studies or compare cases; and at some points, we examine the complex interplay of the different levels of government across actors. Many of the data we use are from primary sources, though some are from secondary ones; we also reanalyze data that other people have collected. Our units of observation and analysis vary throughout the book.

In this appendix, we first describing our primary data collection, then follow with our secondary data. Data collection by type across each of the chapters is summarized table C.1. The most commonly used data across the book come from site visits and interviews with election officials. The election officials whose ideas and actions inform this book are key informants, who are highly engaged in the policy and practice conversations that surround election operations. They are frequent speakers at national, regional, and state conferences of election officials and of other stakeholder groups in the election systems network, and they hold various leadership positions within the network. We find these data the most useful for understanding the complex context in which innovation in election administration occurs, and thus heavily depend on these types of information. At the end of this appendix, we display the actual data tables used to support the analysis in various parts of the book.

Note that all site visits, interviews, focus groups, and surveys were done on a not-for-attribution basis. We have withheld these names and locations, but in some places, where it is obvious to which jurisdictions we refer, we name them. We also have taken the information we have collected to create composite vignettes that begin and end the book, which are used to illustrate the problems and solutions discussed in the chapters. These vignettes are written in a fictional style but are drawn from the perceptions of election administrators and experiences in state and local election offices and poll sites. Their perceptions about the future of elections, the problems that voters encounter, and the issues that they face as election administrators are central to our understanding of the innovations that have evolved to address their concerns. The perceptions of election administrators reveal the relationships and methods of interaction that support cooperation, collaboration, and governance in the innovation network, and they provide context for understanding the influence of professionalism, politics, resources, and needs that are the centerpiece of this study.

TABLE C.1 Data Types and Analysis across This Book's Chapters

	Qualitative				Quantitative		
Chapter	Site Visits	Interview	Focus Groups	Survey	Survey	Document Reviews	Secondary
1	✓	✓	✓	✓	✓		
2						✓	✓
3	✓	✓		✓	✓	✓	✓
4	✓	✓	✓	✓	✓		
5	✓	✓		✓	✓		✓
6	✓	✓				✓	✓
7	✓	✓				✓	✓
8	✓	✓				✓	✓

PRIMARY SOURCE DATA

Primary source data to support the writing of this book come from a variety of sources. These data were collected using (1) site visits to and observations of election offices, polling places, and other election-related locations; (2) focus groups with state and local election officials; (3) interviews with national, state, and local election officials, as well as researchers and advocates; (4) open-ended and close-ended surveys of state and local election officials; (5) intensive case studies; and (6) archival document reviews. Each of these data collection types is discussed below.

It should be noted that in addition to the work we do with undergraduate and graduate students and our research at the university, we are also extensively engaged in the training and certification of election officials from around the country. Our interactions with election officials through these venues have helped us to gain a more comprehensive understanding of the issues faced by practitioners at all levels of elections across the country. We would be remiss not to explain this as well.

Site Visits and Observational Data Collection

We visited state and local election offices around the country, sometimes just one of us, sometimes both, and sometimes with our students or groups of election officials. These visits took place in the Northeast, Mid-Atlantic, South, Midwest, and Western parts of the country. These visits occurred within a variety of time frames, including on Election Day, the days leading up to an election, the days following the election during certification and auditing, and during the relative "quiet" between elections. We also observed poll worker training sessions as well as public hearings convened by local boards of elections.

During these visits, we collected data using a site visit protocol. When possible, we took notes on the facilities and their operations, the people at them, the conversations we held and overheard, the procedures that people followed, their interactions, and outcroppings, or things that were out of place. We focused specifically on voter registration, mail balloting, language assistance, technology, provisional balloting, and data collection; but we also tried to be open to other things that occurred in the offices about which we had not initially planned to collect information.

We also attended scores of national, regional, and state professional meetings of election officials, and in some cases we hosted these meetings. These meetings included presentations from other researchers, advocates, and practitioners. We used the information provided at these meetings, as well as the question-and-answer and discussion periods during these meetings, to help us better understand the nuances of the problems, solutions, and innovations we observed within the election community.

Focus Groups

We conducted two sets of focus groups pertaining to mail ballots. In the first, roughly twenty volunteer participants (all local election officials) were broken into three groups for hour-long conversations about terminology regarding mail ballots; this terminology was used to develop a glossary that we used in conjunction with this and other projects. The terms provided to the groups came from earlier listening sessions that we held with election officials about how they specifically used mail with respect to voting. We then used the focus groups to determine whether common definitions could be developed across states. We found that in most cases they could not.

The second set of focus groups involved about forty election officials and focused on best practices in mail balloting. In this case, we divided election officials into three groups based upon the size of their jurisdictions, and we had them brainstorm to develop their collective opinions about best (or optimal) procedures and policies for mail balloting. Representatives from each group presented their suggestions to all the officials present in a series of feedback loops.

Interviews

Over the past four years, we conducted interviews with election officials from national, state, and local levels about their work generally and about innovation specifically. We conducted the interviews as a team using a semistructured interview protocol, with one person asking the questions and the other typing the answers and contributing as appropriate. We did not record the interviews. In most cases, the interviews took about 45 minutes, but in a few they were much lengthier. Sometimes they occurred over a meal, and sometimes in an office setting. Rarely, but in a few cases, these interviews were conducted over the telephone.

Our interview protocol included questions about voter registration, mail balloting, language assistance, technology, provisional ballots, and data. For each topic, we had a set of predetermined questions that delved into procedures, problems, changes, innovation, best practices, partnerships, information exchanges, networks, need, and resources. Depending upon the person we were interviewing, we selected the questions that were most appropriate. For example, when interviewing state officials, we did not ask questions about their procedures for voter file maintenance, as that would not have been applicable. As new or interesting topics emerged in the conversations, we allowed the experts with whom we spoke to expand on those topics, even if they were not included in the protocols. And at times we were not able to cover all the topics in the protocol.

Open-Ended Informal Surveys

Throughout the period in which we collected data for this book, we conducted informal surveys through both large and small group discussions that were less structured than focus groups. Innovations in election administration, challenges in election operations, and solutions were discussed at nearly every exchange, one way or another. The vision of future elections presented in chapter 1 is a synthesis of these conversations.

Archival Document Review

Where relevant and possible, we used information from election offices to augment our understanding of issues, challenges, and innovation in election offices. In some places, this was, for example, a copy of a training manual, a procedures poster, or a report. In each instance, we treated this as a primary source document used for illustrative purposes. In some cases, the information was provided to us by an election official, and in others the documents were publicly available, either in hard copy or on a website. These written documents provided a check on the perceptions and view of key informant election officials (Stake 1995; Yin 2002).

Case Studies

We used each of these data collection techniques to build case studies about different election issues and offices, whether at the local, state, or national level. For triangulation purposes, we tried to include all types of primary data for each election office, though this was not always possible. In addition, where available and as necessary, we augmented the information we collected through these means with newspaper and other media accounts.

SECONDARY SOURCE DATA

Secondary source data to support the writing of this book come from a variety of public sources, use different units of observation and analysis, and cover a range of years. The sources of these data are indicated in all related data tables. Below, we provide more specific information about the data used in the Election Administration Professionalism Index.

The Election Administration Professionalism Index

To measure professionalism, we compiled information on three preliminary professionalism proxies, and we use these to develop an equally weighted additive index, as follows. The first component is a count of nationally certified election administrators by state, which has been collapsed into an ordinal variable using quartiles. The second component is a state-level indicator of whether election officials are on the boards of key national organizations, including the Election Center, the Democracy Fund, the Bipartisan Policy Center, the Election Assistance Commission, the National Association of State Election Directors, and the National Association of Secretaries of State. In the case of the National Association of Secretaries of State, the measure reflects designation as the chair and co-chair of its Elections Committee. Our approach follows research finding that board membership and service on key committees of local, state, and national organizations are linked to professionalism; the development of new institutional architecture; and innovation across a variety of substantive areas in public service, including criminal justice (Hale 2011), e-government policy (Tolbert, Mossberger, and McNeal 2008), and financial administration (Mintrom and Vergari 1998). The third component captures whether state training programs in election administration are mandated and is generated by Katy Owens Hubler and Wendy Underhill (2018) through their work for the National Conference of State Legislatures.

Data on each component were captured for the fifty states and the District of Columbia. Where applicable, the data were aggregated at the state level. Each component was then compared with the others and equally weighted to create the additive election administrative professionalism index. We then validate the index using the Pew and Stewart Election Performance Index. The correlation between professionalism and the Election Performance Index is fairly strong ($r = .469$; $p < .001$).

DATA TABLES

Several chapters refer to statistical tests. These are captured in tables C.2 through C.13. Using data from many sources at the state level, we display the percentage of states in each relevant category.

We examine the relationship between various topics and a variety of proxies for the major components of innovation: politics, networks, resources, and need. To measure politics, we examine legislative control for 2016 (Republican, Democratic, and split). To measure networks, we use our Professionalism Index. For resources, we created a 3-point ordered scale using the 2010 US Census's median household income. And for need, we created another 3-point ordered scale based on the 2016 turnout figures. We then generated

TABLE C.2 Online Voter Registration Use and Legislation

Level of Use	Percentage of States by Category		Innovation Relationships			
			Politics	Networks	Resources	Need
OVR use in states	Yes	62.7%				
	Updates	5.9%	0.257	0.134	0.256	0.020
	Not required	3.9%				
	Not applicable	27.5%				
OVR legislation passed in states	Yes	37.3%				
	No	23.5%	0.32	0.408*	0.319	0.102
	Not applicable	25.5%				
	No response	13.7%				

Note: $N = 51$; *** = statistically significant at 99 percent confidence; ** = statistically significant at 95 percent confidence; * = statistically significant at 90 percent confidence. Politics: test shown is Cramer's V. Networks: test shown is Kendall's Tau-b using a two-tailed test. Resources: test shown is Kendall's Tau-b using a two-tailed test. Need: test shown is Kendall's Tau-b using a two-tailed test.

chi-squares for each pair (four per variable) and looked at the chi-square extensions, for the nominal variables using a Cramer's V and for the ordinal variables the Kendall's Tau-b (a two-tailed test). We note significance on the tables at 90 percent, 95 percent, and 99 percent significance. The resource and need proxies were not statistically significant in any of the analyses.

Each analysis is based on the fifty states plus the District of Columbia; states that did not respond to the Pew requests for information were dropped from the bivariate analysis; these states vary by measurement item.

The book's chapters also refer to descriptive presentations and data analyses that are a bit unwieldy to display in the body of the book. For chapter 1, the complexity of the election administration environment is illustrated further with table C.14, which presents a typology of national third-party organizations active in the election administration environment. This illustration depicts additional dimensions of the intricate political environment that election officials navigate, and helps frame many of major administrative categories that characterize this field.

In support of the discussion in chapter 5, about the complexities of language assistance, data tables are provided to display census data supporting the Voting Rights Act of 1965 (VRA) Section 203 language coverage by state (table C.15), a count of VRA-covered counties by language group and subgroup (table C.16), and county-level language coverage for California counties (table C.17).

For chapter 7, the broad principles that guide the voluntary federal guidelines for voting systems are provided in table C.18. The array of organizations

TABLE C.3 Requirements to Access Online Voter Registration Systems

Requirement	Percentage of States by Category		Innovation Relationships			
			Politics	Networks	Resources	Need
Date of birth required to access system	Yes	58.8%	0.288	0.255	0.296	0.061
	No	1.9%				
	Not applicable	25.5%				
	No response	13.7%				
Driver's license or state identification required to access system	Yes	50.9%	0.279	0.232	0.265	−0.056
	No	9.8%				
	Not applicable	25.5%				
	No response	13.7%				
Last four SSN required to access system	Yes	19.6%	0.381*	0.036	0.253	−0.100
	No	41.2%				
	Not applicable	25.5%				
	No response	13.7%				
Full SSN required to access system	Yes	5.9%	0.263	0.260	0.250	−0.013
	No	54.9%				
	Not applicable	25.5%				
	No response	13.7%				

Note: SSN = Social Security Number. $N = 51$; *** = statistically significant at 99 percent confidence; ** = statistically significant at 95 percent confidence; * = statistically significant at 90 percent confidence. Politics: test shown is Cramer's V. Networks: test shown is Kendall's Tau-b using a two-tailed test. Resources: test shown is Kendall's Tau-b using a two-tailed test. Need: test shown is Kendall's Tau-b using a two-tailed test.

engaged in election cybersecurity are displayed in table C.19, along with their missions, organizational forms, and primary audience for their efforts.

To support further understanding of the discussion about measurement in chapter 8, table C.20 provides a chronology of contemporary efforts that have been initiated in the modern era of election administration to conceptualize and measure election administration activities.

TABLE C.4 Online Voter Registration Development and Housing

OVR configuration	Percentage of States by Category		Innovation Relationships			
			Politics	Networks	Resources	Need
OVR developed solely by state IT staff	Yes	33.3%	0.293	0.193	0.224	0.034
	No	27.5%				
	Not applicable	25.5%				
	No response	13.7%				
OVR developed solely by vendor	Yes	17.6%	0.296	0.192	0.296	0.031
	No	41.1%				
	Not applicable	25.5%				
	No response	13.7%				
OVR developed by state IT staff and vendor	Yes	9.8%	0.412**	0.215*	0.326	−0.009
	No	51.0%				
	Not applicable	25.5%				
	No response	13.7%				
OVR pilot launch conducted	Yes	31.4%	0.371*	0.170	0.275	0.067
	No	29.4%				
	Not applicable	25.5%				
	No response	13.7%				
OVR resides with CEO	Yes	45.1%	0.342	0.212	0.251	0.016
	No	15.7%				
	Not applicable	25.5%				
	No response	13.7%				
OVR resides with DMV	Yes	2.0%	0.274	0.220	0.313	0.019
	No	58.8%				
	Not applicable	25.5%				
	No response	13.7%				
OVR resides with state IT office	Yes	9.8%	0.300	0.197*	0.326	0.026
	No	51.0%				
	Not applicable	25.5%				
	No response	13.7%				
OVR resides with vendor	Yes	7.8%	0.426**	0.229	0.333	0.061
	No	52.9%				
	Not applicable	25.5%				
	No response	13.7%				

Note: IT = information technology. $N = 51$; *** = statistically significant at 99 percent confidence; ** = statistically significant at 95 percent confidence; * = statistically significant at 90 percent confidence. Politics: test shown is Cramer's V. Networks: test shown is Kendall's Tau-b using a two-tailed test. Resources: test shown is Kendall's Tau-b using a two-tailed test. Need: test shown is Kendall's Tau-b using a two-tailed test.

TABLE C.5 Features of Online Voter Registration Systems

Feature	Percentage of States by Category		Innovation Relationships			
			Politics	Networks	Resources	Need
Confirmation screen	Yes	56.9%				
	No	3.9%	0.379**	0.233	0.332	−0.018
	Not applicable	25.5%				
	No response	13.7%				
Confirmation number	Yes	31.4%				
	No	29.4%	0.286	0.208	0.277	0.034
	Not applicable	25.5%				
	No response	13.7%				
Confirmation email when submitted	Yes	35.3%				
	No	25.5%	0.298	0.047	0.278	−0.058
	Not applicable	25.5%				
	No response	13.7%				
Confirmation email when registration active	Yes	7.8%				
	No	52.9%	0.265	0.209	0.377	−0.011
	Not applicable	25.5%				
	No response	13.7%				
Mobile phone optimized	Yes	39.2%				
	No	21.6%	0.359*	0.235	0.296	0.041
	Not applicable	25.5%				
	No response	13.7%				
Supports multiple languages	Yes	25.5%				
	No	35.3%	0.455***	0.295	0.316	0.031
	Not applicable	25.5%				
	No response	13.7%				
Collects email addresses	Yes	52.9%				
	No	7.8%	0.265	0.285	0.300	0.089
	Not applicable	25.5%				
	No response	13.7%				
Email is public record	Yes	19.6%				
	No	41.2%	0.327	0.185	0.174	0.064
	Not applicable	25.5%				
	No response	13.7%				

Note: $N = 51$; *** = statistically significant at 99 percent confidence; ** = statistically significant at 95 percent confidence; * = statistically significant at 90 percent confidence. Politics: test shown is Cramer's V. Networks: test shown is Kendall's Tau-b using a two-tailed test. Resources: test shown is Kendall's Tau-b using a two-tailed test. Need: test shown is Kendall's Tau-b using a two-tailed test.

TABLE C.6 Processing Online Voter Registration Applications and Updates

Processing Step	Percentage of States by Category		Innovation Relationships			
			Politics	Networks	Resources	Need
Election official reviews all applications	Yes	56.9%	0.257	0.259	0.332	0.095
	No	3.9%				
	Not applicable	25.5%				
	No response	13.7%				
Election official reviews only flagged applications	Yes	5.9%	0.263	0.209	0.281	−0.086
	No	54.9%				
	Not applicable	25.5%				
	No response	13.7%				
Can differentiate between OVR and paper applications	Yes	52.9%	0.279	0.292	0.373	0.124
	No	7.8%				
	Not applicable	25.5%				
	No response	13.7%				
Can differentiate between new and updated applications	Yes	45.1%	0.284	0.192	0.306	0.011
	No	15.7%				
	Not applicable	25.5%				
	No response	13.7%				
Registration transmitted in real time to LEO	Yes	27.5%	0.337	0.240	0.393	0.097
	No	33.3%				
	Not applicable	25.5%				
	No response	13.7%				
Registration transmitted to LEO in batches	Yes	27.5%	0.353*	0.134	0.150	0.002
	No	31.4%				
	Not applicable	25.5%				
	No response	15.7%				
Applicant notified in real time of existing registration	Yes	21.6%	0.389**	0.294	0.278	0.095
	No	39.2%				
	Not applicable	25.5%				
	No response	13.7%				
Can process without DMV record	Yes	19.6%	0.285	0.178	0.360	0.064
	No	41.2%				
	Not applicable	25.5%				
	No response	13.7%				

(*continued*)

TABLE C.6 (*continued*)

Processing Step	Percentage of States by Category		Innovation Relationships			
			Politics	Networks	Resources	Need
DMV record automatically updated with voter information	Yes	7.8%	0.279	0.257	0.373	−0.021
	No	52.9%				
	Not applicable	25.5%				
	No response	13.7%				
Address updated at DMV to match voter record	Yes	9.8%	0.293	0.171	0.328	−0.045
	No	49.0%				
	Not applicable	25.5%				
	No response	13.7%				
Requires some paper printing by state	Yes	7.8%	0.276	0.255	0.189	−0.045
	No	51.0%				
	Not applicable	25.5%				
	No response	15.7%				
Requires some manual data entry	Yes	19.6%	0.360*	0.233	0.293	0.096
	No	41.2%				
	Not applicable	25.5%				
	No response	13.7%				

Note: OVR = online voter registration; LEO = local election official; DMV = Department of Motor Vehicles. $N = 51$; *** = statistically significant at 99 percent confidence; ** = statistically significant at 95 percent confidence; * = statistically significant at 90 percent confidence. Politics: test shown is Cramer's V. Networks: test shown is Kendall's Tau-b using a two-tailed test. Resources: test shown is Kendall's Tau-b using a two-tailed test. Need: test shown is Kendall's Tau-b using a two-tailed test.

TABLE C.7 Electronic Pollbook Use

Use	Percentage of States by Category		Innovation Relationships			
			Politics	Networks	Resources	Need
State uses EPB	Yes	50.9%				
	No	37.3%	0.363	0.156	−0.118	−0.245
	No response	11.8%				
EPBs are used statewide	Yes	11.8%				
	No	43.1%	0.357*	0.134	−0.013	−0.153
	Not applicable	33.3%				
	No response	11.8%				

Note: EPB = electronic pollbook. $N = 51$; *** = statistically significant at 99 percent confidence; ** = statistically significant at 95 percent confidence; * = statistically significant at 90 percent confidence. Politics: test shown is Cramer's V. Networks: test shown is Kendall's Tau-b using a two-tailed test. Resources: test shown is Kendall's Tau-b using a two-tailed test. Need: test shown is Kendall's Tau-b using a two-tailed test.

TABLE C.8 Electronic Pollbook Legislative Requirements

Requirement	Percentage of States by Category		Innovation Relationships			
			Politics	Networks	Resources	Need
Legislation passed on EPBs	Yes	25.5%				
	No	25.5%	0.325	0.289	0.025	−0.085
	Not applicable	35.3%				
	No response	15.7%				
State certification requirements	Yes	15.7%				
	No	29.4%	0.251	0.206	−0.098	−0.193
	Not applicable	37.3%				
	No response	17.6%				

Note: EPB = electronic pollbook. $N = 51$; *** = statistically significant at 99 percent confidence; ** = statistically significant at 95 percent confidence; * = statistically significant at 90 percent confidence. Politics: test shown is Cramer's V. Networks: test shown is Kendall's Tau-b using a two-tailed test. Resources: test shown is Kendall's Tau-b using a two-tailed test. Need: test shown is Kendall's Tau-b using a two-tailed test.

TABLE C.9 Electronic Pollbook Development and Maintenance

Aspect	Percentage of States by Category		Innovation Relationships			
			Politics	Networks	Resources	Need
System designed by the state	Yes	5.9%	0.311	0.171	−0.046	−0.160
	Varies	2.0%				
	No	39.2%				
	Not applicable	37.3%				
	No response	17.6%				
System designed by vendor	Yes	29.4%	0.233	0.058	−0.146	−0.281
	Varies	2.0%				
	No	13.7%				
	Not applicable	37.3%				
	No response	17.6%				
System designed jointly between state and vendor	Yes	9.8%	0.248	0.236	−0.137	−0.099
	No	35.3%				
	Not applicable	37.3%				
	No response	17.6%				
Hardware proprietary to vendor	Yes	9.8%	0.251	0.069	−0.160	−0.198
	Varies	19.%				
	No	15.7%				
	Not applicable	35.3%				
	No response	19.6%				
Hardware off the shelf	Yes	13.7%	0.250	0.100	−0.124	−0.151
	Varies	19.6%				
	No	11.8%				
	Not applicable	37.3%				
	No response	17.6%				
Software proprietary to vendor	Yes	27.5%	0.254	0.101	−0.082	−0.232
	Varies	7.8%				
	No	9.8%				
	Not applicable	37.3%				
	No response	17.6%				
Software off the shelf	Yes	0.0%	0.238	0.186	−0.107	−0.152
	Varies	7.8%				
	No	35.3%				
	Not applicable	37.3%				
	No response	19.6%				

(*continued*)

TABLE C.9 (*continued*)

Software proprietary to state	Yes	9.8%				
	No	35.3%	0.311	0.185	−0.137	−0.152
	Not applicable	37.3%				
	No response	17.6%				
Maintenance done in house by government	Yes	25.5%				
	Varies	0.0%	0.262	0.075	−0.038	−0.030
	No	0.0%				
	Not applicable	56.9%				
	No response	17.6%				
Maintenance done by vendor	Yes	17.6%				
	Varies	3.9%	0.174	0.225	−0.059	−0.164
	No	0.0%				
	Not applicable	60.8%				
	No response	17.6%				

Note: $N = 51$; *** = statistically significant at 99 percent confidence; ** = statistically significant at 95 percent confidence; * = statistically significant at 90 percent confidence. Politics: test shown is Cramer's V. Networks: test shown is Kendall's Tau-b using a two-tailed test. Resources: test shown is Kendall's Tau-b using a two-tailed test. Need: test shown is Kendall's Tau-b using a two-tailed test.

TABLE C.10 Electronic Pollbook Features

Feature	Percentage of States by Category		Innovation Relationships			
			Politics	Networks	Resources	Need
Check	Yes	41.2%				
voters in	Varies	3.9%	0.262	0.165	−0.089	−0.222
	No	0.0%				
	Not applicable	37.3%				
	No response	17.6%				
Verify	Yes	39.2%				
whether vote	Varies	2.0%	0.259	0.184	−0.054	−0.191
was cast	No	3.9%				
	Not applicable	37.3%				
	No response	17.6%				
Ballot	Yes	17.6%				
production	Varies	3.9%	0.235	0.177	−0.169	−0.200
	No	23.5%				
	Not applicable	37.3%				
	No response	17.6%				
Verify ballot	Yes	31.4%				
totals	Varies	3.9%	0.218	0.169	−0.156	−0.177
	No	9.8%				
	Not applicable	37.3%				
	No response	17.6%				
Same-day	Yes	11.8%				
registration	Varies	2.0%	0.260	0.246	0.067	−0.048
	No	33.3%				
	Not applicable	35.3%				
	No response	17.6%				

Note: $N = 51$; *** = statistically significant at 99 percent confidence; ** = statistically significant at 95 percent confidence; * = statistically significant at 90 percent confidence. Politics: test shown is Cramer's V. Networks: test shown is Kendall's Tau-b using a two-tailed test. Resources: test shown is Kendall's Tau-b using a two-tailed test. Need: test shown is Kendall's Tau-b using a two-tailed test.

TABLE C.11 Electronic Pollbook Processes and Security Features

Process	Percentage of States by Category		Innovation Relationships			
			Politics	Networks	Resources	Need
Testing by state before each election	Yes	0.0%	0.267	0.233	−0.098	−0.192
	Varies	17.0%				
	No	27.5%				
	Not applicable	37.3%				
	No response	17.6%				
Testing left up to local offices	Yes	0.0%	0.267	0.069	−0.119	−0.161
	Varies	27.5%				
	No	17.6%				
	Not applicable	37.3%				
	No response	17.6%				
Audit by state after each election	Yes	0.0%	0.241	0.141	−0.030	−0.197
	Varies	9.8%				
	No	33.3%				
	Not applicable	37.3%				
	No response	19.6%				
Audit by state occasionally	Yes	0.0%	0.252	0.184	−0.127	−0.218
	Varies	3.9%				
	No	39.2%				
	Not applicable	37.3%				
	No response	19.6%				
Audits left up to local agency	Yes	0.0%	0.259	0.098	−0.206	−0.228
	Varies	25.5%				
	No	17.6%				
	Not applicable	37.3%				
	No Response	19.6%				
Backup EPBs on election day	Yes	17.6%	0.280	0.155	−0.122	−0.158
	Varies	5.9%				
	No	21.6%				
	Not applicable	37.3%				
	No response	17.6%				
Backup paper rolls on election day	Yes	33.3%	0.332	0.088	−0.117	−0.156
	Varies	5.9%				
	No	5.9%				
	Not applicable	37.3%				
	No response	17.6%				

(*continued*)

TABLE C.11 (*continued*)

Process	Percentage of States by Category		Innovation Relationships			
			Politics	Networks	Resources	Need
Data transmitted from county directly to state	Yes	9.8%	0.269	0.232	−0.060	−0.097
	Varies	3.9%				
	No	27.5%				
	Not applicable	37.3%				
	No response	21.6%				
Data transmitted between counties and to state	Yes	1.9%	0.409**	0.186	−0.112	−0.133
	Varies	3.9%				
	No	35.3%				
	Not applicable	37.3%				
	No response	21.6%				
Data transmitted only between EPBs within local agency	Yes	25.5%	0.258	0.063	−0.167	−0.240
	Varies	3.9%				
	No	11.8%				
	Not applicable	37.3%				
	No response	21.6%				
Written security protocol	Yes	31.4%	0.360*	0.221	−0.090	−0.058
	No	13.7%				
	Not applicable	37.3%				
	No response	17.6%				

Note: $N = 51$; *** = statistically significant at 99 percent confidence; ** = statistically significant at 95 percent confidence; * = statistically significant at 90 percent confidence. Politics: test shown is Cramer's V. Networks: test shown is Kendall's Tau-b using a two-tailed test. Resources: test shown is Kendall's Tau-b using a two-tailed test. Need: test shown is Kendall's Tau-b using a two-tailed test.

TABLE C.12 Electronic Pollbook Data Collected or Held about Voters

Type of Data	Percentage of States by Category		Innovation Relationships			
			Politics	Networks	Resources	Need
Name of voter	Yes	41.2%				
	Varies	3.9%	0.262	0.165	−0.089	−0.222
	No	0.0%				
	Not applicable	37.3%				
	No response	17.6%				
Whether ballot was cast	Yes	41.2%	0.262	0.165	−0.090	−0.222
	Varies	3.9%				
	No	0.0%				
	Not applicable	37.3%				
	No response	17.6%				
Date of birth	Yes	35.3%	0.221	0.163	−0.151	−0.205
	Varies	5.9%				
	No	3.9%				
	Not applicable	37.3%				
	No response	17.6%				
Last four digits of SSN	Yes	11.8%	0.220	0.122	−0.146	−0.231
	Varies	3.9%				
	No	29.4%				
	Not applicable	37.3%				
	No response	17.6%				
Full SSN	Yes	2.0%	0.401**	0.197	−0.107	−0.128
	Varies	3.9%				
	No	39.2%				
	Not applicable	37.3%				
	No response	17.6%				
Driver's license or State identification	Yes	25.5%	0.224	0.189	−0.098	−0.146
	Varies	3.9%				
	No	15.7%				
	Not applicable	37.3%				
	No response	17.6%				
Address	Yes	41.2%	0.262	0.165	−0.089	−0.222
	Varies	3.9%				
	No	0.0%				
	Not applicable	37.3%				
	No response	17.6%				

(*continued*)

TABLE C.12 (*continued*)

Type of Data	Percentage of States by Category		Innovation Relationships			
			Politics	Networks	Resources	Need
Email address	Yes	7.8%	0.271	0.126	−0.096	−0.179
	Varies	3.9%				
	No	33.3%				
	Not applicable	37.3%				
	No response	17.6%				
Absentee ballot / early voting status	Yes	33.3%	0.235	0.203	−0.030	−0.122
	Varies	3.9%				
	No	7.8%				
	Not applicable	37.3%				
	No response	17.6%				
Electronic signature	Yes	19.6%	0.229	0.123	−0.165	−0.255
	Varies	3.9%				
	No	21.6%				
	Not applicable	37.3%				
	No response	17.6%				
Polling place location	Yes	33.3%	0.239	0.106	−0.124	−0.240
	Varies	7.8%				
	No	3.9%				
	Not applicable	37.3%				
	No response	17.6%				
Party identification	Yes	9.8%	0.293	0.231	−0.111	−0.137
	Varies	5.9%				
	No	29.4%				
	Not applicable	37.3%				
	No response	17.6%				
Time of arrival or vote cast	Yes	23.5%	0.236	0.209	−0.101	−0.091
	Varies	3.9%				
	No	17.6%				
	Not applicable	37.3%				
	No response	17.6%				
Type of ballot issued	Yes	31.4%	0.239	0.190	−0.159	−0.177
	Varies	3.9%				
	No	9.8%				
	Not applicable	37.3%				
	No response	17.6%				

(*continued*)

TABLE C.12 (*continued*)

Type of Data	Percentage of States by Category		Innovation Relationships			
			Politics	Networks	Resources	Need
Voter	Yes	35.3%	0.275	0.193	−0.126	−0.153
Eligibility	Varies	3.9%				
	No	5.9%				
	Not applicable	37.3%				
	No response	17.6%				
Voter phone	Yes	9.8%	0.218	0.130	−0.151	−0.121
number	Varies	3.9%				
	No	31.4%				
	Not applicable	37.3%				
	No response	17.6%				
Voting history	Yes	3.9%	0.224	0.150	−0.202	−0.155
	Varies	3.9%				
	No	37.3%				
	Not applicable	37.3%				
	No response	17.6%				

Note: SSN = Social Security Number. $N = 51$; *** = statistically significant at 99 percent confidence; ** = statistically significant at 95 percent confidence; * = statistically significant at 90 percent confidence. Politics: test shown is Cramer's V. Networks: test shown is Kendall's Tau-b using a two-tailed test. Resources: test shown is Kendall's Tau-b using a two-tailed test. Need: test shown is Kendall's Tau-b using a two-tailed test.

TABLE C.13 Convenience Voting and Innovation Relationships

Aspect	Percentage of States by Category		Innovation Relationships			
			Politics	Networks	Resources	Need
Any kind of VBM allowance	Any	41.2%	0.261	0.556	0.125	0.078
	None	58.8%				(0.429***)
VBM by type	All elections and jurisdictions	5.9%				
	Certain elections, all jurisdictions	15.7%	0.301	0.404***	0.235	0.181 (0.323*)
	Certain elections, certain jurisdictions	19.6%				
	None	58.8%				

Note: VBM = voting by mail. N = 51. Numbers in parentheses indicate the second proxy measure for need, a scale accounting for persons per square mile. *** = statistically significant at 99 percent confidence; ** = statistically significant at 95 percent confidence; * = statistically significant at 90 percent confidence. Politics: test shown Cramer's V; Networks: test shown is Cramer's V. Resources: test shown is Cramer's V. Need: test shown is Cramer's V.

TABLE C.14 Typology of National Third-Party Groups That Are Influential in Election Administration

Identity Groups	Professional Associations	Philanthropy and Research	Academic Institutions
American Association of People with Disabilities	National Association of Election Officials/ Election Center	American Civil Liberties Union	Auburn University Election Initiative
Asian American Legal Defense and Education Fund	National Association of Secretaries of State	Bipartisan Policy Center	Ball State University Bowen Center for Public Affairs Voting System Technology Oversight Program
Association of Community Organizations for Reform	National Association of State Election Directors	Brennan Center for Justice	Caltech/MIT Voting Technology Project
Advancement Project	National Conference of State Legislatures	Center for Election Innovation and Research	College of William & Mary Election Law Program
League of Women Voters	Council of State Governments	Common Cause	Harvard University Belfer Center
Mexican American Legal Defense and Education Fund	International Association of Government Officials	Democracy Fund	MIT Election Data and Science Lab
National Association for the Advancement of Colored People	Various State Associations	Demos	The Ohio State University Moritz School of Law
		Fair Elections Legal Network	University of California at Berkeley
National Disabilities Rights Network		Fair Vote	University of Florida United States Elections Project
Project Vote		International Foundation for Electoral Systems	
Verified Voting		Pew Charitable Trusts	University of Minnesota Humphrey School Program for Excellence in Election Administration
			Yale University

TABLE C.15 VRA Language Coverage by Language and Political Subdivision, by Subdivision and State, 2002, 2011, and 2016

State	Language Group	Subdivision 2002	Subdivision 2011	Subdivision 2016	Total 2002	Total 2011	Total 2016
Alaska	American Indian	27	11	19			
	Asian American	1	2	2	14	9	15
	Spanish Heritage	0	1	1			
Arizona	American Indian	16	14	6			
	Asian American	0	0	0	12	10	10
	Spanish Heritage	6	4	4			
California*	American Indian	3	0	2			
	Asian American	15	22	21	25	27	27
	Spanish Heritage*	25	27	26			
Colorado	American Indian	4	0	2			
	Asian American	0	0	0	10	3	6
	Spanish Heritage	8	3	4			
Connecticut	American Indian	0	0	1			
	Asian American	0	0	0	7	9	10
	Spanish Heritage	7	9	9			
Florida*	American Indian	3	0	1			
	Asian American	0	0	0	10	10	13
	Spanish Heritage	8	10	9			
Georgia	American Indian	0	0	0			
	Asian American	0	0	0	0	0	1
	Spanish Heritage	0	0	1			
Hawaii	American Indian	0	0	0			
	Asian American	4	4	2	2	2	1
	Spanish Heritage	0	0	0			
Idaho	American Indian	0	0	0			
	Asian American	5	0	0	5	0	1
	Spanish Heritage	0	0	1			
Illinois	American Indian	0	0	0			
	Asian American	1	2	2	2	4	3
	Spanish Heritage	2	4	3			
Iowa	American Indian	0	0	0			
	Asian American	0	0	1	0	0	2
	Spanish Heritage	0	0	1			
Kansas	American Indian	0	0	0			
	Asian American	0	0	0	6	4	5
	Spanish Heritage	6	4	5			
Louisiana	American Indian	1	0	0			
	Asian American	0	0	0	1	0	0
	Spanish Heritage	0	0	0			
Maryland	American Indian	0	0	0			
	Asian American	0	0	0	1	1	1
	Spanish Heritage	1	1	1			

(continued)

TABLE C.15 (*continued*)

State	Language Group	Subdivision			Total		
		2002	2011	2016	2002	2011	2016
Massachusetts	American Indian	0	0	0			
	Asian American	0	1	3	6	12	12
	Spanish Heritage	6	11	10			
Michigan	American Indian	0	0	0			
	Asian American	0	1	1	1	3	3
	Spanish Heritage	1	2	2			
Mississippi	American Indian	9	10	10			
	Asian American	0	0	0	9	10	10
	Spanish Heritage	0	0	0			
Montana	American Indian	2	0	0			
	Asian American	0	0	0	2	0	0
	Spanish Heritage	0	0	0			
Nebraska	American Indian	1	0	0			
	Asian American	0	0	0	2	3	3
	Spanish Heritage	1	3	3			
Nevada	American Indian	6	0	0			
	Asian American	0	1	1	6	1	1
	Spanish Heritage	1	1	1			
New Jersey	American Indian	0	0	0			
	Asian American	0	1	2	7	8	8
	Spanish Heritage	7	8	8			
New Mexico	American Indian	17	15	12			
	Asian American	0	0	0	26	22	20
	Spanish Heritage	21	16	12			
New York	American Indian	0	0	0			
	Asian American	4	5	5	7	7	7
	Spanish Heritage	7	7	7			
North Dakota	American Indian	2	0	0			
	Asian American	0	0	0	2	0	0
	Spanish Heritage	0	0	0			
Oklahoma	American Indian	0	0	0			
	Asian American	0	0	0	2	0	1
	Spanish Heritage	2	0	1			
Oregon	American Indian	1	0	0			
	Asian American	0	0	0	1	0	0
	Spanish Heritage	0	0	0			
Pennsylvania	American Indian	0	0	0			
	Asian American	0	0	0	1	3	3
	Spanish Heritage	1	3	3			
Rhode Island	American Indian	0	0	0			
	Asian American	0	0	0	2	3	3
	Spanish Heritage	2	3	3			

(*continued*)

TABLE C.15 (*continued*)

State	Language Group	Subdivision			Total		
		2002	2011	2016	2002	2011	2016
South Dakota	American Indian	19	0	0			
	Asian American	0	0	0	18	0	0
	Spanish Heritage	0	0	0			
Texas*	American Indian	2	2	2			
	Asian American	1	2	3	104	89	88
	Spanish Heritage*	104	89	88			
Utah	American Indian	2	1	2			
	Asian American	0	0	0	1	2	1
	Spanish Heritage	0	1	0			
Virginia	American Indian	0	0	0			
	Asian American	0	0	1	0	1	1
	Spanish Heritage	0	1	1			
Washington	American Indian	0	0	0			
	Asian American	1	2	2	4	4	4
	Spanish Heritage	3	3	3			
Wisconsin	American Indian	0	0	0			
	Asian American	0	0	0	0	1	3
	Spanish Heritage	0	1	3			
Totals	American Indian	115	53	57			
	Asian American	32	43	46	296	248	263
	Spanish Heritage	217	212	219			

Source: US Census Bureau (2016), "Voting Rights Determination File," www.census.gov/rdo/data/voting_rights_determination_file.html.

* Denotes state coverage.

Note: Alaskan Native Languages, though a covered category, are not included in this table.

TABLE C.16 Count of VRA-Covered Counties by Bilingual Group and Subgroup, 2002, 2011, and 2016

Group	Subgroup	County, 2002	Total, 2002	County, 2011	Total, 2011	County, 2016	Total, 2016
American	Navajo	13	121	12 (11)	42	11	57
Indian	Pueblo	13	(104)	12 (10)		3	(38)
	Hopi	-		1 (2)		0	
	Yuma	2		3 (4)		0	
	Tohono	-		-		0	
	O'Odham	3		3		0	
	Yaqui	1		10 (1)		0	
	Choctaw	9		1 (10)		10	
	Kickapoo	-				0	
Asian	Filipino	6	27	9	43	8	45
American	Chinese	12		16		18	
	Vietnamese	4		7		9	
	Asian Indian	0		3		3	
	Japanese	2		2		0	
	Korean	3		4		4	
	Bangladeshi	0		1		1	
	Not specified	0		1		0	
Alaskan	Yup'ik	0	17	4	11	9	19
Natives	Inupiat	0		5		6	
	Alaskan	0		-		-	
	Athabascan	5		1		3	
	Not specified	1		1		0	
Spanish Heritage	Not specified	220	220	215 (214)	215	217	217
Total		368	368	310	310	319	319

Sources: US Bureau of the Census, Department of Commerce (2011), *Voting Rights Act Amendments of 2006, Determinations Under Section 302, Federal Register* 76, no. 198 (October 13, 2011) and 2017 ACS Estimates.

Note: Numbers in parentheses indicate the total without Alaskan Native Languages.

TABLE C.17 Comparison of California Language Coverage, VRA Section 203 versus California Elections Code 14201, 2018 Election

Coverage Type	Languages	Number of Counties 203	Number of Counties 14201	Number of Precincts (14201 only)
No coverage		2		
203 or 14201	American Indian	2	0	0
	Cambodian/Khmer	1	6	77
	Chinese	9	9	312
	Filipino	4	22	1,069
	Korean	2	14	366
	Hispanic or Spanish	26	30	3,552
	Vietnamese	5	11	399
14201 only	Arabic	NA	1	180
	Armenian	NA	1	2,139
	Bengali	NA	1	5
	Hmong	NA	5	373
	Panjabi	NA	8	794
	Persian	NA	2	1,388
	Syriac	NA	1	55
Overall		49 (duplicated)	111 (duplicated)	
	14+ languages*	58 counties		10,709

Source: Reyes (2017).

* Some of these are language groups with more than one dialect requiring different sets of materials.

Note: NA = not applicable.

TABLE C.18 Principles and Concepts of Voluntary Voting System Guidelines 2.0

Item	Principle	Concept for Systems/Processes
1	High-quality design	Designed to accurately, completely, and robustly carry out functions
2	High-quality implementation	Implemented using high-quality best practices
3	Transparency	Designed to provide transparency
4	Interoperability	Supports interoperability in its interfaces to external systems and internal components, its data, and its peripherals.
5	Equivalent and consistent voter access	Access and use regardless of ability, without discrimination.
6	Voter privacy	Mark, verify, and cast ballot privately and independently
7	Marked, verified, and cast as intended	Ballots and vote selections presented in a perceivable, operable, and understandable way; can be marked, verified, and cast by all voters
8	Robust, safe, usable, and accessible	Voting system and voting processes provide a robust, safe, usable, and accessible experience
9	Auditable	Auditable and enables evidence-based decisions
10	Ballot secrecy	Protects the secrecy of voters' ballot selections
11	Access control	Authentication of administrators, users, devices, and services before granting access to sensitive functions
12	Physical security	Prevents or detects attempts to tamper with voting system hardware
13	Data protection	Protects sensitive data from unauthorized access, modification, or deletion
14	System integrity	Unimpaired performance, free from unauthorized manipulation of the system, whether intentional or accidental.
15	Detection and monitoring	Mechanisms to detect anomalous or malicious behavior

Source: Adapted from EAC (2017).

TABLE C.19 Characteristics of Organizations Engaged in the Cybersecurity of Elections

Organization Name	Mission	Organization Form	Cybersecurity Audience
US Department of Homeland Security		Executive branch federal agency	
Election infrastructure, subsector government coordinating council	Cross-jurisdictional, interagency, and intergovernmental coordination	Multisector coordinating council	Federal agencies State and local election officials (EOs)
Center for Internet Security	Identify, develop, validate, promote, and sustain best practice solutions for cyber defense; build and lead communities to enable an environment of trust in cyberspace	Private nonprofit with public, private, and nonprofit members	EOs and technical
Multi-State Information Sharing and Analysis Center	Improve the overall cybersecurity posture of the nation's state, local, tribal, and territorial governments through focused cyber threat prevention, protection, response, and recovery	Public private partnership	EOs and technical
National Guard Defensive Cyber Operations Elements	Expansion of 1999 effort related to Y2K		
National Institute of Standards and Technology	Practical cybersecurity and privacy through outreach and effective application of standards and best practices necessary for US to adopt cybersecurity capabilities. to advance collaboration on the unique priorities and challenges that exist regarding cybersecurity and elections. In addition to helping states share information and combat threats, the body is tasked with providing guidance on efforts of Offset National Association of Secretaries of State and fostering effective partnerships with public/private stakeholders, including DHS and other federal government entities.		

Organization	Focus	Type	Members
National Association of Secretaries of State		Nonprofit	Secretaries of state
National Association of State Chief Information Officers		Nonprofit	State chief information officers
National Association of State Technology Directors		Nonprofit	State technology directors
Belfer Center for Science and International Affairs, Harvard University	To provide leadership in advancing policy-relevant knowledge about the most important challenges of international security and other critical issues where science, technology, environmental policy, and international affairs intersect; and to prepare future generations of leaders for these arenas	University research center	Academics, policymakers
US Election Assistance Commission		Independent federal agency	
Election Center (aka National Association of Election Officials)	Professionalization Certification	Nonprofit	State and local EOs
International Association of Government Officials	Professionalization	Nonprofit	
Council of State Governments (January 2018)	Interoperability	Nonprofit	
Aspen Institute Cyber Security Working Group (January 2018)	Translating cybersecurity conversations into action by (1) improving public/private operational collaboration; (2) workforce development to confront cybersecurity needs; and (3) confidence in emerging technologies, including artificial intelligence and the Internet of Things	Public–private forum	

TABLE C.20 The Evolution of Measurement Approaches in Election Administration

Year	Performance Measure/Element	Leadership/Organization	Performance Areas
2004	Election Administration and Voting Survey	Election Assistance Commission	Comprehensive data at the election jurisdiction level on election administration methods including registration, voting methods, and technology deployment
2008	Survey of the Performance of American Elections	Caltech/MIT [Massachusetts Institute of Technology] Voting Technology Project MIT Department of Political Science	Individual level data about voter experience
2009	Democracy Index	Yale University School of Law	Normative list of 10 dimensions of general election operations and voter behavior
2012	Long Lines Project and Polling Place of the Future	Bipartisan Policy Center and Caltech/MIT Voting Technology Project MIT Department of Political Science	Mapping voting line length at precinct level; repeated regularly; 100 precincts in 11 states in 2016
2013	Election Performance Index	PEW Center on the States	Performance in 17 dimensions areas of general election operations and voter behavior; state-level grades
2014	*The American Voting Experience: Report* and recommendations of the Presidential Commission on Election Administration	Presidential Commission on Election Administration	Identification of best practices and recommendations for improving voter experience and further development of the profession

2016	Common Data Format	National Institute of Standards and Technology and partners	Mapping processes and terminology across election technology and election systems
2016	Mail ballot processes	Auburn University Department of Political Science and Election Center	Catalogue of best practices in mail ballot processes, process maps by jurisdiction size; analysis of variance
2017	Election Administration Professionalism Index	Auburn University Department of Political Science	Comprehensive measure of election administration network interconnections and capacity; analysis of variance
2017	Investing in Elections: Professional Measurement Project	Auburn University Department of Political Science and Election Center	Descriptive mapping of election administration finances; analysis of variance
2017	Academic curriculum	Election Administration and Leadership Section Network of Schools of Public Administration and Affairs	Graduate curriculum in election administration Competencies for education in the field Cross-university educational opportunities
2017	Solutions for Securing America's Elections	Center for American Progress	Categories of capacity to address categories of vulnerability; state-level grades
2018	Cybersecurity readiness	State Council of Governments Democracy Fund	Pilot project in 8 states to coordinate state and local offices in election administration and IT to map cybersecurity processes and create capacity
2018	Glossary	Democracy Fund Research partners	Glossary of terms in election technology and election administration
2018	Election Validation Project	Democracy Fund	Verification of accuracy of state and local election operations; analysis of variance

REFERENCES

Abdelall, Brenda Farthy. 2004. "Not Enough of a Minority: Arab Americans and the Language Assistance Provisions (Section 203) of the Voting Rights Act; Note." *University of Michigan Journal of Law Reform* 38: 911–40 .

Abrajano, Marisa, and Zoltan L. Hajnal. 2015. *White Backlash: Immigration, Race, and American Politics*. Princeton, NJ: Princeton University Press.

Adams, Janet, Armen Tashchain, and Ted H. Shore. 2001. "Codes of Ethics as Signals for Ethical Behavior." *Journal of Business Ethics* 29: 199–211.

Agranoff, Robert. 2007. *Managing within Networks: Adding Value to Public Organizations*. Washington, DC: Georgetown University Press.

———. 2012. *Collaborating to Manage*. Washington, DC: Georgetown University Press.

———. 2017. *Crossing Boundaries for Intergovernmental Management*. Washington, DC: Georgetown University Press.

Agranoff, Robert, and Michael McGuire. 1998. "Multinetwork Management: Collaboration and the Hollow State in Local Economic Policy." *Journal of Public Administration Research and Theory* 8: 67–92.

———. 2004. *Collaborative Public Management: New Strategies for Local Governments*. Washington, DC: Georgetown University Press.

Aistrup, Joseph A., Rick Travis, John C. Morris, Kathleen Hale, and David Breaux. 2019. "Voter Photo ID Laws in the US: Back to the Southern Dummy Variable?" Paper presented at Southern Political Science Association annual meeting, Austin.

Alvarez, R. Michael, Lonna Rae Atkeson, and Thad Hall. 2013. *Evaluating Elections: A Handbook of Standards and Methods*. New York: Cambridge University Press.

Alvarez, R. Michael, and Bernard Grofman. 2014. *Election Administration in the United States: The State of Reform after Bush v. Gore*. New York: Cambridge University Press.

Alvarez, R. Michael, and Thad E. Hall. 2003. *Point, Click, and Vote: The Future of Internet Voting*. Washington, DC: Brookings Institution Press.

———. 2008. *Electronic Elections: The Perils and Promises of Digital Democracy*. Princeton NJ: Princeton University Press.

Alvarez, R. Michael, Thad E. Hall, and Morgan Llewellyn. 2008. "Are Americans Confident Their Ballots Are Counted?" *Journal of Politics* 70: 754–66.

Ancheta, Angelo. 2006. *Language Accommodation and the Voting Rights Act*. Legal Studies Research Paper Series, Working Paper 06-21. Santa Clara, CA: Santa Clara University School of Law.

Ansolabehere, Stephen, and Charles Stewart III. 2005. "Residual Votes Attributable to Technology." *Journal of Politics*. 67: 365–89.

Anzia, Sarah F. 2011. "Election Timing and the Electoral Influence of Interest Groups." *Journal of Politics* 73: 412–27.

Ao, Terry M. 2007. "When the Voting Rights Act Became Un-American: The Misguided Vilification of Section 203." *Alabama Law Review* 58: 377–97.

Atkeson, Lonna Rae, and Kyle L. Saunders. 2007. "The Effect of Election Administration on Voter Confidence: A Local Matter?" *PS: Political Science and Politics* 40: 655–60.

Augino, Lori. 2019. "State Support for Local Election Offices." In *The Future of Election Administration: Critical Cases and Conversations*, edited by Mitchell Brown, Kathleen Hale, and Bridgett King. New York: Palgrave.

Austin, James E. 2000. *The Collaboration Challenge: How Nonprofits and Businesses Succeed Through Strategic Alliances*. San Francisco: Jossey-Bass.

Baker, Susan Gonzalez. 1996. "Su Voto Es Su Voz: Latino Political Empowerment and the Immigration Challenge." *PS: Political Science and Politics* 29: 465–68.

Banducci, Susan A., and Jeffrey A. Karp. 2000. "Going Postal: How All-Mail Elections Influence Turnout." *Political Behavior* 22: 223–39.

Barbas, Terin M. 2009. "We Count Too! Ending the Disenfranchisement of Limited English Proficiency Voters." *Florida State University Law Review* 37: 188–214.

Becker, David. 2019. "The Development of the Electronic Registration and Information Center." In *The Future of Election Administration: Critical Cases and Conversations*, edited by Mitchell Brown, Kathleen Hale, and Bridgett King. New York: Palgrave.

Belfer Center for Science and International Affairs. 2018. *The State and Local Election Cybersecurity Playbook*. Cambridge, MA: Harvard Kennedy School of Government.

Bell, Susan, Josh Benaloh, Michael Byrne, Dana DeBeauvior, Bryce Eakin, Gail Fisher, Phillip Kortun, Neal McBurnett, Julian Montoya, Michelle Parker, Olivier Pereria, Philip Stark, Sam Wallach, and Michael Winn. 2014. "STAR-Vote: A Secure, Transparent, and Reliable Voting System." Concept paper presented at multiple election technology conferences. STAR-Vote Team, Travis County, Texas.

Bennett, David A. 2019. "Technology Procurement in Election Systems." In *The Future of Election Administration: Critical Cases and Conversations*, edited by Mitchell Brown, Kathleen Hale, and Bridgett King. New York: Palgrave.

Bennion, Elizabeth, and David Nickerson. 2011. "The Cost of Convenience: An Experiment Showing e-Mail Outreach Decreases Voter Registration." *Political Research Quarterly* 64, no. 4: 858–69.

Bensel, Richard F. 2004. *The American Ballot Box in the Mid-Nineteenth Century*. Cambridge: Cambridge University Press.

Benson, Jocelyn Friedrichs. 2007. "Su Voto Es Su Voz! Incorporating Voters of Limited English Proficiency into American Democracy." *Boston College Law Review* 48: 251–329.

Berardo, Ramiro. 2009. "Generalized Trust in Multi-organizational Policy Arenas: Studying Its Emergence from a Network Perspective." *Political Research Quarterly* 62: 178–89.

Berman, Evan M. 2006. *Performance and Productivity in Public and Nonprofit Organizations*, 2nd ed. Armonk, NY: M. E. Sharpe.

Berry, Frances Stokes, and William D. Berry. 1990. "State Lottery Policy as Innovation: An Event Historical Analysis." *American Political Science Review* 84: 395–416.

———. 1999. "Innovation and Diffusion Models in Policy Research." In *Theories of the Public Policy Process*, edited by Paul A. Sabatier. Boulder, CO: Westview Press.

Berry, Jeffrey M. 1999. *The New Liberalism: The Rising Power of Citizen Groups*. Washington, DC: Brookings Institution Press.

Birkland, Thomas A. 1997. *After Disaster: Agenda Setting, Public Policy, and Focusing Events*. Washington, DC: Georgetown University Press.

———. 2006. *Lessons of Disaster: Policy Change After Catastrophic Events*. Washington, DC: Georgetown University Press.

Bowler, Shaun, and Todd Donovan. 2016. "A Partisan Model of Electoral Reform: Voter Identification Laws and Confidence in State Election." *State Politics & Policy Quarterly* 16: 340–61.

Bowman, Ann O'M. 2002. "American Federalism on the Horizon." *Publius: The Journal of Federalism* 32: 3–22

Bowman, Ann O'M., and James Kearney. 2011. "Second-Order Devolution: Data and Doubt." *Publius: The Journal of Federalism* 41: 563–85.

Brace, Kimball. 2017. *The Election Process from a Data Perspective: Presentation to the Presidential Advisory Commission on Election Integrity*. Manassass, VA: Election Data Services. Available at www.whitehouse.gov.

Bradbury, Bill. 2006. "A Better Way to Vote." *Washington Post*, November 19.

Brians, Craig Leonard, and Bernard Grofman. 2001. "Election Day Registration's Effect on US Voter Turnout." *Social Science Quarterly* 82: 170–83.

Brown, Justin D., and Justin Wedeking. 2006. "People Who Have Their Tickets but Do Not Use Them: 'Motor Voter,' Registration, and Turnout Revisited." *American Politics Research* 34: 479–504.

Brown, Mitchell. 2008. "Improving Organizational Capacity Among Faith- and Community-Based Domestic Violence Service Providers." In *Innovations in Effective Compassion*, edited by Pamela Joshi, Stephanie Hawkins, and Jeffery Novey. Washington, DC: US Department of Health and Human Services.

———. 2012. "Enhancing and Sustaining Organizational Capacity." *Public Administration Review* 72: 506–15.

———. 2016. "Mobilization through Third-Party Groups." In *Why Don't Americans Vote: Causes and Consequences*, edited by Bridgett King and Kathleen Hale. Denver: ABC-CLIO.

Brown, Mitchell, and Kathleen Hale. 2015. *Applied Research Methods in Public and Nonprofit Organizations*. San Francisco: Wiley/Jossey-Bass.

———. 2019. "The Evolution of Professionalism in the Field of Election Administration." In *The Future of Election Administration*, edited by Mitchell Brown, Kathleen Hale, and Bridgett King. New York: Palgrave.

Brown, Mitchell, Kathleen Hale, and Bridgett King, eds. 2019. *The Future of Election Administration: Critical Cases and Conversations*. New York: Palgrave.

Brown, Mitchell, Kathleen Hale, Robert Montjoy, and Mary Afton Day. 2017. *Mail Ballot Pilot Study: A Report of the Professional Measurement Project*. Auburn, AL, and Katy, TX: Auburn University and Election Center.

Brown, William. 2002. "Inclusive Governance Practices in Nonprofit Organizations and Implications for Practice." *Nonprofit Management & Leadership* 12: 369–85.

Bryson, John, Barbara Crosby, and Laura Bloomberg. 2014. "Public Value Governance: Moving Beyond Traditional Public Administration and the New Public Management." *Public Administration Review* 74: 445–56.

———. 2015. *Creating Public Value in Practice: Advancing the Common Good in a Multi-Sector, Shared Power, No One Is Wholly In Charge World.* Boca Raton, FL: CRC Press / Francis Taylor.

Burden, Barry C., David T. Canon, Stéphane Lavertu, Kenneth R. Mayer, and Donald P. Moynihan. 2013. "Selection Method, Partisanship, and the Administration of Elections." *American Politics Research* 41: 903–36.

Burden, Barry C., and Jacob R. Neiheisel. 2013. "Election Administration and the Pure Effect of Voter Registration on Turnout." *Political Research Quarterly* 66, no. 1: 77–90.

Burden, Barry C., and Charles Stewart III, eds. 2014. *The Measure of American Elections.* New York: Cambridge University Press.

Burgess, Phillip M. 1975. "Capacity Building and the Elements of Public Management." *Public Administration Review* 35: 705–16.

Burris, Arthur, and Eric Fischer. 2016. *Help America Vote Act and Election Administration: Overview for 2016.* Washington, DC: Congressional Research Service.

Carter, Jimmy, and James A. Baker. 2005. *Building Confidence in US Elections: Report of the Commission on Federal Election Reform.* Washington, DC: Commission on Federal Election Reform.

Catt, Helena, Andrew Ellis, Michael Maley, Alan Wall, and Peter Wolf. 2014. *Electoral Management Design*, Revised Edition. Stockholm: International IDEA.

Cha, Mijin, and Liz Kennedy. 2014. *Millions to the Polls: Language and Disability Access.* New York: Demos.

Chapin, Doug. 2019. "The Road to Election Administration Professionalism: Follow the Bottom Line." In *Future of Election Administration: Critical Cases and Conversations*, edited by Mitchell Brown, Kathleen Hale, and Bridgett King. New York: Palgrave.

Chisnell, Dana. 2013. *Field Guides to Ensuring Voter Intent, Vols. 1–10 and 100.* Cambridge, MD: Center for Civic Design.

Choate, Judd, and Robert Smith. 2019. "Election Cyber-security." In *The Future of Election Administration*, edited by Mitchell Brown, Kathleen Hale, and Bridgett King. New York: Palgrave.

CIS (Center for Internet Security). 2018. *A Handbook for Elections Infrastructure Security.* New York: Center for Internet Security.

Coleman, Kevin J. 2014. *The Uniformed and Overseas Citizens Absentee Voting Act: Overview and Issues.* Washington, DC: Congressional Research Service.

Comfort, Louise. 1999. *Shared Risk: Complex Systems in Seismic Response.* Bingley, UK: Emerald.

———. 2002. "Managing Intergovernmental Responses to Terrorism and Other Extreme Events." *Publius: The Journal of Federalism* 32: 29–50.

Comfort, Louise, and Naim Kapucu. 2006. "Interorganizational Coordination in Extreme Events: The World Trade Center, September 11, 2001." *Natural Hazards* 39: 309–27.

Comfort, Louise, and Sandra Resolihardjo. 2013. "Leadership in Complex Adaptive Systems." *International Review of Public Administration* 18: 1–15.

Corley, Brian E. 2016. *COOP for Pasco County, Florida*. Dade City, FL: Pasco County Supervisor of Elections.

Council of State Governments. 2016. *Improving Military and Overseas Election Data Collection: Overseas Voting Initiative EAVS Section B Recommendations Report*. Lexington, KY: Council of State Governments.

———. 2017. *FVAP Data Migration Tool: A CSG Overseas Voting Initiative Report*. Lexington, KY: Council of State Governments.

———. 2018a. *Election Cybersecurity Initiative Guide*. Lexington, KY: Council of State Governments.

———. 2018b. *Election Cybersecurity Resource Guide*. Lexington, KY: Council of State Governments.

Creek, Heather, and Kimberly Karnes. 2010. "Federalism and Election Law: Implementation Issues in Rural America." *Publius: The Journal of Federalism* 40: 275–95.

Dahl, Robert A. 1961. *Who Governs? Democracy and Power in an American City*. New Haven, CT: Yale University Press.

Damschroeder, Matt. 2013. "Of Money, Machines, and Management: Election Administration from an Administrator's Perspective." *Election Law Journal* 12: 195–202.

Davidson, Donetta, and Thomas Wilkey. 2019. "Voting System Standards." In *The Future of Election Administration: Critical Cases and Conversations*, edited by Mitchell Brown, Kathleen Hale, and Bridgett King. New York: Palgrave.

de la Garza, Rodolfo O., and Louis DeSipio. 1993. "Save the Baby, Change the Bathwater, and Scrub the Tub: Latino Electoral Participation After Seventeen Years of Voting Rights Act Coverage." *Texas Law Review* 71: 1479–1539.

DHS (US Department of Homeland Security). 2013. *NIPP 2013: Partnering for Critical Infrastructure Security and Resilience*. Presidential Policy Directive 21. www.dhs.gov/sites/default/files/publications/NIPP%202013_Partnering%20for%20Critical%20Infrastructure%20Security%20and%20Resilience_508_0.pdf.

———. 2014. *2014–2017 National Strategy for the National Network of Fusion Centers*. Washington, DC: US Department of Homeland Security.

———. 2017. "Statement of Secretary Jeh Johnson on Designation of Election Infrastructure as a Critical Infrastructure Subsector, January 6." US Department of Homeland Security, Washington, DC.

Donovan, Todd, and Shawn Bowler. 1998. "Direct Democracy and Minority Rights: An Extension." *American Journal of Political Science* 42: 1020–24.

EAC (US Election Assistance Commission). 2007a. *Effective Design for the Administration of Federal Elections*. Washington, DC: US Election Assistance Commission.

———. 2007b. *Quick Start Management Guide: Polling Places and Vote Centers*. Washington, DC: US Election Assistance Commission.

———. 2008a. *Election Administration and Voting Survey*. Washington, DC: US Election Assistance Commission.

———. 2008b. *Poll Worker Best Practices*. Washington, DC: US Election Assistance Commission.

———. 2008c. *Quick Start Management Guide: Canvassing and Certifying an Election*. Washington, DC: US Election Assistance Commission.

———. 2008d. *Quick Start Management Guide: Provisional Ballots*. Washington, DC: US Election Assistance Commission.

————. 2010. *Strengthening the Electoral System One Grant at a Time: A Retrospective of Grants Awarded by EAC April 2003–December 2010.* Washington, DC: US Election Assistance Commission.

————. 2013. *The Impact of the National Voter Registration Act on the Administration of Elections for Federal Office, 2011–2012.* Washington, DC: US Election Assistance Commission.

————. 2014. *Report to Congress on State Expenditures of HAVA Funds.* Washington, DC: US Election Assistance Commission.

————. 2015. *EAC Report to Congress on State Expenditures of HAVA Funds.* Washington, DC: Election Assistance Commission.

————. 2016. *Election Administration and Voting Survey.* Washington, DC: US Election Assistance Commission.

————. 2018. *Election Security Preparedness.* Washington, DC: US Election Assistance Commission. Available at www.eac.gov.

Edelman, Gilad, and Paul Glastris. 2018. "Letting People Vote at Home Increases Voter Turnout: Here Is Proof." *Washington Post*, January 26.

Edelson, Jack, Alexander Alduncin, Christopher Krewson, James A. Sieja, and Joseph E. Uscinski. 2017. "The Effect of Conspiratorial Thinking on Motivated Reasoning on Belief in Election Fraud." *Political Research Quarterly* 70, no. 4: 933–46.

Eggers, William D., and Shalabh Kumar Singh. 2009. *The Public Innovation Playbook: Nurturing Bold Ideas.* Cambridge, MA: Deloitte Research and Ash Institute for Democratic Governance and Innovation at Harvard Kennedy School of Government.

Elazar, Daniel. 1966. *American Federalism: A View from the States.* New York: Crowell.

Election Administration Reports. 2018a. "Research Conducted for STAR Open Source Voting System Provides Opportunities for Voting System Development." *Election Administration Reports* 48: 5–6.

————. 2018b. "States Reconsider Participation in Interstate Voter Registration Crosscheck Program Amid Cybersecurity Concerns." *Election Administration Reports* 48, no. 3: 5–6.

————. 2018c. "US Election Assistance Commission Recognizes Best Practices in Election Administration Field." *Election Administration Reports* 49: 4.

Election Center. 2016. *Elections Security Check List.* Katy, TX: Election Center.

Emerson, Kirk, and Tina Nabatchi. 2015. *Collaborative Governance Regimes.* Washington, DC: Georgetown University Press.

Ewald, Alec C. 2009. *The Way We Vote: The Local Dimension of American Suffrage.* Nashville: Vanderbilt University Press.

Eyestone, Robert 1977. "Confusion, Diffusion, and Innovation." *American Political Science Review* 71: 441–46.

Federal Voting Assistance Program. 2001. "Voting Over the Internet Pilot Project: Assessment Report." June. www.fvap.gov/uploads/FVAP/Reports/voi.pdf.

————. 2015. "Review of FVAP's Work Related to Remote Electronic Voting for the UOCAVA Population." December 29. www.fvap.gov/uploads/FVAP/Reports/FVAP_EVDP_20151229_final.pdf.

Feiock, Richard. 2013. "Institutional Collective Action Theory." *Policy Studies Journal* 41: 397–425.

Feiock, Richard, ed. 2004. *Metropolitan Governance: Conflict, Competition, and Cooperation.* Washington, DC: Georgetown University Press.

Feiock, Richard, and John T. Scholz, eds. 2010. *Self-Organizing Federalism: Collaborative Mechanisms to Mitigate Institutional Collective Action Dilemmas.* Cambridge: Cambridge University Press

Fischer, Eric, and Kevin Coleman. 2008. *Election Reform and Local Election Officials: Results of Two National Surveys.* Washington, DC: Congressional Research Service Report for Congress.

Flack, Oliver, Robert Gold, and Stephan Helbich. 2014. "E-lections: Voting Behavior and the Internet." *American Economic Review* 104: 2238–65.

Flaxman, Seth, Marie-Fatima Hyacinthe, Parker Lawson, and Kathryn Peters. 2012. *Voting by Mail: Increasing the Use and Reliability of Mail-Based Voting Options.* Washington, DC: Presidential Commission on Election Administration.

Florida Department of State. 2017. *Report by the Military and Overseas Voting Assistance Task Force to the Governor, President of the Florida Senate, and Speaker of the Florida House of Representatives.* Tallahassee: Florida Department of State.

Fortier, John C., and Norman J. Ornstein. 2004. "If Terrorists Attacked Our Presidential Election." *Election Law Journal* 3: 597–605.

Fountain, Jane. 2000. *Building the Virtual State: Information Technology and Institutional Change.* Washington, DC: Brookings Institution Press.

Frankovic, Kathleen A. 2003. "News Organizations' Responses to the Mistakes of Election 2000: Why They Will Continue to Project Elections." *Public Opinion Quarterly* 67: 19–31.

Fredrickson, David G., and H. George Fredrickson. 2006. *Measuring the Performance of the Hollow State.* Washington, DC: Georgetown University Press.

Friedson, Eliot. 1960. *Professionalism, the Third Logic: On the Practice of Knowledge.* Chicago: University of Chicago Press.

FSE (Florida Supervisors of Elections). 2018. *Florida Certified Election Professionals Program.* Tallahassee: Florida State Association of Supervisors of Elections. Available from fsase@myflorida.com.

Gamson, William A., and Gadi Wolfsfeld. 1993. "Movements and Media as Interacting Systems." *Annals of American Academy of Political and Social Science* 528: 113–25.

Gargan, John J. 1981. "Consideration of Local Government Capacity." *Public Administration Review* 41: 649–58.

GAO (US Government Accountability Office). 2012. *Elections: Views on Implementing Federal Elections on a Weekend.* GAO-12-69. Washington, DC: Government Accountability Office.

———. 2016. *Elections: Issues Related to Registering Voters and Administering Elections.* GAO-16-630. Washington, DC: Government Accountability Office.

———. 2017. *Voters with Disabilities: Observations on Polling Place Accessibility and Federal Guidance.* GAO-18-4. Washington, DC: Government Accountability Office.

———. 2018. *Elections: Observations on Voting Equipment Use and Replacement.* GAO-18-294. Washington, DC: Government Accountability Office.

Gerber, Alan S., Gregory A. Huber, and Seth J. Hill. 2013. "Identifying the Effect of All Mail Elections on Turnout: Staggered Reform in the Evergreen State." *Political Science Research and Methods* 1: 91–116.

Gerken, Heather. 2009. *The Democracy Index.* Princeton, NJ: Princeton University Press.

Glaser, Max P. 2005. "Humanitarian Engagement with Non-State Armed Actors: The Parameters of Negotiated Access." Humanitarian Practice Network Policy Group, Network Paper 51. http://odihpn.org/wp-content/uploads/2005/06/networkpaper051.pdf.

Goggin, Malcolm, Ann O'M. Bowman, James J. Lester, and Lawrence J. O'Toole Jr. 1990. *Implementation Theory and Practice: Toward a Third Generation.* Glenview, IL: Scott Foresman / Little-Brown.

Goldfeder, Jerry H. 2005. "Could Terrorists Derail a Presidential Election?" *Fordham Urban Law Journal* 32: 523–52.

Gore, Al. 1993. *National Performance Review.* Washington, DC: US Government Printing Office.

Government Accountability Board. 2013. *Final Report on the Impacts and Costs of Eliminating Election Day Registration in Wisconsin.* Madison: State of Wisconsin.

Gray, Virginia A. 1973. "Innovation in the States: A Diffusion Study." *American Political Science Review* 67: 1174–85.

Greene, Sean. 2019. "The Value of the Election Administration and Voting Survey." In *The Future of Election Administration: Critical Cases and Conversations,* edited by Mitchell Brown, Kathleen Hale, and Bridgett King. New York: Palgrave.

Gregorowicz, Krysha, and Thad E. Hall. 2016. "Digitizing Democracy: Online Voter Registration." In *Why Don't Americans Vote: Causes and Consequences,* edited by Bridgett King and Kathleen Hale. Denver: ABC-CLIO.

Gronke, Paul, Evan Galanes-Rosenbaum, Peter A. Miller, and Daniel Toffey. 2008. "Convenience Voting." *Annual Review of Political Science* 11: 437–55.

Gronke, Paul, and Peter Miller. 2012. "Voting by Mail and Turnout in Oregon: Revisiting Southwell and Burchett." *American Politics Research* 40: 976–97.

Gronke, Paul, and Charles Stewart III. 2013. "Early Voting in Florida." Political Science Department of Massachusetts Institute of Technology, Research Paper 2013-12. dx.doi.org/10.2139/ssrn.2247144.

Hale, Kathleen. 2011. *How Information Matters: Networks And Public Policy Innovation.* Washington, DC: Georgetown University Press.

Hale, Kathleen, and Mitchell Brown. 2013. "Adopting, Adapting, and Opting Out: State Response to Federal Voting System Guidelines." *Publius: The Journal of Federalism* 43: 428–51.

———. 2016. "Inter-Local Diffusion and Difference: How Networks Are Transforming Public Service." In *Transforming Government Organizations: Fresh Ideas and Examples from the Field,* edited by William Sauser. Charlotte: Information Age.

———. 2019. "Investing in Elections." Presentation to Joint Election Officials Liaison Council Annual Meeting, January 11, Washington.

Hale, Kathleen, and Ramona McNeal. 2010. "Election Administration Reform and State Choice: Voter Identification Requirements and HAVA." *Policy Studies Journal* 38: 281–302.

Hale, Kathleen, Robert Montjoy, and Mitchell Brown. 2015. *Administering Elections: How American Elections Work.* New York: Palgrave-Macmillan.

Hale, Kathleen, and Christa Slaton. 2008. "Building Capacity in Election Administration: Responses to Complexity and Interdependence." *Public Administration Review* 68: 839–49.

Hall, Thad E. 2003. "Public Participation in Election Management: The Case of Language Minority Voters." *American Review of Public Administration* 33: 407–22.

Hall, Thad E., Lonna Atkeson, and Michael Alvarez. 2012. *Confirming Elections: Creating Confidence and Integrity through Election Auditing.* New York: Palgrave.

Hall, Thad E., and Kathleen Moore. 2011. *Poll Workers and Polling Places.* VTP Working Paper 104. Pasadena and Cambridge: Caltech/MIT Voting Technology Project.

Hamilton, Charles V. 1977. "Voter Registration Drives and Turnout: A Report on the Harlem Electorate." *Political Science Quarterly* 92: 43–46.

Hamner, Michael, and Paul Herrnson. 2014. "Provisional Ballots." In *The Measure of American Elections*, edited by Barry Burden and Charles Stewart III. New York: Cambridge University Press.

Harris, Joseph P. 1928. "Permanent Registration of Voters." *American Political Science Review* 22: 349–53.

———. 1929. "The Progress of Permanent Registration of Voters." *American Political Science Review* 23: 908–14.

———. 1934. *Election Administration in the United States.* Washington, DC: Brookings Institution Press.

Hawkins, Ernie. 2019. "Creating Professionalism in the Field." In *The Future of Election Administration: Critical Cases and Conversations*, edited by Mitchell Brown, Kathleen Hale, and Bridgett King. New York: Palgrave.

Hayes, Christina D., and Erika Bryant. 2002. *Sustaining Comprehensive Community Initiatives: Key Elements for Success.* New York: Finance Project.

Hernandez, Miriam. 2018. "A Week After a Huge Glitch during the California Primary, Los Angeles County Moved to Modernize Its Voting System." KABC-TV, Los Angeles.

Hero, Rodney. 1998. *Faces of Inequality: Social Diversity in American Politics.* New York: Oxford University Press.

Hero, Rodney, and Caroline Tolbert. 1996. "A Racial/Ethnic Diversity Interpretation of Politics and Policy in the States of the US." *American Journal of Political Science* 40: 851–71.

Herrnson, Paul S. 2009. "The Role of Party Organizations, Party-connected Committees, and Party Allies in Elections. *Journal of Politics* 71: 1207–24.

Herrnson, Paul S., Richard G. Niemi, Michael J. Hanmer, Benjamin B. Bederson, Frederick C. Conrad, and Michael W. Traugott. 2008. *Voting Technology: The Not-So-Simple Act of Counting a Ballot.* Washington, DC: Brookings Institution Press.

Herron, Erik, Nazav Boyko, and Michael Thunberg. 2017. "Serving Two Masters: Professionalism and Corruption in Ukrainian Election Administration." *Governance: An International Journal of Policy and Administration* 30: 601–19.

Herron, Michael, and Daniel A. Smith. 2016. "Precinct Resources and Voter Wait Times." *Electoral Studies* 42: 249–63.

Hicks, Thomas. 2019. "Accessible and Secure: Improving Voter Confidence by Protecting the Right to Vote." In *The Future of Election Administration*, edited by Mitchell Brown, Kathleen Hale, and Bridgett King. New York: Palgrave.

Highton, Benjamin. 2004. "Voter Registration and Turnout in the United States: How Voter Registration Laws Influence Practice." *PS: Perspectives on Politics* 2: 507–15.

Hill, Sarah A. 2011. "Election Administration Finance in California Counties." *American Review of Public Administration* 42, no. 5: 606–28.

Hitt, Lorin, Simran Ahluwalia, Matthew Caulfield, Leah Davidson, Mary Margaret Diehl, Alina Ispas, and Michael Windle. 2016. *The Business of Voting: Market Structure and Innovation in the Election Technology Industry.* Philadelphia: Penn Wharton Public Policy Initiative at University of Pennsylvania.

Honadle, Beth Walter. 1981. "A Capacity-Building Framework: A Search for Concept and Purpose." *Public Administration Review* 41: 575–80.

Hopkins, Daniel J. 2011. "Translating into Votes: The Electoral Impacts of Spanish-Language Ballots." *American Journal of Political Science* 55: 814–30.

Horwitz, Sari. 2016. "More Than 30 States Offer Online Voting, but Experts Warn It Isn't Secure." *Washington Post*, May 17.

Humanitarian Practice Network. 2010. *Operational Security Management in Violent Environments: Good Practice Review 8.* London: Overseas Development Institute.

Jefferson, David, Aviel Rubin, Barbara Simons, and David Wagner. 2004. "A Security Analysis of the Secure Electronic Registration and Voting Experiment (SERVE)." http://servesecurityreport.org/.

Jupp, James, and Juliet Pietsch. 2018. "Migrant and Ethnic Politics in the 2016 Election." In *Double Disillusion: The 2016 Australian Federal Election*, edited by Anika Gauja, Peter Chen, Jennifer Curtin, and Juliet Pietsch. Canberra: ANU Press.

Kansas Secretary of State. 2006. "Thornburgh Signs Four-State Agreement." *Canvassing Kansas*, March. Topeka: Office of Kansas Secretary of State.

Kent, Randolph. 2011. "Planning from the Future: An Emerging Agenda." *International Review of the Red Cross* 93: 939–64.

Kettl, Donald. 2002. *The Transformation of Governance: Public Administration for the Twenty-First Century.* Baltimore: Johns Hopkins University Press.

Kettl, Donald, and John J. DiIulio. 1995. *Inside the Reinvention Machine: Appraising Government Reform.* Washington, DC: Brookings Institution Press.

Keyssar, Alexander. 2000. *The Right to Vote: The Contested History of Democracy in the United States.* New York: Basic Books.

Kimball, David C., and Brady Bayback. 2013. "Are All Jurisdictions Equal? Size Disparity in Election Administration." *Election Law Journal* 12: 130–45.

Kimball, David C., and Martha Kropf. 2006. "The Street-Level Bureaucrats of Elections: Selection Methods for Local Election Officials." *Review of Policy Research* 23: 1257–68.

King, Bridgett A. 2016. "Policy and Precinct: Citizen Evaluations and Electoral Confidence." *Social Science Quarterly* 98: 566–83.

Kopko, Kyle C., Sarah McKinnon Bryner, Jeffrey Budziak, Christopher J. Davine, and Steven P. Nawara. 2011. "In the Eye of the Beholder? Motivated Reasoning in Disputed Elections." *Political Behavior* 33: 271–90.

Kousser, Thad, and Megan Mullin. 2006. *Will Vote-by-Mail Increase Participation? Evidence from California Counties.* Los Angeles: John Randolph Haynes & Dora Haynes Foundation.

———. 2007. "Does Voting by Mail Increase Participation? Using Match to Analyze a Natural Experiment." *Political Analysis* 15: 428–55.

Kreutzer, Karin. 2009. "Nonprofit Governance during Organizational Transition in Voluntary Associations." *Nonprofit Management & Leadership* 20: 117–33.

Kropf, Martha, and JoEllen V. Pope. 2019. "Election Costs: A Study of North Carolina." In *The Future of Election Administration*, edited by Mitchell Brown, Kathleen Hale, and Bridgett King. New York: Palgrave.

Kubisch, Anne C., Patricia Auspos, Prudence Brown, Robert Chaskin, Karen Fulbright-Anderson, and Ralph Hamilton. 2002. *Voices from the Field II: Reflections on Comprehensive Community Change*. Washington, DC: Aspen Institute.

Kubisch, Anne C., Patricia Auspos, Prudence Brown, and Tom Dewar. 2010. *Voices from the Field III: Lessons and Challenges from Two Decades of Community Change Efforts*. Washington, DC: Aspen Institute.

Larimer County. 2014. "Vote Center History." www.co.larimer.co.us/elections/vote-center/votecenters_history.htm.

Lausen, Marcia. 2007. *Design for Democracy: Ballot and Election Design*. Chicago: University of Chicago Press.

Lavine, Jill, and Alice Jarboe. 2019. "Assisting Voters with Language Access." In *Future of Election Administration: Critical Cases and Conversations*, edited by Mitchell Brown, Kathleen Hale, and Bridgett King. New York: Palgrave.

Lawson, Connie. 2013. *Vote Center Report*. Indianapolis: Office of Indiana Secretary of State.

Lewis, Doug. 2019. "Parties and Politics: The Evolution of Election Administration." In *The Future of Election Administration*, edited by Mitchell Brown, Kathleen Hale, and Bridgett King. New York: Palgrave.

Lichtenheld, Peter. 2019. "The Role of Election Vendors in Election Administration." In *The Future of Election Administration*, edited by Mitchell Brown, Kathleen Hale, and Bridgett King. New York: Palgrave.

Lieberman, Robert C. 1998. *Shifting the Color Line: Race and the American State*. San Francisco: Wiley & Sons.

Lieberman, Robert C., and Greg M. Shaw. 2000. "Looking Inward, Looking Outward: The Politics of State Welfare Innovation Under Devolution." *Political Research Quarterly* 53: 215–40.

Light, Paul. 1998. *Sustaining Innovation: Creating Nonprofit and Government Organizations That Innovate Naturally*. San Francisco: Jossey-Bass.

———. 2004. *Sustaining Nonprofit Performance: The Case for Capacity Building and the Evidence to Support It*. Washington, DC: Brookings Institution Press.

Logan, Dean. 2019. "Special Elections Costs: Filling Legislative and Congressional Vacancies." In *The Future of Election Administration*, edited by Mitchell Brown, Kathleen Hale, and Bridgett King. New York: Palgrave.

Love, Margaret Colgate. 2005. *Relief from the Collateral Consequences of a Criminal Conviction*. Washington, DC: Sentencing Project.

Lynn, Laurence, Jr. 1997. "Innovation and the Public Interest: Insights From the Private Sector." In *Innovations in American Government: Opportunities, Challenges, and Dilemmas*, edited by Alan Altshuler and Robert Behn. Washington, DC: Brookings Institution Press.

———. 2013. "Innovation and Reform in Public Administration: One Subject or Two?" In *Handbook of Innovation in Public Services*, edited by Stephen P. Osborne and Louise Brown. Cheltenham, UK: Edward Elgar.

Martinez, Michael D., and David Hill. 1999. "Did Motor Voter Work?" *American Politics Quarterly* 27: 296–315.

Martinez, Ray, III. 2013. "Is the Election Assistance Commission Worth Keeping?" *Election Law Journal* 12: 190–94.

Massicote, Louis, Andre Blais, and Antoine Yoshinaka. 2004. *Establishing the Rules of the Game: Election Laws in Democracies.* Toronto: University of Toronto Press.

Masterson, Matthew. 2019. "Protecting Election Infrastructure and the View from the Federal Level." In *The Future of Election Administration: Critical Cases and Conversations,* edited by Mitchell Brown, Kathleen Hale, and Bridgett King. New York: Palgrave.

Matland, Richard E., and Gregg R. Murray. 2012. "An Experimental Test of Mobilization Effects in a Latino Community." *Political Research Quarterly* 65: 192–205.

Mattice, Tim. 2019. "The Role of Professional Associations in Supporting Election Administration." In *The Future of Election Administration: Critical Cases and Conversations,* edited by Mitchell Brown, Kathleen Hale, and Bridgett King. New York: Palgrave.

Mauer, Mark. 1999. *Race to Incarcerate.* New York: New Press.

McCabe, Barbara Coyle, Branco Ponomariov, and Fabyan Estrada. 2017. "Professional Cities, Accredited Agencies, Government Structure and Rational Choice." *Public Administration Review* 78: 295–304.

McCormick, Christy. 2019. "Election Integrity in Ensuring Accuracy." In *The Future of Election Administration,* edited by Mitchell Brown, Kathleen Hale, and Bridgett King. New York: Palgrave.

McDonald, Michael P. 2014. "Voter Turnout." US Elections Project. www.election-project.org.

Miles, Matthew B., and A. Micheal Huberman. 1994. *Qualitative Data Analysis: An Expanded Sourcebook, Second Edition.* Thousand Oaks, CA: Sage

Miller, Judith L. 2002. "The Board as a Monitor of Organizational Activity: The Applicability of Agency Theory to Nonprofit Boards." *Nonprofit Management and Leadership* 12: 429–50.

Miller-Millesen, Judith L. 2003. "Understanding the Behavior of Nonprofit Boards of Directors: A Comparative Theory-Based Approach." *Nonprofit and Voluntary Sector Quarterly* 32: 521–47.

Mintrom, Michael. 1997. "Policy Entrepreneurs and Diffusion of Innovation." *American Journal of Political Science* 41: 738–70.

Mintrom, Michael, and Sandra Vergari. 1998. "Policy Networks and Innovation Diffusion: The Case of State Education Reform." *Journal of Politics* 60: 126–48.

Mitchell, Daniel. 2006. *Policy Implications for NGOs and Contractors in Permissive and Non-Permissive Environments.* Washington, DC: Army War College.

Mohr, Zachary, JoEllen V. Pope, Martha E. Kropf, and Mary Jo Shepherd. 2019. "Strategic Spending: Does Politics Influence Election Administration Expenditure?" *American Journal of Political Science* 63: 427–38.

Monroe, Nathan W., and Dari E. Sylvester. 2011. "Who Converts to Vote-by-Mail? Evidence from a Field Experiment." *Election Law Journal* 10: 15–37.

Montjoy, Robert S. 2008. "The Public Administration of Elections." *Public Administration Review* 68: 788–99.

———. 2010. "The Changing Nature . . . and Costs . . . of Election Administration." *Public Administration Review* 70: 867–75.

Montjoy, Robert S., and Christa Daryl Slaton. 2002. "Interdependence and Ethics in Election Administration: The Case of the Butterfly Ballot." *Public Integrity* 4: 195–210.

Montjoy, Robert, and Lawrence O'Toole Jr. 1979. "Toward a Theory of Policy Implementation: An Organizational Perspective." *Public Administration Review* 38: 465–76.

Mooney, Christopher Z., and Mei-Hsien Lee. 1995. "Legislating Morality in the American States: The Case of Pre-*Roe* Abortion Regulation Reform." *American Journal of Political Science* 39: 599–627.

Moore, Mark. 1995. *Creating Public Value: Strategic Management in Government.* Cambridge, MA: Harvard University Press.

Morrell, Jennifer. 2019. "Election Audits." In *The Future of Election Administration,* edited by Mitchell Brown, Kathleen Hale, and Bridgett King. New York: Palgrave.

Mossberger, Karen. 2000. *The Politics of Ideas and the Spread of Enterprise Zones.* Washington, DC: Georgetown University Press.

Mossberger, Karen, and Kathleen Hale. 2002. "Polydiffusion in Intergovernmental Programs: Information Diffusion in School-to-Work Programs." *American Review of Public Administration* 32: 398–422.

Mossberger, Karen, Caroline Tolbert, and William Franko. 2012. *Digital Cities: The Internet and the Geography of Opportunity.* New York: Oxford University Press.

Moynihan, Donald P. 2004. "Building Secure Elections: E-Voting, Security and Systems Theory." *Public Administration Review* 64: 515–28.

Moynihan, Donald P., and Sanjay K. Pandey. 2010. "The Big Question for Performance Management: Why Do Managers Use Performance Information?" *Journal of Public Administration Research and Theory* 20: 849–66.

Moynihan, Donald P., and Carol L. Silva. 2008. "The Administrators of Democracy." *Public Administration Review* 68: 816–27.

National Commission on Terrorist Attacks Upon the United States. 2004. *The 9/11 Commission Report.* Washington, DC: US Government Printing Office.

National Conference of State Legislatures. 2014a. "Absentee and Early Voting (February 26, 2014)." http://ncsl.org/research/elections-and-campaigns/absentee-and-early-voting.aspx.

———. 2014b. "Same Day Registration." www.ncsl.org/research/elections-and-campaigns/same-day-registration.aspx.

———. 2015. "Provisional Ballots." http://www.ncsl.org/research/elections-and-campaigns/provisional-ballots.aspx.

———. 2018a. "Election Costs: What States Pay." August 3.

———. 2018b. "Electronic Transmission of Ballots." February 28.

National Performance Management Advisory Commission. 2010. *A Performance Management Framework for State and Local Governments: From Measurement and Reporting to Management and Improving.* Chicago: Government Finance Officers Association.

Nickerson, David W. 2014. "Do Voter Registration Drives Increase Participation?" *Journal of Politics* 77: 88–101.

Nickerson, David W., Ryan D. Friedrichs, and David C. King. 2006. "Partisan Mobilization Campaigns in the Field: Results from a Statewide Turnout Experiment in Michigan." *Political Research Quarterly* 59: 85–97.

NIST (National Institute of Standards and Technology). 2016. *Election Results, Common Data Format Specification Version 1.0.* NIST Special Publication 1500-100. Washington, DC: US Department of Commerce.

———. 2018. *Security Considerations for Remote Electronic Voting.* Washington, DC: US Department of Commerce.

Norden, Lawrence, and Wilfred U. Codrington III. 2015. *America's Voting Machines at Risk.* New York: Brennan Center for Justice at New York University School of Law.

———. 2018. *America's Voting Machines at Risk: An Update.* New York: Brennan Center for Justice at New York University School of Law.

Norden, Lawrence, and Andrea Cordova. 2019. Voting Machines at Risk: Where We Stand Today. New York: Brennan Center for Justice at New York University School of Law.

Norden, Lawrence, Christopher R. Deluzio, and Gowri Ramachandran. 2019. *A Framework for Election Vendor Oversight.* New York City: Brennan Center for Justice at New York University School of Law.

Norris, Pippa. 2004. *Electoral Engineering: Voting Rules and Political Behavior.* Cambridge: Cambridge University Press.

———. 2014. *Why Electoral Integrity Matters.* New York: Cambridge University Press.

Norris, Pippa, Richard W. Frank, and Ferran Martine i Coma. 2014. *Advancing Electoral Integrity.* New York: Oxford University Press.

North, Douglass C. 1990. *Institutions, Institutional Change, and Economic Performance.* Cambridge: Cambridge University Press.

Ochs, Holona Leigh. 2006. "'Colorblind' Policy in Black and White: Racial Consequences Of Disenfranchisement Policy." *Policy Studies Journal* 34: 81–93.

OJP (Office of Justice Programs). 2006. *Fusion Center Guidelines: Developing and Sharing Information and Intelligence in a New Era.* Washington, DC: US Department of Justice.

———. 2011. *What's Being Said about Fusion Centers.* Washington, DC: US Department of Justice.

Oregon Secretary of State. No date. "Oregon Vote-by-Mail Timeline." http://sos.oregon.gov/voting-elections.

Osborne, David, and Ted Gaebler. 1992. *Reinventing Government: How the Entrepreneurial Spirit Is Transforming the Public Sector.* Boston: Addison-Wesley.

Osborne, Stephen P., and Louise Brown, eds. 2013. *Handbook of Innovation in Public Services.* Cheltenham, UK: Edward Elgar.

Ostrower, Francie, and Melissa Stone. 2009. "Moving Governance Research Forward: A Contingency-Based Framework and Data Application." *Nonprofit and Voluntary Sector Quarterly* 39: 901–24.

O'Toole, Lawrence J. Jr. 1988. "Strategies for Intergovernmental Management: Implementing Programs in Intergovernmental Management." *International Journal of Public Administration* 11: 417–41.

Owens Hubler, Katy, and Tammy Patrick. 2019. "Process Maps and the Common Data Format." In *The Future of Election Administration*, edited by Mitchell Brown, Kathleen Hale, and Bridgett King. New York: Palgrave.

Owens Hubler, Katy, and Wendy Underhill. 2018. *Election Costs: Who Pays and with Which Funds?* Legisbrief. Denver: National Conference of State Legislatures.

Palazzolo, Daniel J., and Vincent G. Moscardelli. 2006. "Policy Crisis and Political Leadership: Election Law Reform in the States after the 2000 Presidential Election." *State Politics and Policy Quarterly* 6: 300–321.

Palazzolo, Daniel J., Vincent G. Moscardelli, Meredith Patrick, and Doug Rubin. 2008. "Election Reform after HAVA: Voter Verification in Congress and the States." *Publius: The Journal of Federalism* 38: 515–37.

Palmer, Donald, Justin Reimer, and Matthew Davis 2014. *Annual Report on Voter Registration List Maintenance Activities*. Richmond: Virginia State Board of Elections.

Parsons, Talcott. 1960. *Structure and Process in Modern Societies*. Glencoe, IL: Free Press.

Pellissier, Allyson. 2014. *In Line or Online? American Voter Registration in the Digital Era*. VTP Working Paper 33. Pasadena and Cambridge: Caltech/MIT Voting Technology Project.

Pettus, Katherine I. 2013. *Felony Disenfranchisement in America: Historical Origins, Institutional Racism, and Modern Consequences*. 2nd ed. Albany: State University of New York Press.

Pew Center on the States. 2012. *Inaccurate, Costly, and Inefficient: Evidence That America's Voter Registration System Needs an Upgrade*. Washington, DC: Pew Charitable Trusts.

———. 2015. "Survey Summary: State Online Voter Registration." Available at www.pewtrusts.org.

———. 2018. "Online Voter Registration: Trends in Development and Implementation." Available at www.pewtrusts.org.

Pew Charitable Trusts. 2016a. "Data Visualization: Election Performance Index." Available at www.pewtrusts.org.

———. 2016b. "Data Visualization: State Online Voter Registration Systems." Available at www.pewtrusts.org.

———. 2017. "Data Visualization: A Look at How—and How Many—States Adopt Electronic Poll Books." Available at www.pewtrusts.org.

Pew Research Center. 2012. "Precincts or Vote Centers." www.pewstates.org/research/analysis/precincts-or-vote-centers-85899401301#.

Pierson, Paul. 2000. "Increasing Returns, Path Dependence, and the Study of Politics." *American Political Science Review* 94: 251–67.

Praetz, Noah. 2019. "Election Security in Large Counties." In *The Future of Election Administration: Critical Cases and Conversations*, edited by Mitchell Brown, Kathleen Hale, and Bridgett King. New York: Palgrave.

Presidential Commission on Election Administration. 2014. *The American Voting Experience: Report and Recommendations of the Presidential Commission*. Washington, DC: Presidential Commission on Election Administration.

Provan, Keith G., and H. Brinton Milward. 2001. "Do Networks Really Work? A Framework for Evaluating Public Sector Organizational Networks." *Public Administration Review* 61: 414–23.

Quarantelli, Enrico L. 1991. "Disaster Response: Generic or Agent-Specific?" In *Managing Natural Disasters and the Environment*, edited by A. Kreimer and M. Munasinghe. Washington, DC: Environmental Department of World Bank.

Radin, Beryl. 1998. "The Government Performance and Results Act: Hydra-Headed Monster or Effective Policy Tool?" *Public Administration Review* 58: 307–16.

———. 2000. "The Government Performance and Results Act and the Tradition of Federal Management Reform: Square Pegs in Round Holes." *Journal of Public Administration Research and Theory* 11: 111–35.

———. 2006. *Challenging the Performance Movement: Accountability, Complexity, and Democratic Values.* Washington, DC: Georgetown University Press.

Rainey, Hal G., and Paula Steinbauer. 1999. "Galloping Elephants: Developing Elements of a Theory of Effective Public Organizations." *Journal of Public Administration Research and Theory* 9: 1–32.

Ramchandani, Taaps, Dana Chisnell, and Whitney Quesenbery. 2017. *The Next Generation of Accessible Voting: Designing Election Systems for Language Access.* High Bridge, NJ: Center for Civic Design.

Reilly, Shauna. 2015. *Language Assistance Under the VRA: Are Voters Lost in Translation?* New York: Lexington Books.

Renz, David O., ed. 2016. *The Jossey-Bass Handbook of Nonprofit Leadership and Management, 4th Edition.* San Francisco: Jossey-Bass.

Reyes, Steve. 2017. "Language Requirements: 14201, Language Minority Determinations." California Secretary of State Elections Division. http://elections.cdn.sos.ca.gov/ccrov/pdf/2017/december/17148sr.pdf.

Rhodes, Mary Lee. 2013. "Innovation in Complex Public Service Systems." In *Handbook of Innovation in Public Services,* edited by Stephen P. Osborne and Louise Brown. Cheltenham, UK: Edward Elgar.

Rogers, Everett. 1995. *Diffusion of Innovation. 4th Edition.* New York: Free Press.

Rosenstone, Steven J., and Raymond E. Wolfinger. 1978. "The Effect of Registration Laws on Voter Turnout." *American Political Science Review* 72: 22–45.

Rozell, Mark, Clyde Wilcox, and Michael M. Franz. 2011. *Interest Groups in American Campaigns: The New Face of Electioneering. 3rd Edition.* Oxford: Oxford University Press.

Rugeley, Cynthia, and Robert A. Jackson. 2009. "Getting on the Rolls: Analyzing the Effects of Lower Barriers in Voter Registration." *State Politics and Policy Quarterly* 9: 56–78.

Saltman, Roy. 2006. *The History and Politics of Voting Technology.* New York: Palgrave Macmillan.

Scheele, Raymond H., Joe Losco, Gary Crawley, and Sally Jo Vasicko. 2009. "Improving Election Administration with Vote Centers: Toward a National Model." Paper presented at Western Political Science Association Annual Meeting, Vancouver.

Schneider, Marian K. 2019. "Election Security: Increasing Election Integrity by Improving Cyber Security." In *The Future of Election Administration,* edited by Mitchell Brown, Kathleen Hale, and Bridgett King. New York: Palgrave.

Scholz, John, Ramiro Berardo, and Brad Kile. 2008. "Do Networks Enhance Cooperation? Credibility, Search, and Collaboration." *Journal of Politics* 70: 393–406.

Schorr, Lisbeth, Kathleen Sylvester, and Margaret Dunkle. 1999. *Strategies to Achieve a Common Purpose: Tools for Turning Good Ideas into Good Policies.* Washington, DC: Institute for Educational Leadership.

Selznick, Philip. 1949. *TVA and the Grass Roots: A Study in the Sociology of Formal Organization.* Berkeley: University of California Press.

Shaw, Daron, and Vincent Hutchings. 2013. *Report on Provisional Ballots and American Elections*. Washington, DC: US Election Assistance Commission.

Shin, Hyon B., and Rosalind Bruno. 2003. *Language Use and English-Speaking Ability: 2000*. Washington, DC: US Census Bureau.

Showalter, Amelia. 2017. "Colorado 2014: Comparisons of Predicted and Actual Turnout." Pantheon Analytics. https://washingtonmonthly.com/wp-content/.../01/colorado2014voterfileanalysis.pdf.

Shrestha, Manoj, Ramiro Berardo, and Richard Feiock. 2014. "Institutional Collective Action Dilemmas, Multiplex Networks, and Collaborative Governance." *Complexity, Governance & Networks* 1: 49–60.

Simon, Herbert A. 1947. *Administrative Behavior: A Study of Decision-Making Processes in Administrative Organization*. New York: Macmillan.

Smith, Daniel A., and Caroline Tolbert. 2007. "The Instructional and Educative Effects of Ballot Measures: Research on Direct Democracy in the American States." *State Politics & Policy Quarterly* 7: 416–45.

Soss, Joe, Richard C. Fording, and Sanford Schram. 2008. "The Color of Devolution: Race, Federalism, and the Politics of Social Control." *American Journal of Political Science* 52: 536–53.

Soss, Joe, Sanford F. Schram, Thomas P. Vartanian, Erin O'Brien. 2010. *The Hard Line and the Color Line Race, Welfare, and the Roots of Get-Tough Reform*. Ann Arbor, MI: University of Michigan Press.

Southwell, Priscilla L. 2004. "Five Years Later: A Re-Assessment of Oregon's Vote by Mail Electoral Process." *PS: Political Science and Politics* 37: 89–93.

———. 2010. "Voting Behavior in Vote-by-Mail Elections." *Analyses of Social Issues and Public Policy* 10: 106–15.

Southwell, Priscilla L., and Justin Burchett. 1997. "Survey of Vote-by-Mail Senate Election in the State of Oregon." *PS: Political Science and Politics* 30: 53–57.

Squire, Peverill. 1992. "Legislative Professionalization and Membership Diversity in State Legislatures." *Legislative Studies Quarterly* 17: 69–79.

———. 2007. "Measuring State Legislative Professionalism: The Squire Index Revisited." *State Politics & Policy Quarterly* 7: 211–27.

Staggenborg, Suzanne. 1988. "The Consequences of Professionalization and Formalization in the Pro-Choice Movement." *American Sociological Review* 63: 585–605.

Stake, Robert E. 1995. *The Logic of Case Study Research*. Thousand Oaks, CA: Sage.

Stein, Robert, Charles Stewart III, and Christopher Mann. 2019. "Polling Place Quality and Access." In *The Future of Election Administration*, edited by Mitchell Brown, Kathleen Hale, and Bridgett King. New York: Palgrave.

Stein, Robert M., and Greg Vonnahme. 2008. "Engaging the Unengaged Voter: Vote Centers and Voter Turnout." *Journal of Politics* 70: 487–97.

———. 2011. "Voting at Non-Precinct Polling Places: A Review and Research Agenda." *Election Law Journal* 10: 307–11.

———. 2012. "When, Where, and How We Vote: Does It Matter?" *Social Science Quarterly* 93: 692–711.

Stevens, Daniel, and Benjamin G. Bishin. 2011. "Getting Out the Vote: Minority Mobilization in a Presidential Election." *Political Behavior* 33: 113–38.

Stewart, Charles, III. 2010. "Losing Votes by Mail." *Legislation and Public Policy* 13: 573–601.

———. 2013. "Waiting in Line to Vote." *Journal of Law & Politics* 28: 439–63.

———. 2019. "The Elections Performance Index: Past, Present, and Future." In *The Future of Election Administration*, edited by Mitchell Brown, Kathleen Hale, and Bridgett King. New York: Palgrave.

Stone, Deborah. 2011. *The Policy Paradox: The Art of Political Decision-Making, 3rd Edition*. New York: W. W. Norton.

Stoneburner, Gary, Alice Goguen, and Alexis Feringa. 2002. *Risk Management Guide for Information Technology Systems: Recommendations of the National Institute of Standards and Technology*. Special Publication 800-30. Washington, DC: US Department of Commerce.

Taylor, Mark Zachary. 2016. *The Politics of Innovation: Why Some Countries Are Better Than Others at Science & Technology*. New York: Oxford University Press.

Thompson, James D. 1967. *Organizations in Action: Social Science Bases of Administrative Theory*. New York: McGraw-Hill.

Tokaji, Daniel P. 2009. "The Future of Election Reform: From Rules to Institutions." *Yale Law & Policy Review* 28: 125–54.

Tolbert, Caroline, and Rodney Hero. 1996. "Race/Ethnicity and Direct Democracy: An Analysis of California's Illegal Immigration Initiative." *Journal of Politics* 58: 806–18.

Tolbert, Caroline, Karen Mossberger, and Ramona McNeal. 2008. "Institutions, Policy Innovation, and E-Government in the American States." *Public Administration Review* 68: 549–63.

Torfing, Jacob. 2016. *Collaborative Innovation in the Public Sector*. Washington, DC: Georgetown University Press.

Torfing, Jacob, B. Guy Peters, Jon Pierre, and Eva Serensen. 2012. *Interactive Governance: Advancing the Paradigm*. London: Oxford University Press.

Tucker, James Thomas. 2006. "Enfranchising Language Minority Citizens: The Bilingual Election Provisions of the Voting Rights Act." *Legislation and Public Policy* 10: 195–260.

———. 2016. *The Battle over Bilingual Ballots: Language Assistance and Political Access under the VRA*. New York: Routledge.

Tucker, James Thomas, and Rodolfo Espino. 2007. "Government Effectiveness and Efficiency? The Minority Language Provisions of the VRA." *Texas Journal on Civil Liberties & Civil Rights* 12: 163–232.

Uggen, Christopher, and Jeff Manza. 2002. "Democratic Contraction? Political Consequences of Felon Disenfranchisement in the United States." *American Sociological Review* 67, no. 6: 777–803.

———. 2006. *Locked Out: Felon Disenfranchisement and American Democracy*. New York: Oxford University Press.

Uggen, Christopher, Ryan Larson, and Sarah Shannon. 2016. *6 Million Lost Voters: State-Level Estimates of Felony Disenfranchisement*. Washington, DC: Sentencing Project.

Uggen, Christopher, Jeff Manza, and Melissa Thompson. 2006. "Citizenship, Democracy, and the Civic Reintegration of Criminal Offenders." *Annals of the American Academy of Political and Social Science* 605: 281–310.

Underhill, Wendy. 2019. *All-Mail Elections (aka Vote-by-Mail)*. Available at www
.ncsl.org.

US Bureau of the Census. 2011. *Voting Rights Act Amendments of 2006, Determinations
under Section 203*. Washington, DC: US Department of Commerce.

——. 2016. *QuickFacts: Travis County, Texas*. Available at www.census.gov.

US Department of the Army. 2003. *Stability and Support Operations, Field Manual
3-07*. Washington, DC: Headquarters of Department of the Army.

US Department of Defense. 2009. *Department of Defense Instruction 3000.05; Stability
Operations*. www.dtic.mil/whs/directives/corres/pdf/300005p.pdf.

Valelly, Richard M. 2004. *The Two Reconstructions: The Struggle for Black Enfranchise-
ment*. Chicago: University of Chicago Press.

Vanderleeuw, James, Baodong Liu, and Erica Williams. 2008. "The 2006 New Orleans
Mayoral Election: The Political Ramifications of a Large-Scale Natural Disaster."
PS: Political Science and Politics 41: 795–801.

Vander Roest, Virginia. 2019. "State Training Initiatives." In *Future of Election Administration: Critical Cases and Conversations*, edited by Mitchell Brown, Kathleen
Hale, and Bridgett King. New York: Palgrave.

Vedlitz, Arnold. 1985. "Voter Registration Drives and Black Voting in the South." *Journal of Politics* 47: 643–51.

Verified Voting Foundation. 2019. *Verified Voting 2019*. Philadelphia: Verified Voting
Foundation. Available at www.verifiedvoting.org/verifier.

Vote at Home. 2019. *Success Stories: Security, Convenience, and Cost Savings*. Denver:
Vote at Home. Available at www.voteathome.org.

Walker, Jack L. 1969. "The Diffusion of Innovations among the American States."
American Political Science Review 63, no. 3: 880–99.

Walker, Richard M. 2013. "Internal and External Influences on the Capacity for
Innovation in Local Government." In *Handbook of Innovation in Public Services*,
edited by Stephen P. Osborne and Louise Brown. Cheltenham, UK: Edward
Elgar.

Weimer, David L. 2010. *Medical Governance: Values, Expertise, and Interests in Organ
Transplantation*. Washington, DC: Georgetown University Press.

Weinberg, Barry H., and Lyn Utrecht. 2002. "Problems in America's Polling Places:
How Can They Be Stopped?" *Temple Policy and Civil Rights Law Review* 11:
401–29.

Weiser, Wendy R. 2006. *Are HAVA's Provisional Ballots Working?* New York: Democracy Program of Brennan Center for Justice at New York University School of
Law.

Weiser, Wendy R., and Alicia Bannon. 2018. *Democracy: An Election Agenda for Candidates, Activists, and Legislators*. New York: Brennan Center for Justice at New
York University School of Law.

Wilson, James Q. 1989. *Bureaucracy: What Government Agencies Do and Why They Do
It*. New York: Basic Books.

Wogan, J. B. 2014. "LA County Designs a Whole New Voting System." July 7. Available at www.governing.com.

Wolfinger, Raymond E., and Steven J. Rosenstone. 1980. *Who Votes?* New Haven, CT:
Yale University Press.

Wolff, T. No date. "Coalition Building Tip Sheets." AHEC/Community Partners, Amherst, MA. www.tomwolff.com/healthy-communities-tools-and-resources .html#pubs.

Xu, Yang. 2011. "Entrepreneurial Social Capital and Cognitive Models of Information." *Management Research Review* 34: 910–26.

Yin, Robert K. 2002. *Case Study Research: Design and Methods.* Thousand Oaks, CA: Sage.

INDEX

ABOUT THE AUTHORS

Kathleen Hale is a professor of political science at Auburn University, where she directs the Graduate Program in Election Administration. Her research focuses on interorganizational relationships and information exchanges that build public-sector capacity. She is the author of *How Information Matters: Networks and Public Policy Innovation,* the 2012 winner of the Academy of Management's Best Book Award in the Public and Nonprofit Division.

Mitchell Brown is a professor of political science at Auburn University. Her research focuses on the civic and political empowerment of marginalized groups, which she approaches through applied research.

Hale and Brown work extensively with election administration practitioners around the country, and they are coauthors of *Administering Elections: How American Elections Work* (with Robert Montjoy; Palgrave Macmillan 2015) and are the editors of two academic-practitioner compendiums of research and reflections under the title *The Future of Election Administration* (with Bridgett King; Palgrave Macmillan 2019).

Thomas R. Wilkey, the author of the foreword, has had a distinguished career in public service, including serving as the public information officer of the Erie County (New York) Board of Elections; the executive director of the New York State Board of Elections; a founding member and president of the National Association of State Election Directors; and as the first executive director of the US Election Assistance Commission. Today, he serves as a member of the Board of Directors of the Election Center.